DALKEY

AN ILLUSTRATED HISTORY

JOHN MARTIN

EASTWOOD

First published 2025 by Eastwood Books
Dublin, Ireland
www.eastwoodbooks.com
www.wordwellbooks.com

Eastwood Books is an imprint of the Wordwell Group

First edition

Eastwood Books
The Wordwell Group
Suite 5
Hub 17
17 Corrig Rd
Sandyford Business Park
Dublin 18, Ireland

The Wordwell Group is a member of Publishing Ireland,
the Irish Publishers' Association.

978-1-916742-68-0 (Paperback)
978-1-916742-89-5 (ePub)

Typesetting and design by the Wordwell Group
Printed in Ireland by SprintBooks

DALKEY

AN ILLUSTRATED HISTORY

Contents

Introduction

I have lived in Dalkey for over forty years and gradually got to know its long and fascinating history, helped in no small way by the guided walks led by the late Harry Latham. Notes of those walks were written up in the Dalkey Community Council Newsletter, and he himself prepared a number of short books, notably on St Patrick's church. These provided the nucleus of a small library on local history, which expanded during the Covid lockdown thanks to a wide range of online sources.

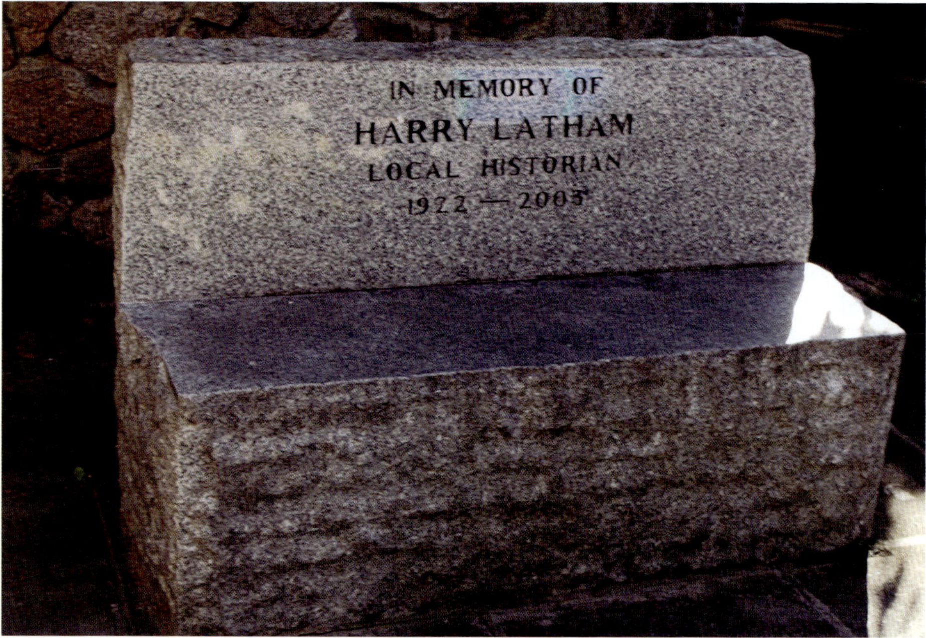

Harry Latham memorial, Castle Street.

This book is aimed at both the general reader and those with a particular interest in the local history of the area. The period covered extends from the earliest settlement about 5000 BC to the present day, taking in Dalkey, Bullock and Dalkey Island. The second part deals with the urban development of Dalkey in the nineteenth and twentieth centuries in relation to topics such as housing, transport and services. The final two chapters provide brief pen-portraits of people who either helped shape its development or made a mark in their chosen careers. Each chapter is illustrated with historic maps, engravings, paintings and photos.

While my research is based on a wide variety of primary and secondary sources, I owe a huge debt of gratitude to my fellow local historians in Dalkey, notably Brian Meyer, Dermot O'Riordan, Michael McShane, Charles Smith and Dr Arnold Horner, who not only shared their knowledge but also commented on draft chapters at informal seminars in Dalkey Library. Peter Pearson, who has written several books on the architectural heritage of the wider Dún Laoghaire area and who has amassed a treasure trove of source material, has generously provided several images used in this book. Brian Porter kindly made his family papers available to me; his ancestors William Edward Porter senior and junior played a prominent role in the development of the town in the nineteenth century. I am grateful to various librarians and archivists who assisted my research, including the Lexicon Local Studies section, the National Library, the National Archives, the Royal Irish Academy, the Registry of Deeds and the library of the Representative Church Body. John Kelleher of the National Transport Museum in Howth generously provided photos of the Dalkey trams.

Finally, this book is dedicated to my wife Mary, who shares my interest in local history and whose own research into the history of Bullock Castle was of considerable value.

John Martin
April 2025

List of illustrations

1.
Dalkey Island

D alkey Island, just over 11ha in area, is the largest of a group of rocky outcrops off the coast of Dalkey. The others are Maiden Rock and Lamb Island to the north and the Muglins to the east; the latter has a distinctive conical-shaped lighthouse, erected in 1880 after several ships were wrecked in the vicinity. Dalkey Sound, which separates Dalkey Island from the mainland, is over 200m wide and up to 12m deep; despite its strong tidal currents, it served as an outport for Dublin during the later Middle Ages, resulting in the construction of Dalkey's famous 'seven castles'.[1]

There are two reasons why any history of Dalkey should begin with Dalkey Island. First, the island contains the site of the earliest known settlement in the wider Dalkey area, dating back about 8,000 years. Second, the place-name itself derives from the Norse *Dalk Ei*, a direct translation of the older Irish name *Deilg Inis*, meaning 'Thorn or Dagger Island'. Visitors arriving at the landing-pier on the west side of the island could be forgiven, however, for overlooking such a historic site, as the grassy promontory on their left at the north-west tip of the island offers no visible evidence of its past.

Prehistory

Following the end of the Ice Age in Ireland, the first settlers arrived around 8000 BC, probably from Britain, settling on the coast and using rivers to explore inland. They were known as hunter-gatherers, living off nearby natural resources such as fish. Sea levels were lower then than they are now, making it likely that more of Dalkey Island constituted dry land and that it was easier to cross the Sound to the mainland. In the late 1950s, archaeologists led by G.D. Liversage carried out a series of excavations within the promontory area (Fig. 1.1), which showed that it had been occupied at different times from about 6000 BC (Mesolithic) to the Iron Age.[2] The earliest material included pottery and implements, some with radiocarbon dates from 5970–5560 BC. Finds from the later Neolithic period included implements known as 'Bann flakes', dated to around 3340 BC; a human skeleton from that era was also found under a refuse heap of sea shells. While a number of stake-holes (for wooden

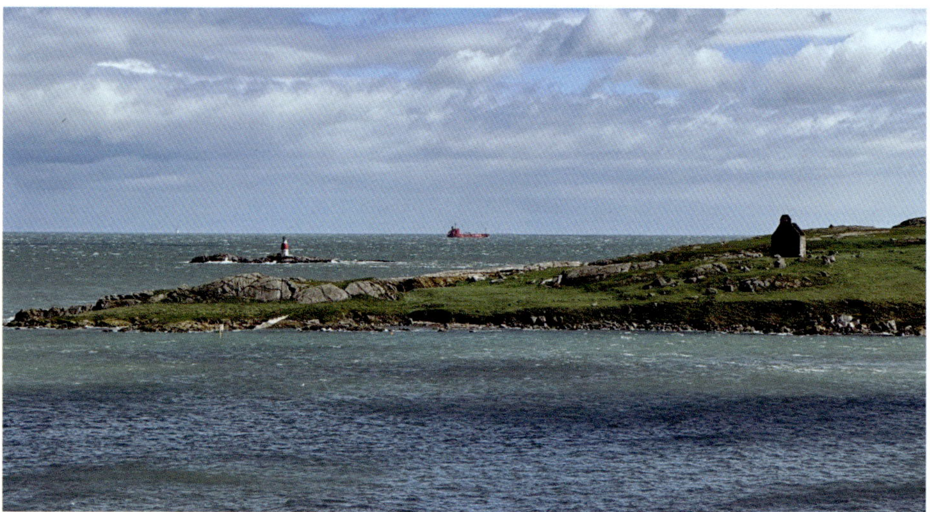

Fig. 1.1—View over the promontory site at the western end of Dalkey Island.

posts) were also uncovered, there is a consensus among archaeologists that the island was not continuously settled over thousands of years; rather there were periods of activity, perhaps of a ritual or ceremonial nature at times. However, despite the rocky character of the island, the well near the landing-pier provided a source of drinking-water which could have helped to sustain a small population.

The discovery of flint tools indicates that the island was used for the production of arrowheads and axeheads, especially in the later Neolithic period and the Bronze Age. A distinctive type of pottery known as Beaker pottery together with clay moulds found within the excavated area provided evidence of early metal-working. Given the island's prominent location at the entrance to Dublin Bay, finds of imported goods suggest that it may also have been used as a base for overseas trading. Those finds included a type of pottery known as E-ware, probably used to contain wine from Britain or France, and a flake of green glass from a late Roman vessel.[3] These artefacts were buried under an earthen bank which, together with an adjoining ditch, constituted the defences of a promontory fort built around the seventh or eighth century AD.

The Early Christian and Viking era
In the early medieval period, parts of south County Dublin (including the Dalkey area) and north County Wicklow formed the kingdom of Cualu, ruled first by Dál Messin Corb and later by the Uí Briúin Chualann dynasty. This coincided with the

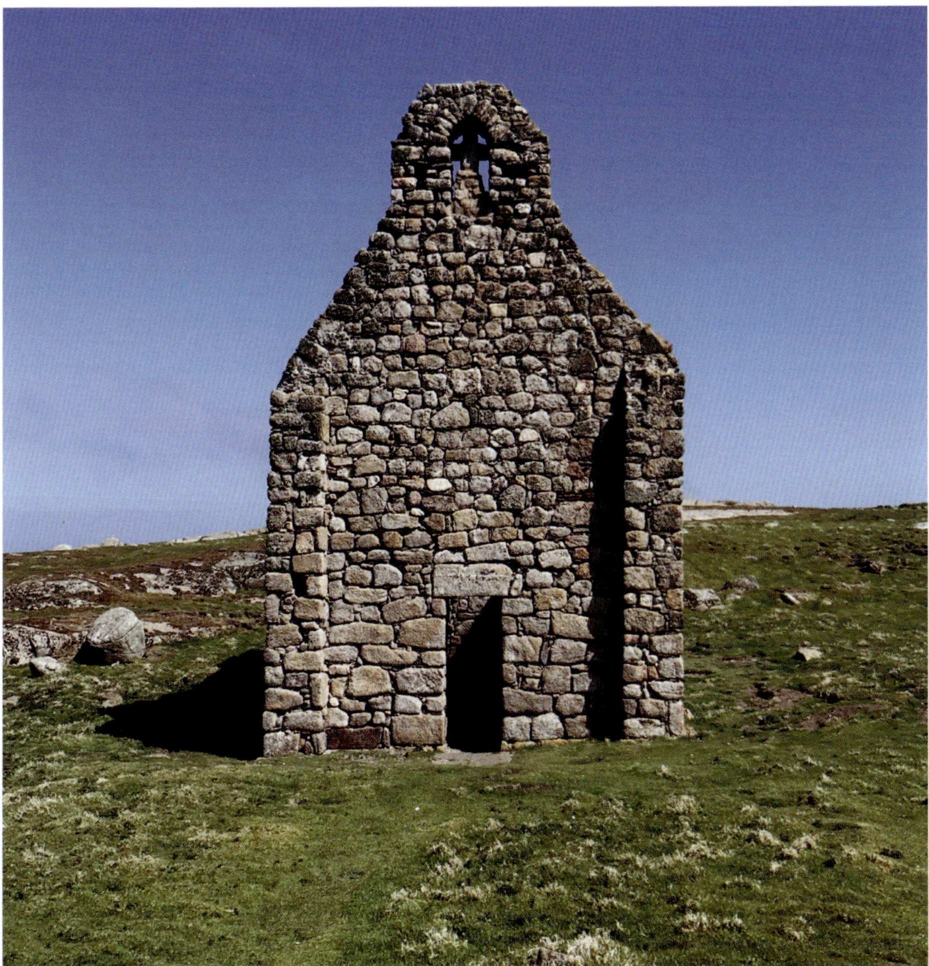

Fig. 1.2—St Begnet's church, Dalkey Island.

spread of Christianity from the fifth century onwards. On Dalkey Island, this was reflected in a stone church (Fig. 1.2), a cross inscribed on a rock face and a holy well, although the latter may have derived its origins from pre-Christian practice. Up to the nineteenth century the 'Scurvy Well' was believed to cure eye conditions.[4]

It is difficult to date the church with precision, but it has certain characteristics pointing to a tenth-century origin, such as the extensions of the side walls to the front and the massive lintel stone over the entrance. There is some evidence from changes to the building that it was still in use in the Anglo-Norman period, such as the bell-cote on the west gable, the now-boarded-up window in the east wall and the remains of glazed ridge tiles, medieval pottery and a fragment of a window

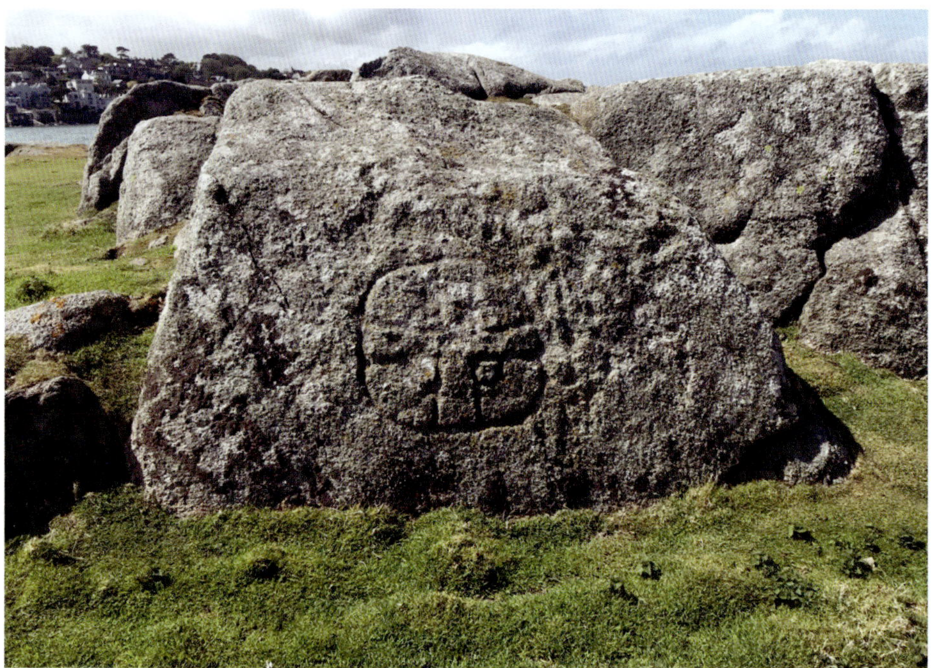

Fig. 1.3—Inscribed cross, Dalkey Island.

moulding made of Dundry stone from near Bristol.[5] The building was also slightly modified in 1804–5 by workmen lodged there during the construction of the Martello tower (see below).

Both the island church and the stone church in Dalkey were dedicated to St Begnet, about whom little is known. It is possible that she came from the ruling dynasty in Cualu, which would help to explain why she was venerated in this area. To the west of the church there is an 'eastern' cross inscribed on the face of a granite rock (Fig. 1.3), probably dating from the eighth or ninth century.[6]

The Vikings captured Dublin in AD 849. While they were defeated by the Irish in 902, the city was retaken in 914 by Ragnall, king of Danish Northumbria, who established a powerful kingdom straddling the Irish Sea. The Dalkey area was located within the zone of influence of Viking Dublin, known as *Dyflinarskiri*, and Dalkey Island appears to have been used for a time as a Viking slave-camp. During the ninth century the Vikings raiding Ireland began to seize captives, some of whom were sold off as slaves, while high-status prisoners were held for ransom. One of the latter was Coibhdeanach, abbot of Killeigh, Co. Offaly; according to the Annals of the Four Masters, he was drowned in 938 off the coast of Deilginis while fleeing from the foreigners.

The quiet centuries from *c.* 1200 to 1800

Dalkey Island, along with Dalkey itself, came into the possession of the archbishop of Dublin in the early twelfth century;[7] both formed part of the archbishop's manor of Shankill in 1326, when the value of the annual rental of grazing on the island was estimated at 12*d.* It is interesting to note that when the Board of Ordnance acquired ownership of the island in 1807 in order to build a Martello tower and a gun battery (see below) the archbishop was still listed as one of the owners. The island appears to have been uninhabited and used for grazing throughout the intervening centuries. While aerial photos show the outline of field boundaries in the vicinity of St Begnet's church, it is not known whether this signified habitation.

It was reputed that many citizens of Dublin fled to the island for safety during the plague of 1575.[8] The quarantine issue re-emerged in 1710, as there were reports

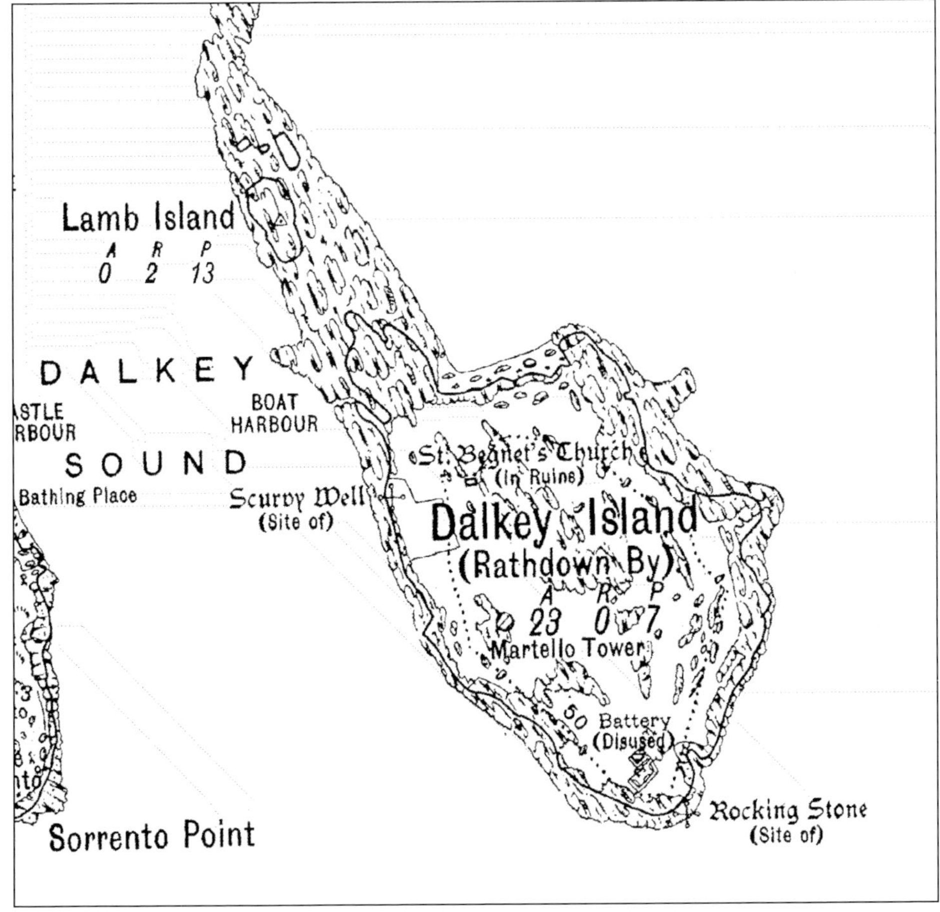

Fig. 1.4—Ordnance Survey six-inch map (Tailte Éireann permit no. 50450108 © Tailte Éireann).

that a ship from Danzig had brought the plague to Kerry. Captain Thomas Burgh, the Surveyor General, was asked to report on the anchorage at Dalkey Sound with a view to its being used as quarantine quarters for ships coming from plague-stricken countries. He found that it was unfit for such a purpose, as no ship could lie there with safety, and the sum of £4,311 was his estimate for the construction of a safe harbour.[9] As a crude measure of inflation, this equates to over £430,000 today.

The island featured in early navigation maps, as it was located at the entrance to Dublin Bay and because the adjoining rocky outcrops posed a hazard to sailors. There was some confusion among early map-makers as to its name, however, probably because St Begnet was not widely known outside Ireland. Thus John Speed's map of Leinster in 1610, followed by de Gomme in 1673, called it St Bennet's Isle. John Bowles named it Dalkey Island in 1728, and this was adopted by John Rocque in 1760. While Samuel Lewis's *Topographical Dictionary of Ireland* (1837) followed suit, he referred to the ruined church as St Benedict's.

On 1 March 1766, four pirates were tried in the Dublin Admiralty Court and found guilty of murdering Captain Cochrane, Captain Glass and others on the high seas, and of plundering and scuttling the ship *Lord Sandwich*. A few days later, they were executed in St Stephen's Green. As the court had ordered that their bodies should be 'hanged in chains' as a deterrent to piracy, two of the corpses were hung near Poolbeg and the other two on the new South Wall. The latter, however, proved a disagreeable sight to the Dublin citizens who walked there for amusement and health, and they called for the removal of the corpses. Their request was granted, and on 1 April the offending bodies were removed to the Muglins off Dalkey Island, where they were fixed in 'new irons'.[10]

The King of Dalkey

Any tranquillity experienced by the island was shattered in the closing decades of the eighteenth century, at least for one Sunday each year at the end of August or in early September. At some time in the 1780s, and certainly by 1787, a fleet of boats carrying the 'King of Dalkey' and his retinue sailed from the Liffey quays to Dalkey Island, where his coronation took place amidst lavish festivities. The event was witnessed by thousands of people crowding both the island and the opposite shoreline; as Dalkey was only a tiny village at the time, most were visitors from the city and suburbs.

When the royal barge arrived with flags flying and music playing, his majesty inspected his territory, surrounded by his dukes, generals, bishops and courtiers, many of them inebriated from the celebrations which had begun the previous evening in the city centre. Divine service took place in the ruined church, where a sermon was preached by the lord primate of Dalkey. Following speeches and debates on the political topics of the day, the king's health was drunk and a festive meal was served outdoors.

An account of the proceedings was published as the *Dalkey Gazette* in some of the Dublin newspapers shortly afterwards. The whole event, while mainly convivial, had a political undertone; the American and French revolutions had sparked intense debate in Ireland, and the mock ceremony on Dalkey Island satirised the extravagant pomp of the British monarchy. The last King of Dalkey was Stephen Armitage, a popular Dublin bookseller. His speech in 1797 made it clear that his office was elective and that it was for his people to decide whether he was worthy of another year:

> 'The crimes of royalty, its tyrannies, its treacheries, and its rapacities, have rendered it suspicious everywhere—from that suspicion it is my wish to vindicate for ever him who wears the crown of Dalkey'. [11]

A major uprising against British rule in Ireland, led by the United Irishmen, took place in 1798 but was suppressed with considerable force, with the death-toll exceeding 10,000. A French expeditionary force that landed in County Mayo was also defeated. In those circumstances, the revelries on Dalkey Island did not take place that year, and the ceremony lapsed until August 1850, when it was briefly revived:

> 'The novelty of this splendid pageant attracted an immense concourse of spectators … the Kingstown railway trains and the carriages of the Atmospheric [railway] were crowded. The rocky shore on the mainland was densely crowded with fashionables. The sound of trumpet and the beat of drum announced the approach of the King of Dalkey; on landing he was received by the nobles and great officers of state. King Henry [Hughes] was proposed as the successor to the late King Stephen. He called for three cheers for Queen Victoria. His majesty then announced he would hold his first levee on Sunday next and his coronation would take place on Monday. He then returned to the mainland. There followed rural games of all sorts, running matches, wheelbarrow races, etc.'[12]

More modest ceremonies took place on the island from time to time during the twentieth century.

The Martello tower and gun battery

The French landing in Killala and the attempted landing in County Donegal (which led to the capture of Wolfe Tone) in 1798 demonstrated the possibility that Napoleon could attack Britain by invading Ireland. The threat appeared to diminish in the following years, but the British military authorities decided to strengthen their coastal defences in both the UK and Ireland. This included the building of 130 Martello towers on the southern coasts of England; the name, though not the design, derived from a Royal Navy attack on a tower at Mortello Point in Corsica in 1794. Following the Act of Union in 1800, responsibility for Irish coastal defences lay with the Board of Ordnance in London, which had a substantial budget. In late 1803 the new military commander of Ireland, Lieutenant General Cathcart, toured the coastal defences with Captain Birch, an officer with experience of the Martello towers in Minorca. About the same time, intelligence was received that suggested a threat of invasion of Ireland by landings on the east coast, and in June 1804 Lieutenant-Colonel Benjamin Fisher, Royal Engineers, was authorised 'to superintend the construction of all such towers, field or other works as may be undertaken', and the construction of the Martello towers to defend the coast of Dublin and north Wicklow began.[13] In all, twenty-eight towers, some with separate gun batteries, were built to defend the capital city.

The tower on Dalkey Island was no. 9 in a series that began at Bray (Fig. 1.5). It occupied a particularly strategic location, as the field of fire from the adjacent gun battery covered both the entrance to Dublin Bay and Killiney Bay. As early as 1797 the authorities had commissioned an émigré French royalist, Major La Chaussée, to

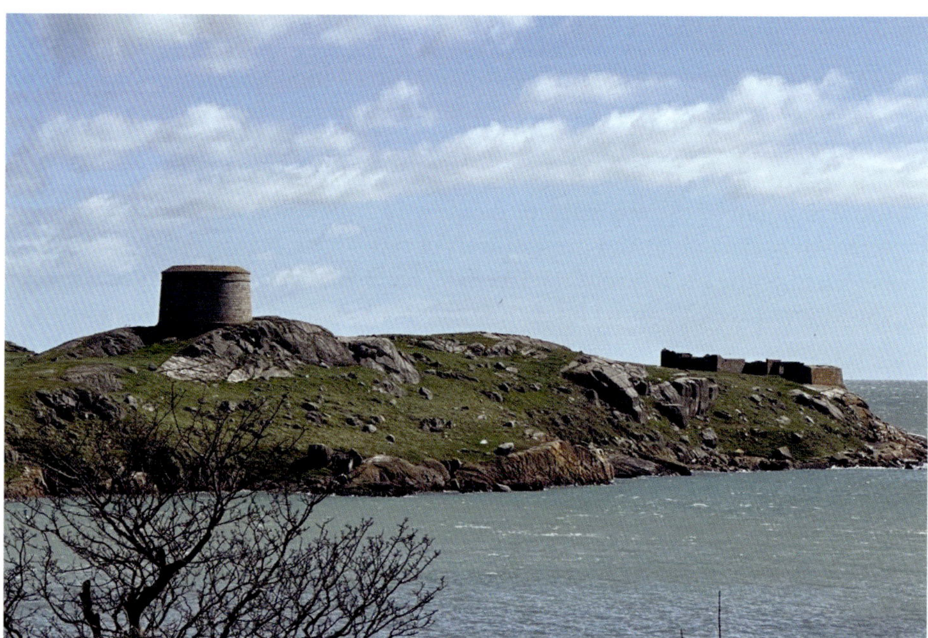

Fig. 1.5—Martello tower and gun battery, Dalkey Island.

examine the terrain around the bay and make recommendations for its defence. It is not clear whether any of his recommended works were actually carried out, but his analysis fed into the location of the Martello towers and batteries. In particular, one of the places considered a possible target was Killiney Bay—a deep-water bay within easy reach of the capital.[14]

The twenty-eight towers and batteries were completed by mid-1805. This was a remarkable achievement by any standard, considering the need to assemble stone contractors and masons, bring the stone to the sites and, in the case of the towers to the south of Dublin, carve the granite ashlar and assemble it with a high degree of precision and craftsmanship. While some stone was quarried on Dalkey Island itself, more is likely to have been brought from the numerous small quarries in the Dalkey and Bullock areas. According to Lewis's *Topographical Dictionary of Ireland* (1837),

> 'About the commencement of the present century, a circle of granite blocks
> enclosing a cromlech was standing on the common; but the cromlech and
> the stones surrounding it were blasted with gunpowder and carried away, to
> furnish materials for the erection of a Martello tower on the coast'.[15]

It is not known whether the 'tower on the coast' was on the island or at Bartra, Harbour Road.

Workmen were accommodated in the ruins of St Begnet's church, where they made some alterations to the structure, including the addition of a fireplace. They also built the small boat pier to facilitate the landing of men and supplies. The average cost of constructing a tower was put at £1,200, and a battery at £1,800,[16] but the costs at Dalkey Island were likely to be higher; when the War Department invited contractors to tender for repair works to seven of the towers in 1867, it offered an extra 10 per cent in relation to the island.[17] While tower no. 9 was broadly similar in appearance to other towers, its potential vulnerability to attack from land led to an unusual design feature: the original entrance was via the roof. The existing first-floor doorway appears to be a later insertion. The tower was equipped with two 24-pounder guns, while the battery had three. It will be seen from the gun-carriage rails within the battery that each cannon could be moved to cover an arc of fire (Fig. 1.6).

Each Martello tower was within sight of the next; in the case of Dalkey Island, the nearest towers were no. 8, overlooking Killiney Bay, and no. 10 (Harbour Road), which protected the small harbour at Bullock. It was initially envisaged that signal-towers, such as that on Dalkey Hill, would also serve as communication links between the towers, but this role appears to have diminished within a few years.

Following the defeat of Napoleon at Waterloo in 1815, the threat of invasion by

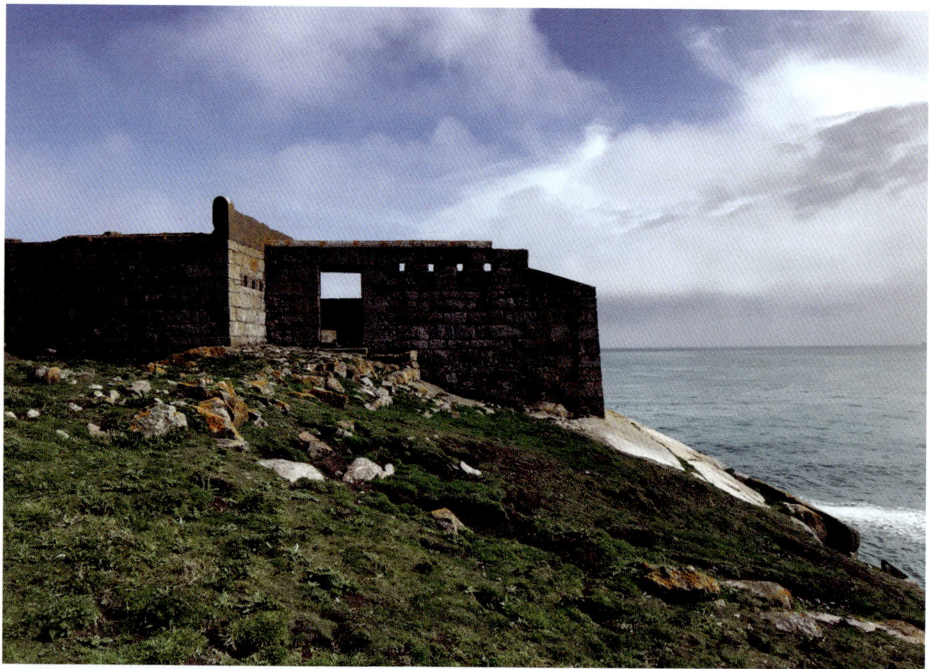

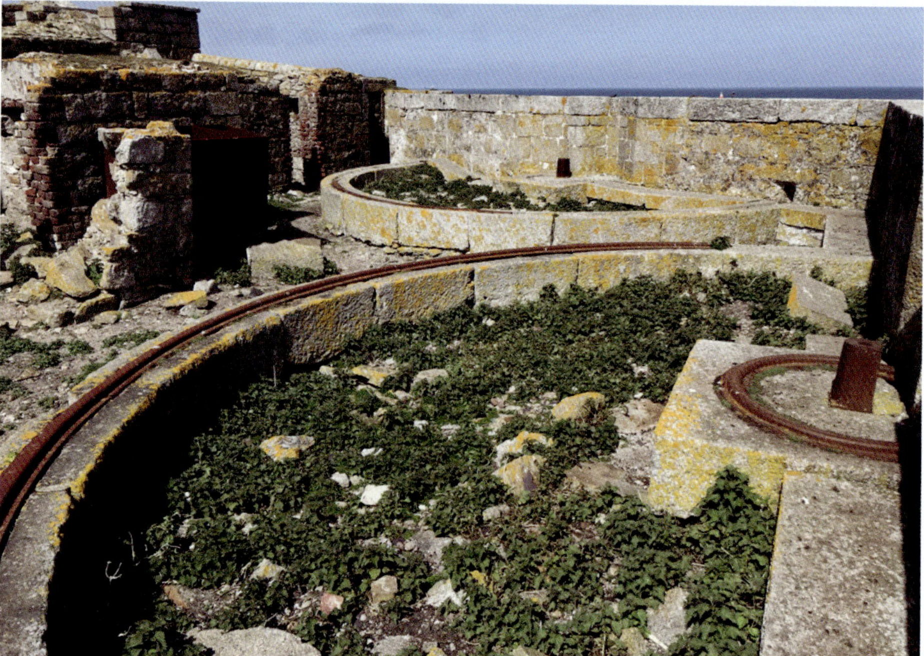

Fig. 1.6—Gun battery, Dalkey Island.

French forces evaporated only ten years after the completion of the network of Martello towers and batteries. Nonetheless, the towers continued to be manned for some time by 'invalid' artillery men; the census recorded a population of eight on the island in 1841, none in 1851 and three in 1861. The battery, where the soldiers lived, was exposed to gales coming in from the Irish Sea, and the cost of maintaining the buildings increased. Once again the island was let out for grazing and the garrison was withdrawn in 1886, one of the last towers to be vacated. The buildings were considered for possible use by the Coast Guard in the 1850s, but instead a decision was made to build a new station at Beacon Hill off Nerano Road, Dalkey, in 1863.[18]

Dalkey Island remained in the ownership of the War Department (which replaced the former Board of Ordnance) after 1886, although public access was permitted. In 1907 Dalkey Urban District Council (UDC) made an offer to the War Department to rent the island as a public park; the Department, however, did not consider the offer sufficient and indicated their intention to advertise the letting of the island to the highest bidder as a yearly tenancy. The island was a popular destination for visitors during the summer, and the UDC was concerned that such visits might be prevented if the island went into private ownership. Discussions with the War Department continued, and in June 1913 the UDC succeeded in buying the island outright for £525. The Commissioners of Irish Lights used the island until 1933 for the storage of explosives.

Dalkey Island today

Although the UDC owned the island from 1913, it was not actually within their administrative area. When their predecessors, the Dalkey Town Commissioners, were established in 1863, their main function was to provide services such as street lighting, water and drainage for the rapidly growing population (see Chapter 12). At that time the sole occupants of the island were a handful of old soldiers, and so it was not included within the boundaries of the new township. Instead, it came within the area of Dublin County Council when that body was created in 1898, and it was not until 1994, with the abolition of the council and its replacement in this area by Dún Laoghaire–Rathdown County Council, that the island was owned and administered by the same body.

The council is charged with protecting the built and natural heritage of the group of islands, including Dalkey Island. The islands are collectively designated as a Special Protection Area under the EU Birds Directive, with a particular focus on conserving the tern population on Maiden Rock. The seals that are often seen basking on the rocks around the islands are also a protected species. The architectural heritage includes St Begnet's church, the Martello tower and the gun battery, while the 'Scurvy Well' is protected as a holy well. The challenge identified in the council's *Dalkey Islands Conservation Plan 2014–2024*[19] is how to balance protecting this multifaceted heritage with facilitating public access, as Dalkey Island is a popular amenity, with regular licensed ferry trips from Coliemore harbour. The sound attracts a variety of boats, and the island waters are popular with divers. For day-trippers, there are superb 360-degree views over Dublin and Killiney bays, as well as towards the mainland, and it is an ideal picnic spot. While the Martello tower is not safe for public access, as the main floor has collapsed, visitors are free to wander inside the remains of both the stone church and the gun battery and to imagine what daily life was like for the 'invalid' garrison who lived in the guardhouse for most of the nineteenth century.

Overall, Dalkey Island offers today's visitors both a sense of tranquillity and a sense of its long history; while three historic structures are clearly visible, other evidence lies buried under the grass at the promontory fort. The island's apparent isolation from the mainland belies the role played by Dalkey Sound as an important landing-place for merchant ships for about 400 years after the Anglo-Norman invasion—but that is a story for the next chapter.

2.
Dalkey *c*. AD 800 to 1800

Origins

The prehistoric peoples who left evidence of their existence on Dalkey Island also settled on the adjoining mainland. While there are Neolithic dolmens in south County Dublin (such as at Ballybrack), none survive near Dalkey. It appears, however, that there had been one on Dalkey Commons until it was destroyed in the early nineteenth century.[1]

There has been some form of settlement based around the modern Castle Street for over a thousand years. Like its namesake on Dalkey Island, the parish church of St Begnet pre-dates the arrival of the Anglo-Normans in 1171. An Early Christian 'tau' cross was carved on the exterior wall.

The first Viking settlement in Dublin was established in the ninth century, and its hinterland (*Dyflinarskiri*) extended as far south as Dalkey. In 1838, workmen at the site of the Queen's Hotel in Castle Street found a hoard of Anglo-Saxon silver

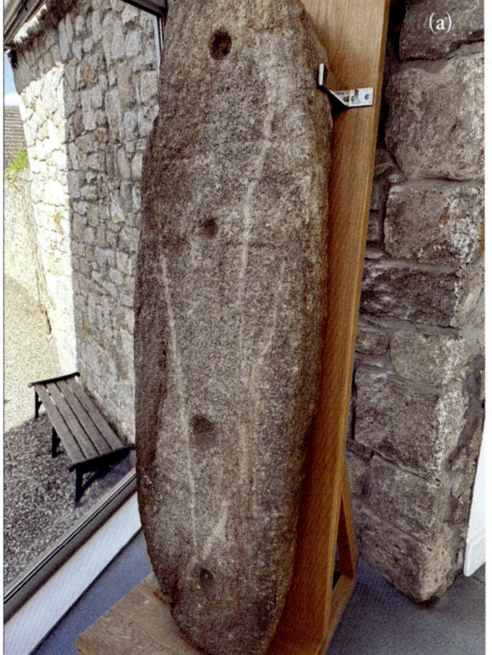

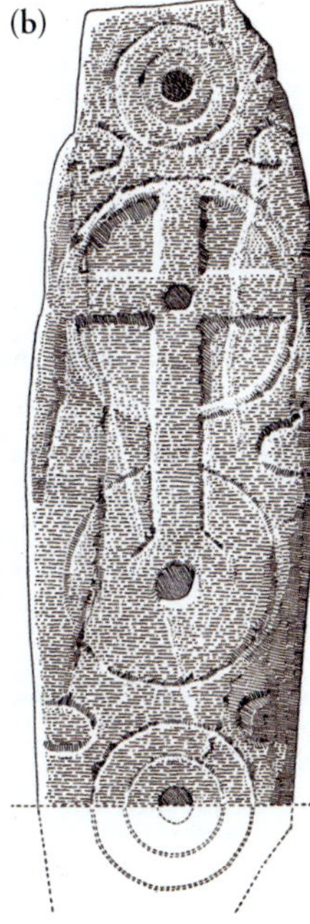

Fig. 2.1—(a) Dalkey Rathdown slab (courtesy of Dalkey Castle Heritage Centre). (b) Drawing from P. Ó hÉailidhe, 'The Rathdown slabs', *Journal of the Royal Society of Antiquaries of Ireland*, vol. 87, no. 1 (1957), p. 83 (courtesy of the Royal Society of Antiquaries of Ireland).

coins, which have been dated to *c.* AD 970; these represented a concession granted by King Eadgar to meet the special requirements of trade between Chester (where some of the coins were minted) and the Ostmen of Dublin, who preferred coins which did not feature the king's portrait.[2] The find suggests that Scandinavian merchants were living in Dalkey by the tenth century, perhaps in a small settlement near St Begnet's church. In the church graveyard there is a cross-inscribed slab, one of ten 'Rathdown slabs' found in south County Dublin (Fig. 2.1). These are often interpreted as marking the graves of Christians of Viking descent.

As shown in the previous chapter, the name 'Dalkey' derives from the Norse *dalk ei* ('thorn or dagger island'), which in turn is a translation of the older Irish *deilg inis.* It is not known how the name of the island came to be associated with a place on the nearby mainland.

St Begnet's parish church

The church, on the north side of Castle Street, is Dalkey's oldest building, with some of the fabric dating back to at least the eleventh century. Parts of the north wall of the church, containing some primitive masonry and a round-headed window, have been identified as pre-dating the Anglo-Norman invasion.[3] The archbishop of Dublin, Laurence O'Toole, laid claim to lands in and around Dalkey, a claim upheld by the pope and Prince John shortly after the invasion; subsequent archbishops appear to have sublet both the church and some adjoining lands to the priory of Holy Trinity (later Christ Church cathedral). The Anglo-Normans often adopted Gaelic churches as their parish churches, enlarging them to meet the needs of the growing population. St Begnet's church consisted of a substantial thirteenth-century nave and a later chancel. The affluence of Dalkey's mercantile families in the sixteenth century is reflected in the elegant stone window inserted into the eastern end of the chancel.[4] St Begnet's served as the parish church until the early seventeenth century; the chaplain, appointed by the prior of Holy Trinity up to the Reformation, lived nearby.

Anglo-Norman Dalkey

In the century or so after the invasion, Dalkey (and Dalkey Island) formed part of the archbishop of Dublin's manor of Shankill. Although Shankill itself came under attack from the native Irish tribes on the border of the Pale in the early fourteenth century, the settlement at Dalkey began to prosper and grow, owing in part to its role as an outport for Dublin (see below). A survey or 'extent' of the archbishop's lands in 1326 showed that there were thirty-nine burgage holdings in Dalkey, although in troubled times it was difficult to collect the rent due from the tenants.[5]

Not all of the land in Dalkey was owned by the archbishop; for example, a prominent Dublin merchant family called the Stakebols[6] also owned a plot near the 'royal road' (probably Castle Street).

The Anglo-Normans introduced a new type of agriculture, based on long, rectangular open fields. Burgesses would have owned a house facing the single street (now called Castle Street) and a patchwork of arable fields, with grazing on the common land to the east of the village. This field pattern persisted in Dalkey until the late eighteenth century, as can be seen on Reading's map of 1765 (see Chapter 6). Fishermen and farm labourers would have had small houses scattered among the fields; fishing was an important part of the local economy from the outset. Castle Street widens into a rough triangle at the eastern end; this may have been the site of the medieval market-place.[7] The right to hold an annual fair was transferred from the archbishop's failed settlement near Powerscourt, Co. Wicklow, to Dalkey in 1482.

The total population in the Middle Ages would have been a few hundred, with the Black Death causing substantial mortality in the fourteenth century.

The medieval port of Dalkey

There were two ports near medieval Dalkey, at Dalkey Sound and Bullock, which differed in their characteristics, ownership and functions. The word 'port' did not imply the presence of stone piers such as we see today; rather it was a place where ships could anchor safely while goods or passengers were brought ashore and new cargoes loaded.

While the port of Dalkey was sometimes referred to as the archbishop's port, the small and tidal creek at Bullock was controlled by the Cistercian abbey of St Mary in Dublin; it was mainly a fishing port, but sometimes officials from England landed there on their way to Dublin Castle (see Chapter 13). Dalkey Sound, about 0.5km to the south-east of the town, provided a deep-water anchorage in the lee of Dalkey Island, and served as an outport of Dublin for over three centuries because of a sand bar in the Liffey estuary. 'The port of Dalkey' was referred to in official documents as early as 1244 without specifying its exact site. In all probability this would have been at Coliemore, a small cove at the lowest point of the rocky shoreline and almost directly opposite the landing-place on the island. The present alignment of Coliemore Road mirrors the likely route from the port to Dalkey.

A court case in 1304–5 heard that 'no large ships laden with wine or other merchandise can touch at the port of Dublin until they are partly discharged whereby, according to a custom which has hitherto prevailed, ships laden with wine were wont to touch at Dalkey and there partly discharge, and the wines so discharged were wont to be conveyed to the city of Dublin in small barks without payment of prisage [tax]'.[8] In response to a 1358 petition, the king granted the merchants of Dublin licence to buy and sell in Dalkey. The petition referred to 'the archbishop's harbour of Dalkey', while in 1419 the king granted that the archbishop's bailiff of Dalkey 'may exercise on the manor and its port all that pertains to the office of Admiral and Water-Bailiff and receive the fees and profits'.[9]

Dalkey on the edge of the Pale
Although the mainly English settlers who established the medieval village of Dalkey were the dominant force in the area, they came under growing threat of attack from the native Irish in the nearby Wicklow hills from the fourteenth century onwards. Dalkey was at the edge of the area known as the Pale which the colonists controlled. It is likely that the settlement had some defences of its own; it has been suggested that an earthen bank was created to the south of Castle Street, on the field boundary to the rear of Melrose and Tudor House running from Dalkey Avenue to Cunning-ham Road.[10] The Pale itself consisted of a series of fortifications such as Carrickmines Castle (owned by the Walsh family, who also held property in Dalkey) and a series of earthen banks and ditches, whose location may have altered over time in response to changing political circumstances. In 1488 an act of the parliament in Drogheda defined the borders of 'the four obedient shires' constituting the Pale (Dublin, Meath, Kildare and Louth) as follows:

> 'From Merrion … by the new ditch to Saggart … thence to the county of Kildare … in such manner that the towns of Dalkey, Carrickbrennan … and Bullock, were in the Dublin shire'.[11]

Dalkey's trade extended as far as Spain in the fifteenth century, the goods landed being sold to Dublin merchants. A reference in 1463 to the highway between the ports of Dublin and Dalkey reflected the growing volume of vehicular traffic. Dalkey's prosperity diminished, however, as its role as an outport ended towards the end of the sixteenth century, when larger ships bound for Dublin berthed in the Liffey estuary at Ringsend rather than in Dalkey Sound.

Dalkey 1600–1800
When Dalkey Sound ceased to act as an outport for Dublin by around 1600, the village lost its main trading *raison d'être*, and its seven castles were no longer required for the storage of goods in transit. Moreover, the impact of the Reformation meant that parish tithes were withheld by Catholic landowners such as Henry Walsh, who

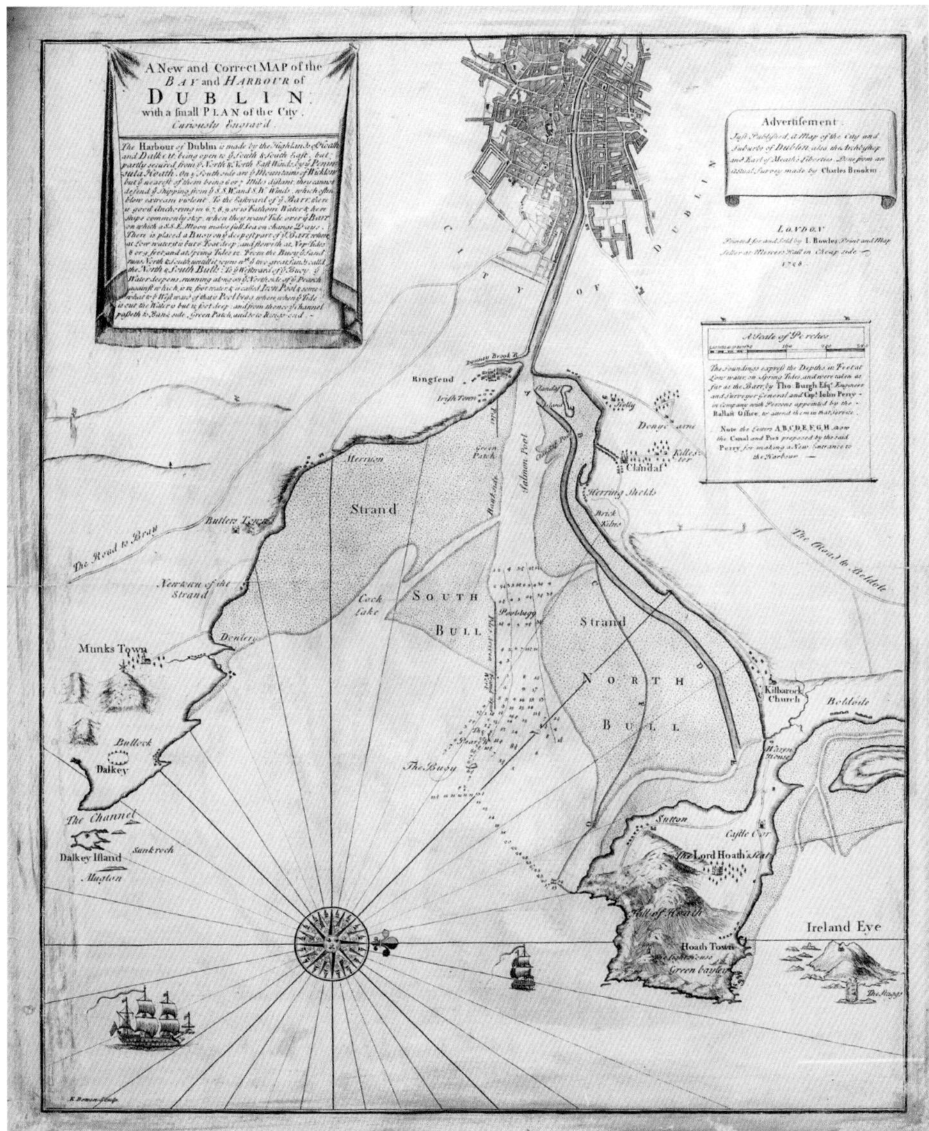

Fig. 2.2—Chart of Dublin Bay by J. Bowles, 1728 (courtesy of Dublin Port Archive).

instead permitted Mass to be said in their houses and castles. A visitation by the Protestant Archbishop Bulkeley in 1630 found that St Begnet's parish church was ruinous and that 'the chancel has no roof … William Morris Lloyd, curate, is allowed but £3 per annum for serving the cure. There is not one that comes to church but the said curate's family, saving that in fishing time there are many English and Scots

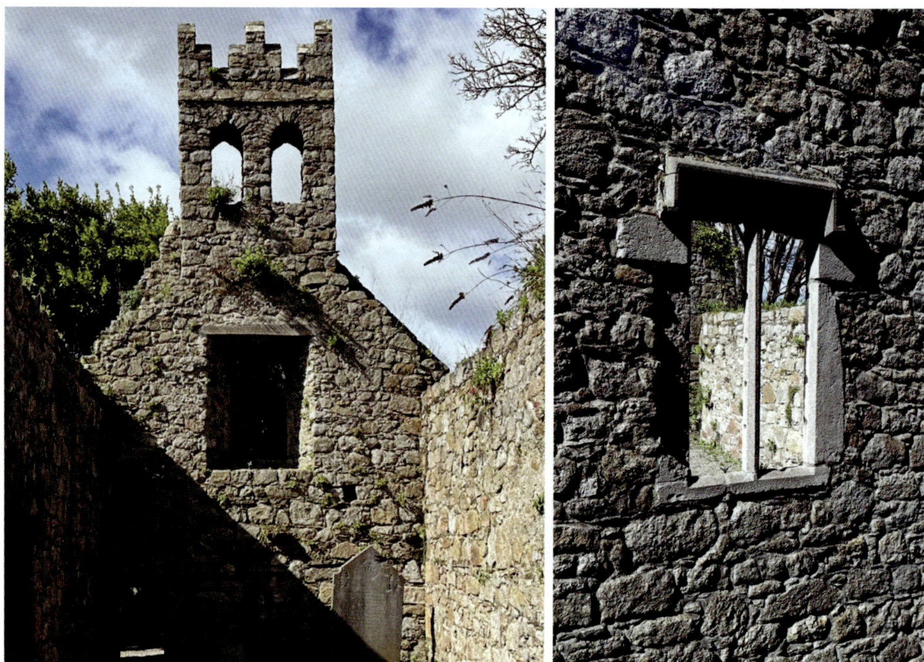

Fig. 2.3—St Begnet's church, Castle Street.

that come to morning and evening prayers.'[12] The church has remained unroofed since then (Fig. 2.3), although burials continued to take place in the adjoining graveyard until the nineteenth century, when it was officially closed.

In the absence of any accurate or comprehensive census, it is difficult to estimate the population of Dalkey in the mid-seventeenth century. Following the Cromwellian invasion, Captain Richard Newcomen was the main landowner in the area; a list of his tenants in 1650 recorded a total of 84 persons, excluding children under the age of 12. All but two of the heads of household were described as 'husbandman', suggesting rural occupations; the other two were described as 'gent'. Most of the surnames were Irish, such as Byrne, Walsh, Doyle and Standon. However, the so-called 'census' of 1659 recorded a total of 44 households, all but three being described as 'Irish'; using an average of three persons per household, the total population in the village and surrounding farmlands would have been about 130.[13]

It is quite likely that many members of the farming population around Dalkey spoke Irish, as some of the field names reflected Irish-language origins. Thomas Reading surveyed landowners and tenants in 1765 and listed field names such as Parkmore ('the big field') and Farranahaslanivee (*Fearann a chaisleán bhuídhe*, 'ground of the

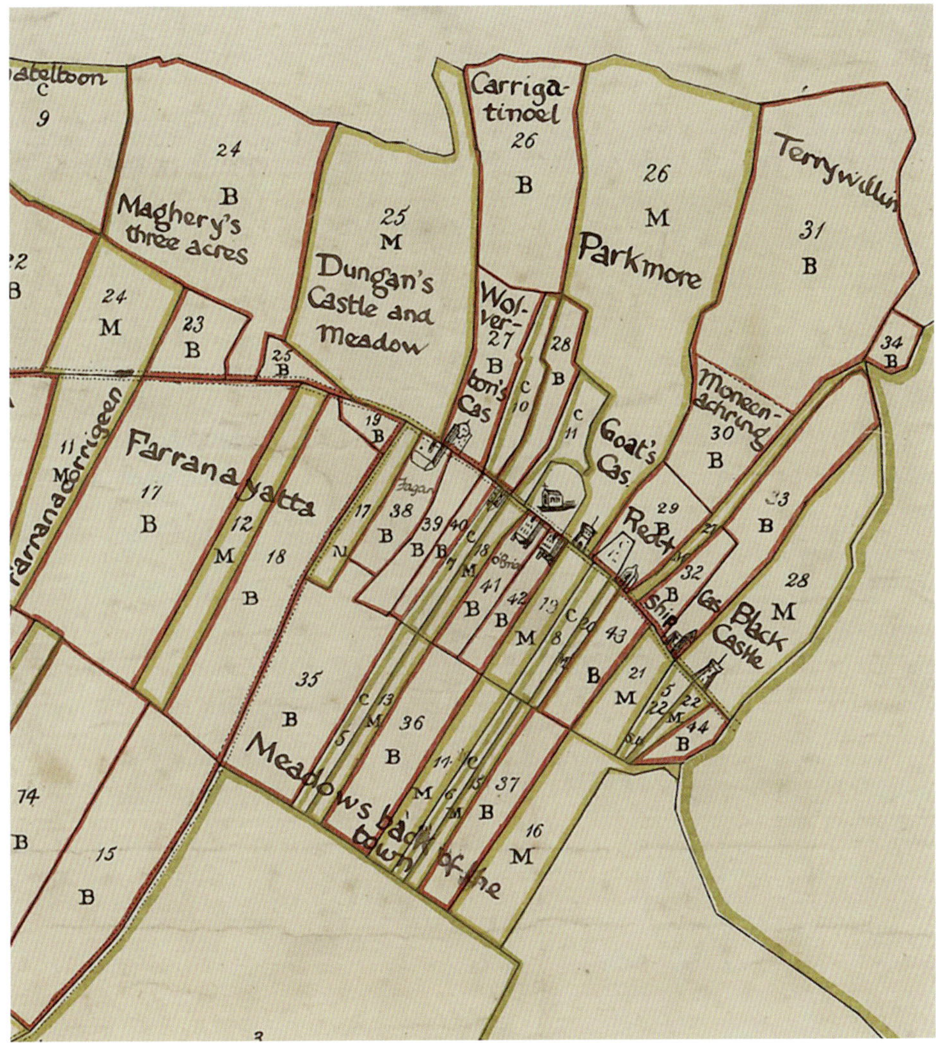

Fig. 2.4—Reading's map of Dalkey, 1765 (courtesy of the Royal Society of Antiquaries of Ireland).

yellow castle'); the strip field patterns themselves dated from the medieval era (Fig. 2.4).

Reading also showed two inns on the north side of Castle Street: the Red Cross Inn near the present Queen's Hotel and the Ship Inn a little further to the east. Castle Street itself was unnamed, but Barnhill Road was shown as Dublin Road and Dalkey Avenue as the road from Rochestown to Dalkey. At the rear of the Ship Inn stood a cotton factory belonging to a Mr Costelloe, one of the earliest in Ireland. Little is known about it other than that it burned down in 1781.[14]

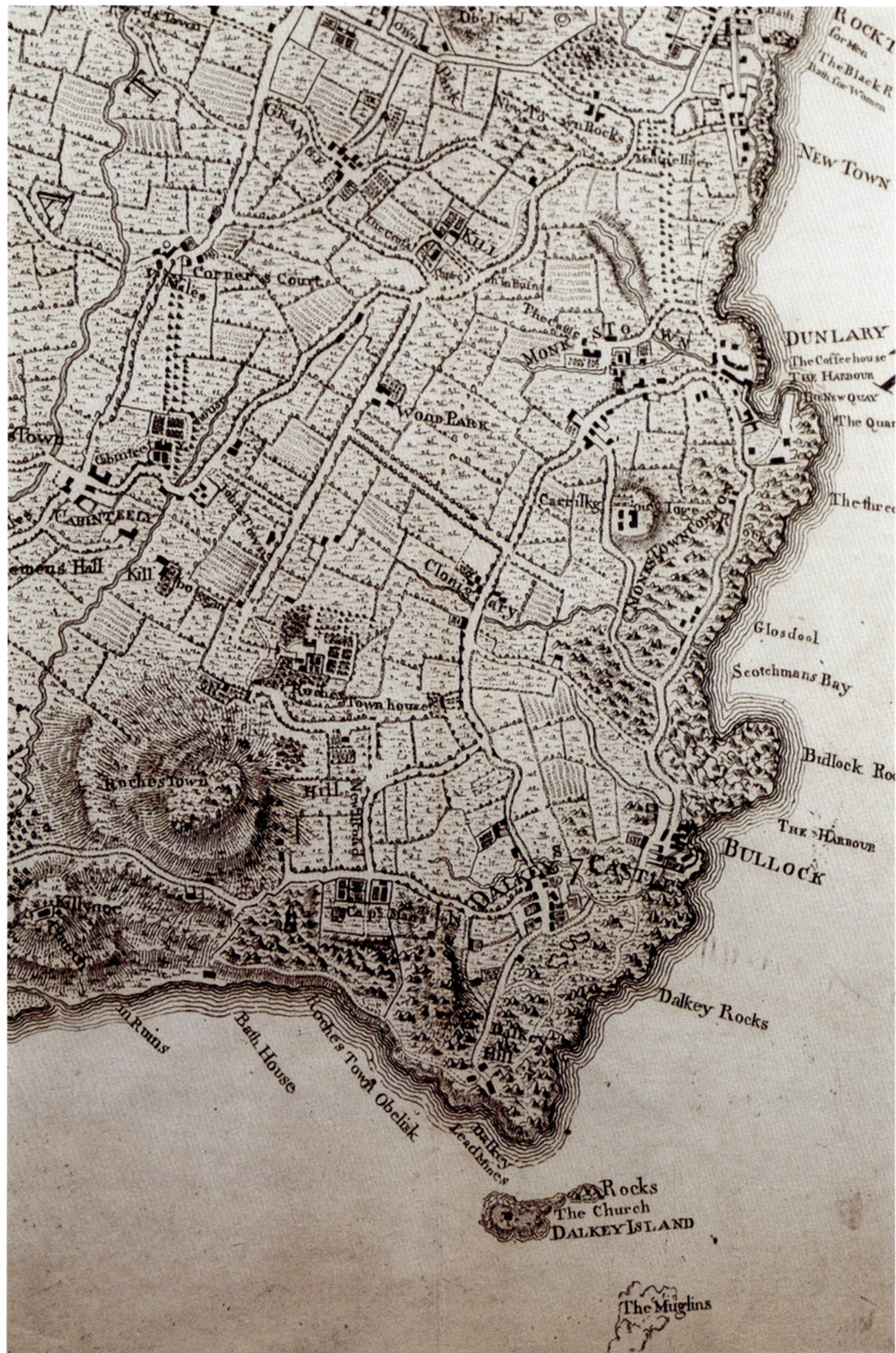

Fig. 2.5—Extract from Rocque's map of County Dublin, 1760 (courtesy of the Royal Irish Academy).

A combination of contemporary sources—Reading's survey map of 1765, Beranger's drawings of three of the castles in 1766 and a long descriptive letter by Peter Wilson in 1768—facilitates a reasonably clear picture of what Dalkey looked like in the 1760s. According to Wilson, Dalkey consisted of

> 'the venerable remains of some old castles, the ruins of an ancient church, some good dwelling houses, and about twenty cabins, for the most part occupied by poor labouring people … At the east end of the town, adjoining the common, is a summer lodge belonging to Robert Barry. This house, being partly ancient and partly modern … has a pleasing view to the sea at the rear and a garden laid out with skill and taste. Opposite the church, and near the centre of the town, is Dalkey House [which] looks directly into the churchyard. The garden is well-furnished with fruit trees, etc. … Adjoining the town, on the east side, is a large common [where] the poorer inhabitants of the town graze their cattle.'[15]

Dalkey seems to have descended into a state of torpor until the middle of the eighteenth century, when new signs of life began to appear. Lead-mines are shown on the shore just west of Sorrento Point on Rocque's map of County Dublin in 1760 (Fig. 2.5), although John Barrett, a geologist, suggested a location further west, at White Rock on Killiney beach.[16] However, whether as a result of an inadequate seam of ore or the difficulty of mining the lead at such a location, the enterprise failed within a few years and the mines were put up for sale in 1774, with twenty years of the lease unexpired.[17] Rocque's map indicates that some kind of road or track existed between Dalkey and the lead-mines; it is likely that the present Sorrento Road followed that alignment when developed for housing in the nineteenth century.

In the second half of the century Dalkey began to attract wealthy residents from Dublin. Peter Wilson was a bookseller who rented Dalkey Lodge on Barnhill Road (still extant) as a summer home in the late 1760s. Sir John Hasler, a senior official in Dublin Castle, lived in a large house on Castle Street, where he entertained his friends; Castle House became Rockview Lodge in the 1820s and the Queen's Hotel in the 1830s. This trend accelerated in the first half of the nineteenth century, led initially by the professional and mercantile élite of the city but followed shortly afterwards by the middle classes, who could commute to work by train. Dalkey Commons, a largely empty and rocky space on Reading's map in 1765, was transformed a century later into a dense maze of expensive villas and elegant terraces.

3.
Bullock to 1800

The medieval era

Church authorities in medieval Ireland, including archbishops and monasteries, accumulated large landholdings as a result of donations by local kings and princes, both Irish and Anglo-Norman. The manor of Blowike (Bullock) was part of an extensive estate held by the Cistercian abbey of St Mary in Dublin pre-dating the Anglo-Norman invasion of 1169, although the first written record of the place-name dates from 1345. The monks exercised the right to claim tolls on all fish landed at Bullock harbour; they built a castle overlooking it, in which they offered hospitality to important English visitors *en route* to Dublin.

The earliest known image of both castle and harbour is a pen-and-wash drawing made by Francis Place in 1698 (Fig. 3.1). As fish had been landed at Bullock since

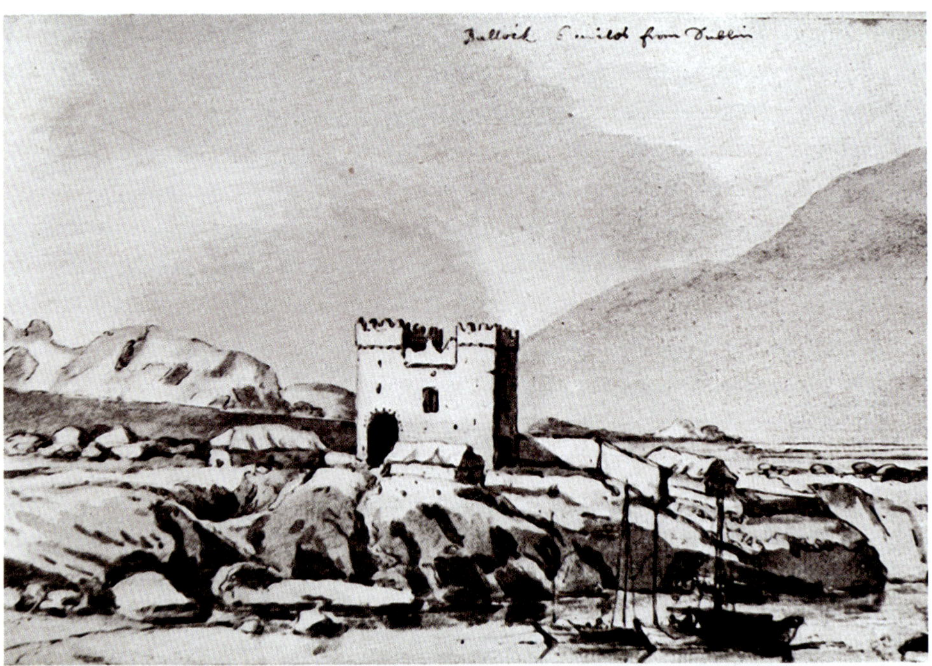

Fig. 3.1—Bullock Castle as drawn by Francis Place, 1698 (courtesy of the Royal Society of Antiquaries of Ireland).

at least the fourteenth century, it is probable that there were crude stone piers in the lee of the large granite outcrop, which would have given some shelter from easterly gales. On the other hand, the harbour is tidal, and Bullock could not compete with Dalkey Sound in terms of mercantile shipping. It is interesting to note that the distinctive battlemented profile of the castle, as illustrated by Place, existed as early as the late seventeenth century, although the earlier Norman structure is likely to have been simpler. A small fishing village developed around the castle and the harbour. Bullock was also noted for its pilots, who guided ships into Dublin port, a tradition which continued into the nineteenth century.

Bullock from 1600 to 1800

St Mary's Abbey was dissolved by Henry VIII in 1540, and its lands were seized by the Crown. At the time of the dissolution, the abbey's lands at Bullock amounted to 60 arable acres.[1] The castle and lands were assigned first to the Talbots of Fassaroe, Co. Wicklow, and then to the Fagans of Feltrim, north Co. Dublin, in the early seventeenth century. In 1611 John Fagan obtained a royal patent for the town and lands of Bullock, comprising one castle, one ruinous tower, thirty messuages (possibly cottage plots), 10 acres of meadow and 200 acres of pasture and furze, with the fishing and harbour.[2]

The Fagans, a family of Catholic merchants, took part in the 1641 rebellion against the Crown. Bullock Castle was captured by Crown forces and some of the local inhabitants were put to death. The English garrison consisted of seven officers and sixty men, and in 1644 the defences of the castle were strengthened by the construction of a rampart, furnished with three cannons, and the erection of a guardhouse.[3] The Fagans regained their property at Bullock following the restoration of Charles II in 1660.

Various contemporary records from the mid-seventeenth century give us a rough picture of what Bullock was like at that time, and its approximate size. The Civil Survey of 1654 stated that Christopher Fagan of Feltrim, an Irish papist, owned 90 acres at Bullock, of which 60 were arable; the castle was slated and had a bawn (walled grounds), while the buildings were valued at £100.[4] The Down Survey of 1656–8 reported that 'there stands in Bullocke a fair ancient town and fishing'; Christopher Fagan of Feltrim was recorded as owner of 123 arable acres. According to the so-called 'census' of 1659, Bullock had 110 households, of which ninety-five were Irish and fifteen English; by comparison, neighbouring Dalkey had only forty-four households, of which forty-one were Irish.[5] At that time Bullock formed part of Monkstown parish (Dalkey was a separate parish); the parish records show that there were thirteen households in Dalkey in 1664 and seventeen households in Bullock, while in 1666–7 there were ten households in Dalkey and thirty-nine in Bullock, including that of John Desmineer, who was mayor of Dublin in 1666–7.[6] These figures should not be treated as exact statistics, but they do indicate that around that time Bullock was a larger settlement than Dalkey.

Christopher Fagan died in 1683 and was succeeded by his son, Richard Fagan, who was attainted for treason after the Revolution of 1688; all his property, including Bullock, was confiscated. Bullock and its lands were purchased from the Crown for £1,750 by Colonel John Allen of Stillorgan around 1703. His father, Joshua Allen, had been sheriff, alderman and lord mayor of Dublin, and was knighted. Joshua died in 1691 and was survived by five of his fifteen children, including John, his heir. Colonel Allen was later ennobled as Baron Allen of Stillorgan. A daughter of the second Baron Allen married Sir John Proby, who became the first Baron Carysfort, hence the Carysfort estate included the lands at Bullock.

Beranger's images of Bullock Castle around 1766 (Fig. 3.2a and b) show that the

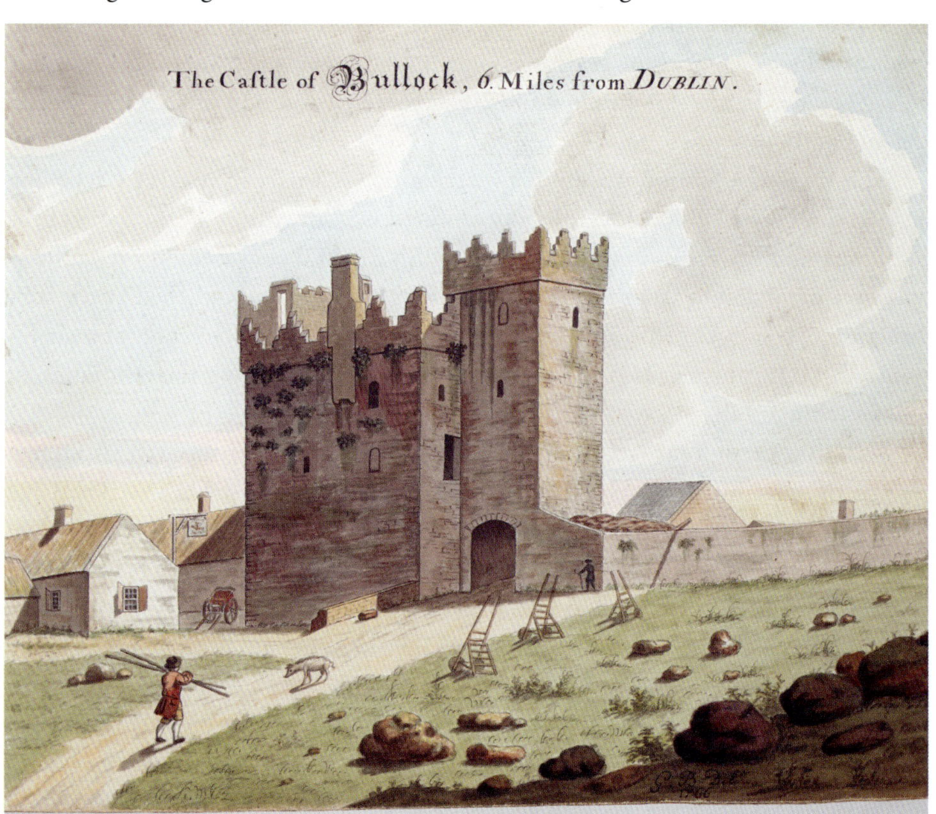

Fig. 3.2a—Bullock Castle by Gabriel Beranger, *c.* 1766 (courtesy of the National Library of Ireland).

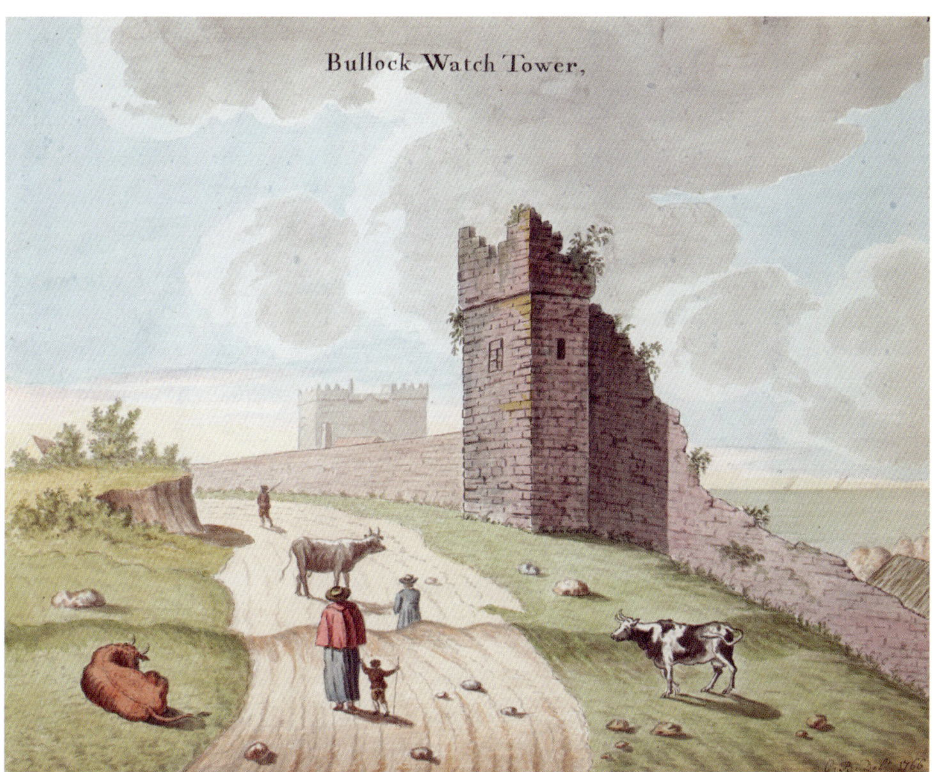

Fig. 3.2b—Bullock watch-tower by Gabriel Beranger, *c.* 1766 (courtesy of the National Library of Ireland).

structure was in good repair at that time, with a cluster of small buildings around it. The castle battlements are clearly defined. The castle bawn was enclosed by a stone wall, seen also on the image of the watch-tower. It is not clear whether the latter was the 'ruinous tower' referred to in John Fagan's patent of 1611. The track shown outside the wall roughly matches the current line of Ulverton Road.

Serres's painting of about twenty years later (Fig. 3.3) shows a substantial three-storey house attached to Bullock Castle, in addition to the other outbuildings. The large house was built by John Watson and remained in residential use until the late twentieth century. The watch-tower can also be seen in the background, although its condition deteriorated further in the nineteenth century and it was demolished around 1880. Serres depicted some houses adjoining the harbour, which was crowded with fishing vessels. A stone pier can be seen on the right-hand side of the harbour entrance. Writing in 1768, Peter Wilson described Bullock harbour:

'A new quay, faced with hewn stone, has lately been built for conveying stone to the lighthouse works. The rest of the town consists of the very small remains

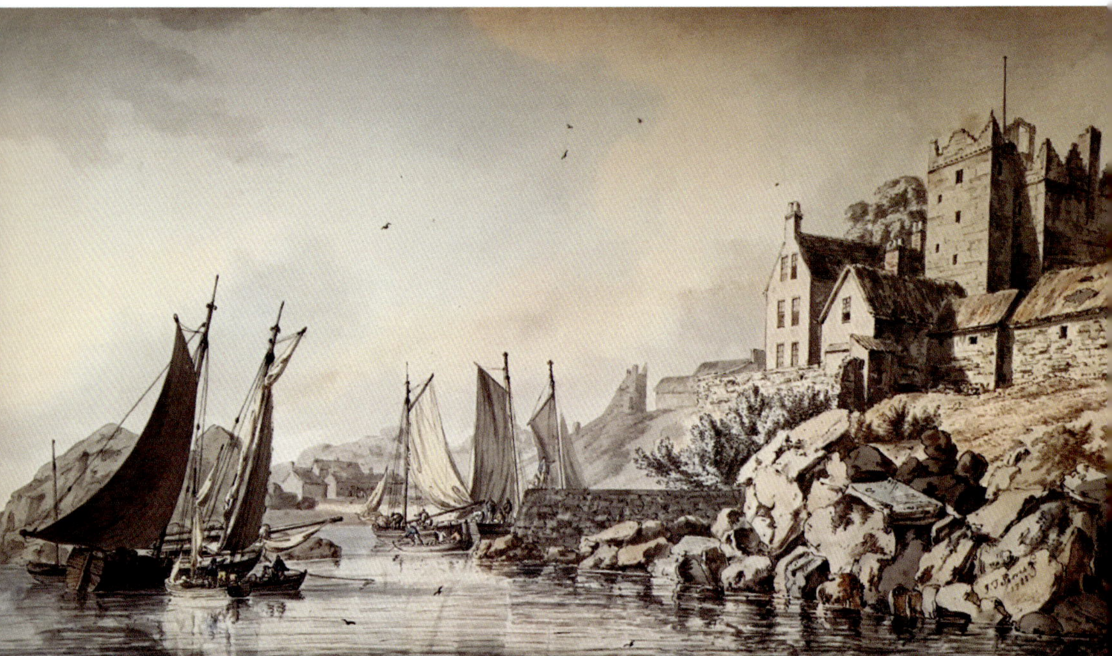

Fig. 3.3—*Bullock Castle and Harbour,* 1788, by John Thomas Serres (1759–1825), ink and watercolour, NGI 19216 (courtesy of the National Gallery of Ireland).

of an old church and a number of cabins, mainly inhabited by fishermen.'[7]

The 'lighthouse' refers to the newly built structure at Poolbeg; the granite stone came from local quarries, which became more important in the following century. It is not known where the ruins of the old church were, although, according to Ball, in 1658 Revd Nathaniel Hoyle, a fellow of Trinity College, was paid £100 a year by the parliament for acting as minister of Bullock.[8]

Towards the end of the eighteenth century, Lord Newhaven, who had married Frances Allen, co-heir of the Allen estate with her sister Elizabeth, began advertising building land for sale around Bullock. A notice in *Saunders's News-Letter* in February 1793 read:

'To be let for building leases, the town and lands of Bullock, also the castle of Bullock. The lands are laid out in convenient lots for building; the situation for bathing lodges, and also the rocks of stone in great demand for public works, are well known. Apply to Lord Newhaven.'

While the castle continued to be let, there was no great demand yet for building land in the area, and when Lady Newhaven died childless in 1801 ownership of Bullock passed back to her sister's family. In 1750 Elizabeth Allen had married John Proby, who was raised to an Irish barony of Carysfort in that year; their son was created Earl of Carysfort in 1789. The Proby/Carysfort lands around Bullock were gradually developed as the nineteenth century progressed.

Bullock since 1800

The name 'Bullock' is associated today with just the small harbour and the adjoining castle, but at the end of the eighteenth century and the beginning of the nineteenth the 'Lands of Bullock' were much more extensive. Reading's map of 1765 shows those lands covering large tracts to the north and west of Dalkey, somewhat similar in extent to the modern townland of Bullock, which has an area of 142ha. Another reflection of the past is that Bullock townland is in Monkstown civil parish, whereas the townlands of Dalkey and Dalkey Commons are in Dalkey civil parish. Towards the middle of the nineteenth century, however, there was a boom in housing development in Dalkey which encompassed Bullock; when Dalkey township was established in 1863, the coastline near Bullock harbour formed its northern boundary, and its western boundary ran along Castlepark Road. Since then, Bullock (or at least that part east of Castlepark Road) has been an integral part of Dalkey.

Taylor's map (Fig. 3.4) shows the very limited extent of development around Bullock in 1816, clustered in the vicinity of the castle. It also shows that, prior to the construction of Ulverton Road in the 1840s, the only link with Dalkey village was via Castlepark Road and Barnhill Road/Castle Street; Harbour Road only extended as far as Bullock harbour, while a track led to Castle Street. The map includes the Martello tower near 'Bartra', but the origin of the tower shown to the north-east of the village is not known; it is unlikely that Taylor would have surveyed all of the environs of Dublin depicted on his map, particularly as cartographers at that time were known to have copied features from their predecessors.

Greig's engraving (Fig. 3.5) shows how the harbour and the new road from Breffni Road appeared in 1820, together with the three-storey house attached to Bullock Castle. William Hutchison, who was appointed harbour-master and inspector of the quarries at Bullock in 1817, may have lived in the house for some time before he moved later in his career to the harbour-master's house in Kingstown in the 1840s.

Ten families lived in the pilots' cottages,[9] while another four lived in Perrin's cottages on the other side of Harbour Road, near the foot of the present steps beside Our Lady's Manor. The cottages were built by Alderman Arthur Perrin, owner of local quarries and a large mansion at Castle Park. John Golden ran a public house in

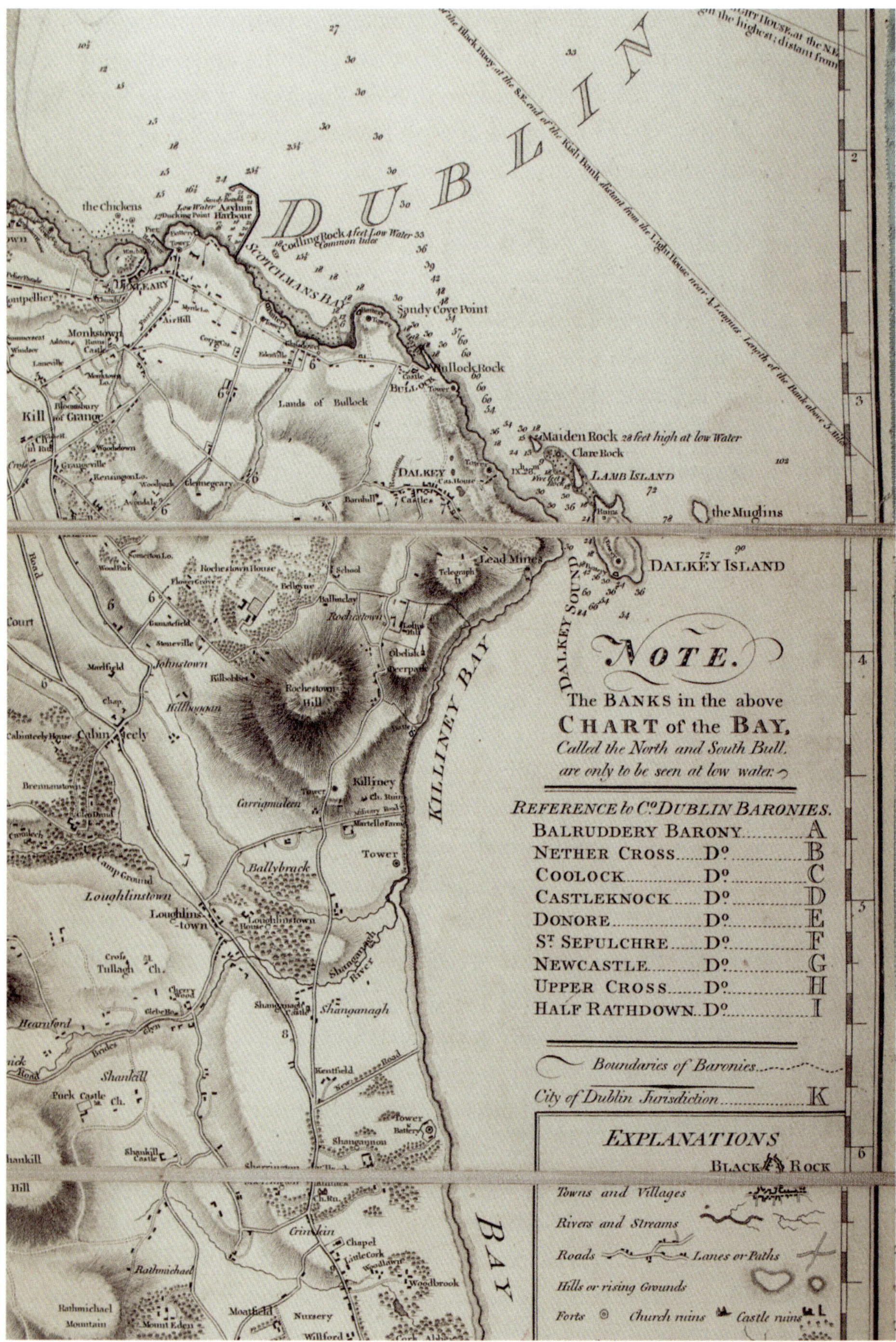

Fig. 3.4—Extract from Taylor's map of the environs of Dublin, 1816 (courtesy of the Royal Irish Academy).

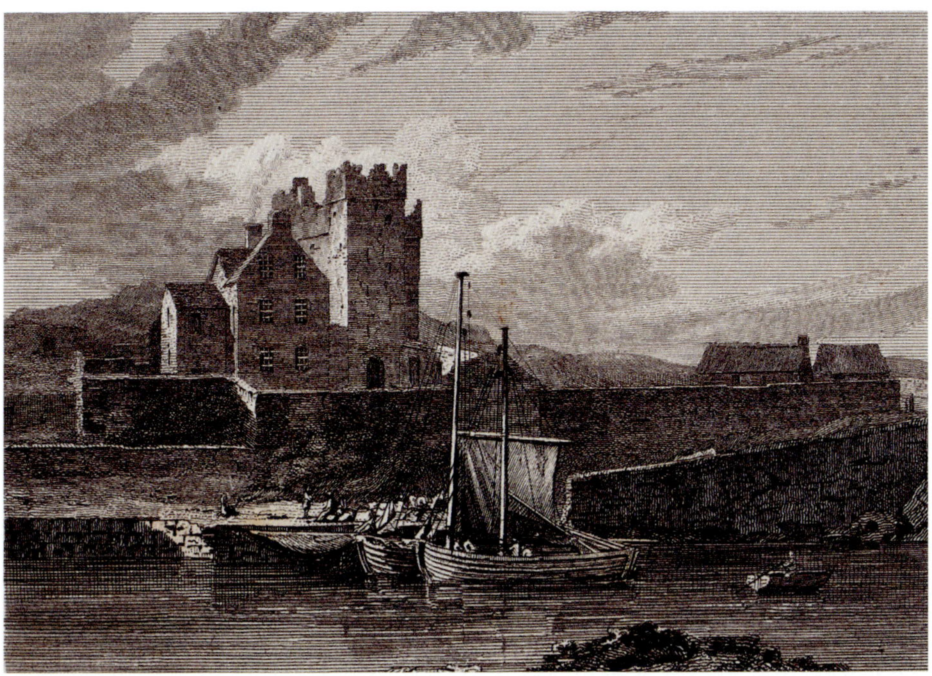

Fig. 3.5—Engraving of Bullock Castle by J. Greig, 1820 (courtesy of the National Library of Ireland).

one of the cottages around the 1840s and 1850s.[10]

Harbour Road was known as the Ballast Office Road in the early 1800s, as it was essentially a private road leading to granite quarries in the locality and to the Martello tower built in 1804. The road was originally gated at the eastern end, but the Ballast Office leased sites for large private houses such as Beulah and Bartra and donated a site for the Anglican church. Ulverton Road, linking Breffni Road with Castle Street in Dalkey, was opened around 1844, thus facilitating the development of housing lands between Harbour Road and the village. Ulverton Road was also a tram route between 1879 and 1949, with extra horses being required to pull trams up the steep hill near Bullock Castle prior to electrification of the route in 1896. The 'turret' on Ulverton Road was demolished in the late nineteenth century and was replaced first by terraced housing and then by Our Lady's Manor nursing home, which was developed in the 1960s; subsequent expansion led to the demolition of the eighteenth-century house beside the medieval castle the early 1980s.

4.
Dalkey's seven castles

Dalkey's seven 'castles' probably date from the fifteenth or early sixteenth century, when Dalkey Sound was in its heyday as the outport of Dublin. Because the sand bar at the mouth of the Liffey prevented heavily laden ships from entering Dublin port, it became the practice to offload some of the cargo at Dalkey and to bring it by cart or barge to the city. Dublin merchants are likely to have built many of the fortified town houses along the single street in the village, later known as Castle Street. These three- to four-storey towers, built of local granite, were used to store the goods in safety, as Dalkey was on the frontier of the Pale and at risk of attack from Irish 'rebels'. It is probable that the Walsh family, who had a similar castle at Carrickmines, Co. Dublin, owned two of the Dalkey castles. It is unlikely that the original castles were used for habitation, although some were adapted as living quarters in the eighteenth century.

When Dalkey port's fortunes declined by around 1600, however, the need for the castles also disappeared, and by 1627 at least one of them was ruinous. The Down Survey found that only one of the seven castles was habitable by 1656–8.[1] There are numerous references to the castles in property deeds of the sixteenth and seventeenth centuries but, frustratingly for historians, these deeds frequently merely mention a castle or castles in Dalkey without being more specific. One exception, as will be seen below, was Dungan's Castle, on the western side of the village.

While eighteenth-century maps of County Dublin and Dublin Bay tended to refer to Dalkey's seven castles (Fig. 4.1), or even to depict them in an oval ring, in reality they were beginning to disappear, so that only three remained by the 1830s: Goat Castle, Archbold's Castle and Wolverton Castle, which itself was demolished by around 1840, leaving just two standing today. The main street began to be called Castle Street around the 1840s.

The history of each castle is outlined below, starting with Dungan's Castle on the north side of the street and ending with the 'lost' seventh castle on the south side.

Dungan's (or Dongan's) Castle
In 1662 William Dongan (later Earl of Limerick) was granted 7 arable acres, two

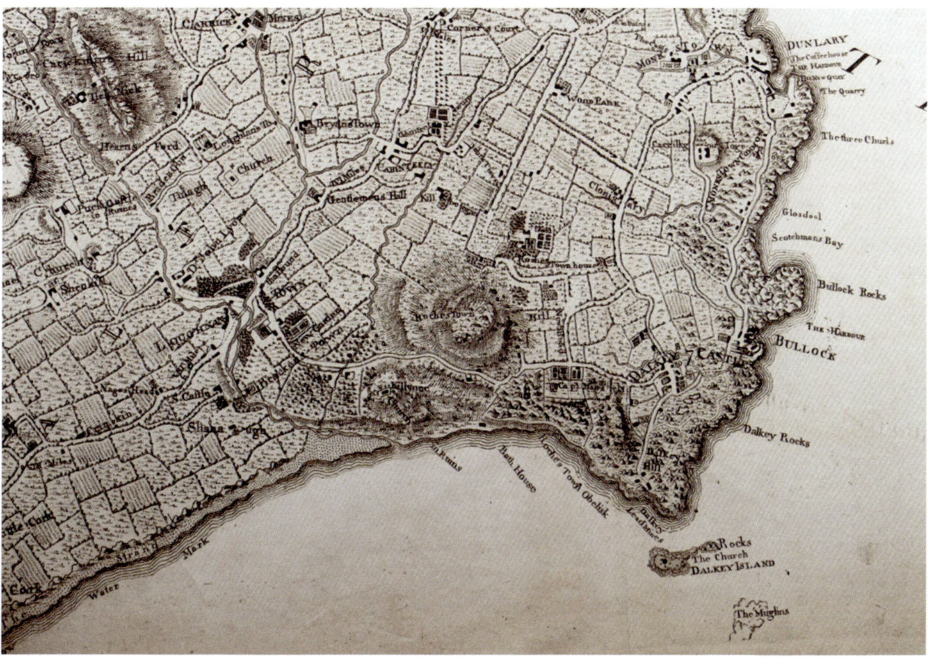

Fig. 4.1—Extract from Rocque's map of County Dublin, 1760, referring to the seven castles (courtesy of the Royal Irish Academy).

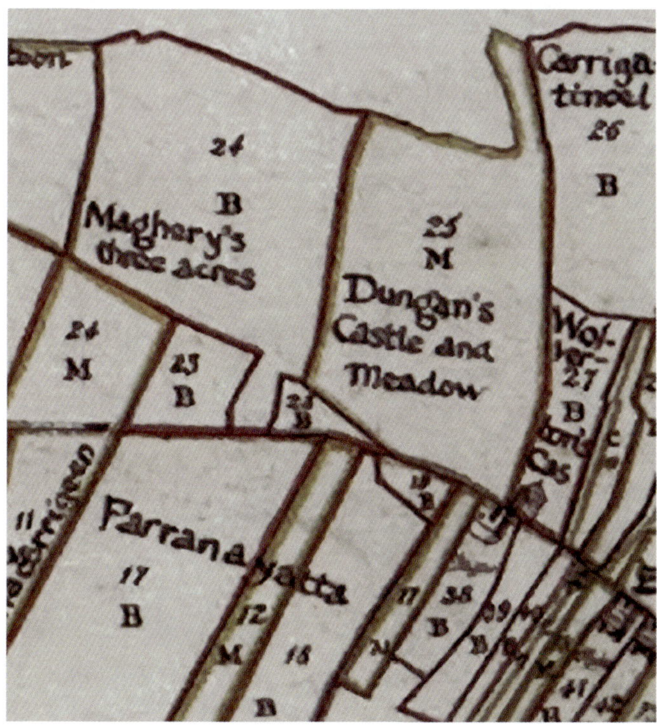

Fig. 4.2—Extract from Reading's map of Dalkey, 1765 (courtesy of the Royal Society of Antiquaries of Ireland).

castles, six houses with gardens and 74 acres of meadow, pasture and common in the town and fields of Dalkey.[2] The first castle (Dungan's) was on the north side of Barnhill Road, while the second is likely to have been Archbold's Castle on the south side of Castle Street (see below). Dungan's Castle and meadow were named on Thomas Reading's map of property holdings in Dalkey in 1765 (Fig. 4.2).

The exact site of the castle—which may not have survived in 1765—was probably opposite Kent Terrace, facing the junction with Dalkey Avenue. Dungan's Castle and the seventh castle, located on the south side of Castle Street (see below), are likely to have formed the 'west gate' in medieval Dalkey.[3] Dungan's meadow was then owned by Sir William Mayne, who married into the Allen family, later ennobled as the Earls of Carysfort. The site was built over by the time of the first draft of the 6in. Ordnance Survey map in 1837.

Wolverton Castle

In 1611 Patrick Barnewall held from the see of Dublin a ruined castle, which was acquired by William Wolverston (d. 1644). Francis Wolverston, who died in Dalkey in 1681, was probably the last of his family to live there.[4] The castle passed through various hands; by 1765 it was owned by William Bull, having been mortgaged by Thomas Archbold. According to Reading's map of that year (Fig. 4.2), Wolverton Castle was located at the present junction of Ulverton Road (the name is a corruption of Wolverton) and Castle Street, and it can also be seen to the west of the ruins of St

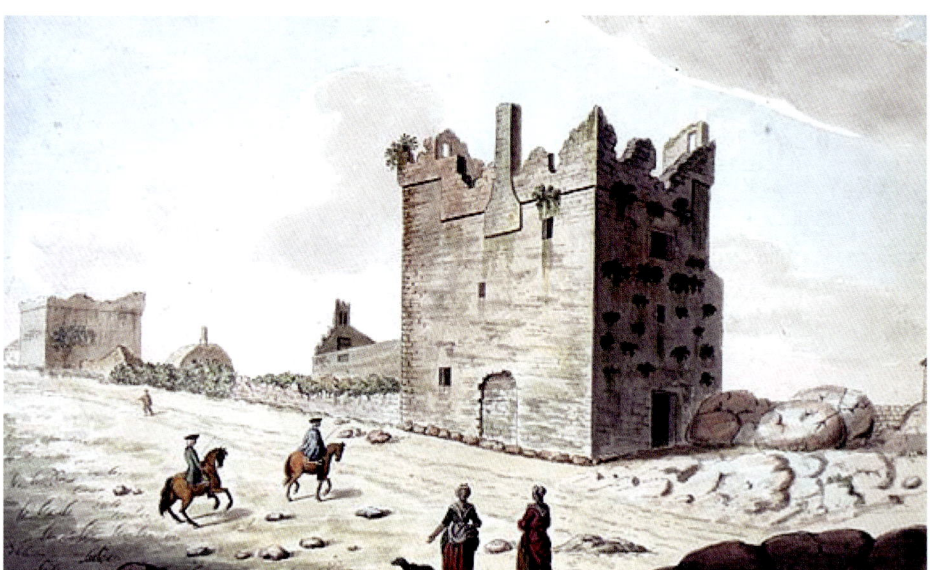

Fig. 4.3—Wolverton Castle is depicted on the left of Beranger's drawing, 1766 (courtesy of the National Library of Ireland).

Begnet's church in a drawing made by Gabriel Beranger in the mid-eighteenth century (Fig. 4.3).

Wolverton Castle was used as a forge in the early nineteenth century.[5] Gaskin, writing in 1869, claimed that it had been taken down by W.E. Porter senior,[6] probably prior to the construction of Ulverton Road around 1844. The first-edition Ordnance Survey map in 1843 merely records the site of a castle. Local legend has it that stones from the castle were acquired by Dr James Parkinson, a Dublin surgeon, for use in the construction of Tudor House on the opposite side of Castle Street later in the decade.

Goat Castle (Town Hall)

Goat Castle, just east of the medieval St Begnet's church and graveyard on the north side of Castle Street, is one of two surviving castles and the only one in use, formerly as Dalkey Town Hall and now the home of the Dalkey Castle Heritage Centre (Fig. 4.4). It was shown on both the 1765 Reading map (Fig. 4.2) and in Beranger's image (Fig. 4.3). The name derives from its association with the Cheevers family, whose emblem included a goat (*chèvre* in French).

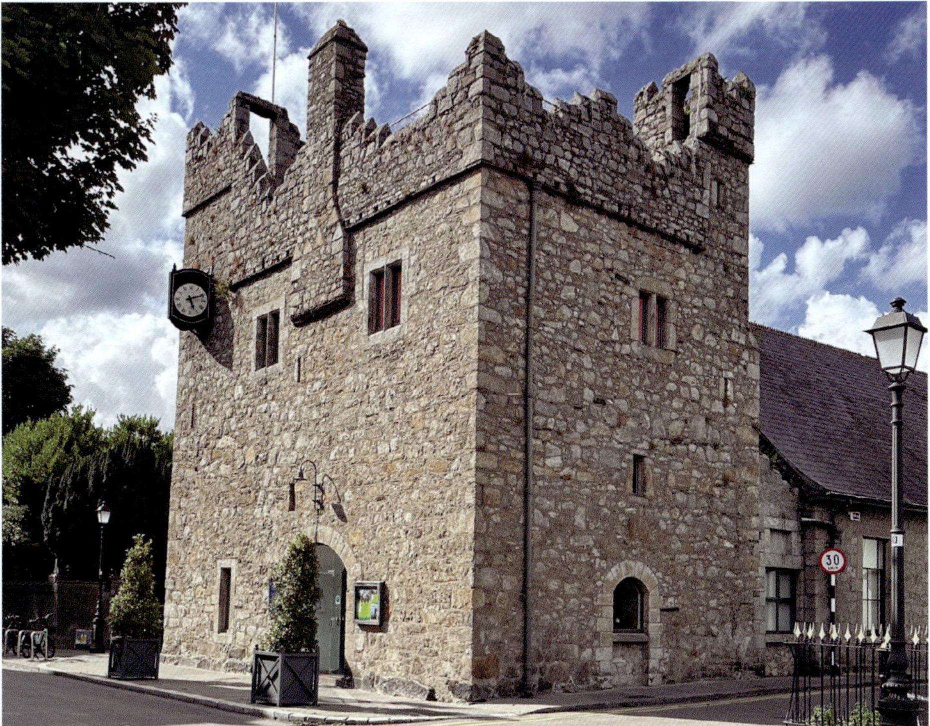

Fig. 4.4—Goat Castle (former Town Hall).

It is likely to have been known before 1660 as the Castle of Dalkey. In the first half of the sixteenth century the owner was probably John Fitzsimmons, whose grandson Walter in 1589 granted a castle and certain messuages and lands in Dalkey to Thomas Gerot, alderman of Dublin, and his heirs. Ownership later passed to Laurence Allen, who perhaps leased or sold it to Henry Cheevers (d. 1640) of Monkstown Castle. In 1750 it was in the possession of James Brennan, the owner being the dowager Lady Allen, to whom it descended from John Allen of Stillorgan. It was leased around 1793 to Sir John Hasler,[7] chamberlain to the lord lieutenant of Ireland.

The Dalkey Town Commissioners, established in 1863, leased the castle as their Town Hall in 1870. The *Irish Builder* reported in July 1872 that 'an ancient building in the Township of Dalkey known as Goat's Castle has been for some time in the course of repair for the purpose of being utilised as a town hall. We are informed that the cost was about £500. The work was executed by a local builder under the direction of Mr J.S. Fuller, architect.'

A hall, used for public meetings, concerts and exhibitions, was later added. The Town Hall continued in use until 1930, when the Dalkey Urban District Council was disbanded and the former township came under the aegis of Dún Laoghaire Borough Corporation. That body in turn was dissolved in 1994, to be replaced by Dún Laoghaire–Rathdown County Council, which carried out extensive renovations to the castle and added a new heritage centre adjoining the old graveyard.

House Castle

The House Castle (Fig. 4.5) was located near the junction of Castle Street and St Patrick's Road. In 1641 it probably belonged to Richard Walshe.[8] The 1765 Reading map (Fig. 4.2) showed that it was owned by William Bull, having been mortgaged a few years earlier by Thomas Archbold. It was situated then between the Ship Inn and the Black Castle. Shortly afterwards it was acquired by Robert Barry, who also held the Black Castle and connected the two buildings. He extended the House Castle and installed a billiard-table before selling it on to Sir John Hasler, who also owned the nearby Goat Castle. Hasler was in charge of ceremonial events, such as balls, at Dublin Castle and was noted for his hospitality. The House Castle was in good condition in 1818 but appears to have then fallen into decay and was demolished before the first draft of the Ordnance Survey map in 1837.

Black Castle

Reading's map showed the Black Castle at the eastern end of Castle Street (Fig. 4.6), adjoining the Commons of Dalkey, which in 1765 consisted of rocky pasturage and

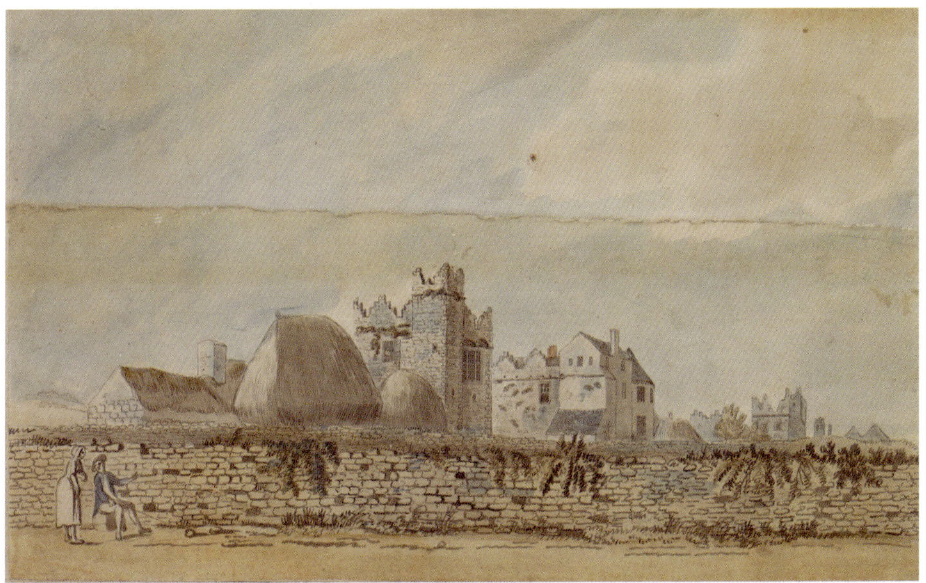

Fig. 4.5—The Black Castle, the House Castle and Goat Castle, *c.* 1770 (courtesy of the National Library of Ireland).

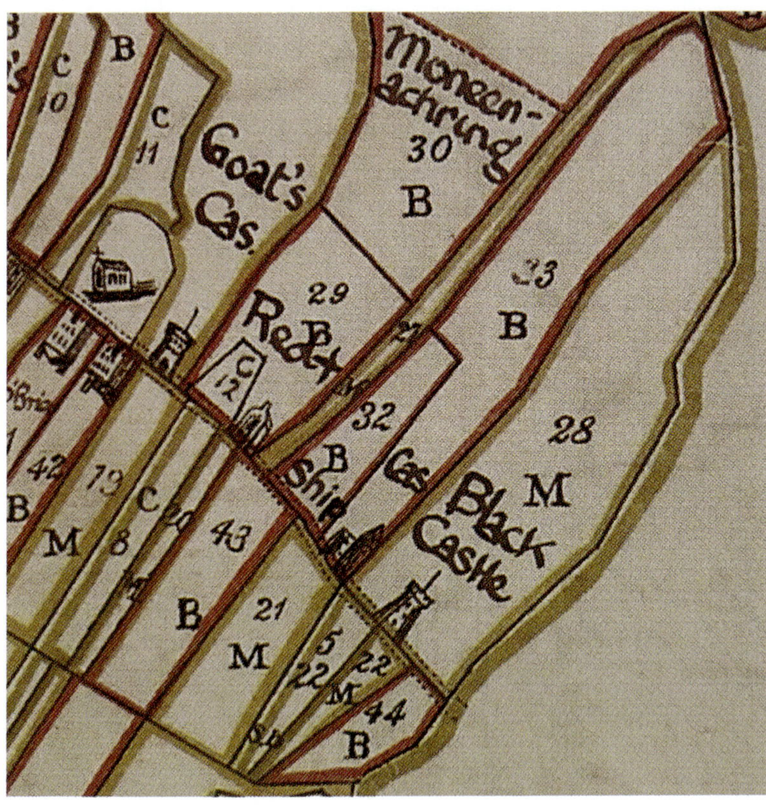

Fig. 4.6—The Black Castle as shown on Reading's map, 1765 (courtesy of the Royal Society of Antiquaries of Ireland).

few inhabitants. Peter Wilson, a Dublin bookseller who wrote a long letter about Dalkey in 1768, described the Black Castle as 'a summer lodge belonging to Robert Barry. This house, being partly ancient and partly modern … has a pleasing view to the sea at the rear and a garden laid out with skill and taste.'[9] Barry himself advertised his property for sale in 1773:

> 'To be sold, Mr Barry's interest in his house and lands at Dalkey, near Dunleary; the house is completely furnished, and the garden in full bearing. There are a few acres of excellent meadow, and an unlimited right of commonage on above 300 acres of good land adjoining the meadow grounds. Or the house will be let for a term of years.' [10]

The Black Castle had disappeared by the early years of the nineteenth century.

Archbold's Castle

Archbold's Castle (Fig. 4.7) still survives on the south side of Castle Street, opposite St Begnet's churchyard. It is in the care of the Office of Public Works and is not open to the public. In 1585 John Dungan was given a lease by Christ Church of the castle,[11] the only castle it owned in Dalkey. In 1684 Michael Archbold was granted a castle and 40 acres in Dalkey;[12] this may have been how the castle acquired its name. Reading's map of 1765 showed that the site was still owned by Christ Church; while the castle was not named, the map indicated a substantial building. Ball de-

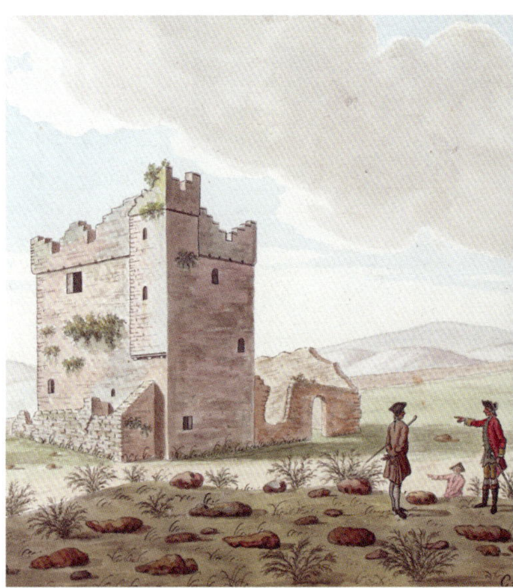
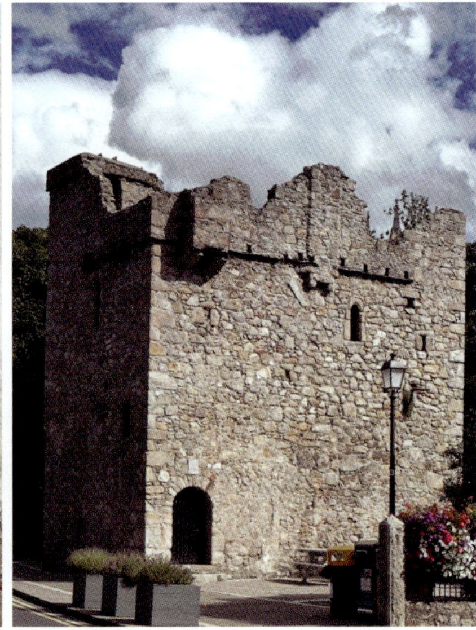

Fig. 4.7—Left: Archbold's Castle by Gabriel Beranger, 1766 (courtesy of the National Library of Ireland). Right: Archbold's Castle as it appears today.

scribed it as being in a ruinous state in 1902, but the OPW carried out repairs in 1948.[13]

The seventh castle

The seventh castle was probably the first to be demolished; it was neither shown nor recorded on Reading's map of 1765. It is likely, however, that the site—presently occupied by an apartment complex at the junction of Castle Street and Dalkey Avenue (Fig. 4.8)—was discovered during pre-development excavations by the archaeologist John Kavanagh in 2002.[14] Peter Wilson wrote in 1768 that 'the entrance [to Dalkey from] the west was through a gateway, secured by two castles, of which few or no traces remain'.[15] If that was the case, it is plausible to suggest that the two castles were Dungan's Castle to the north and the seventh castle to the south.

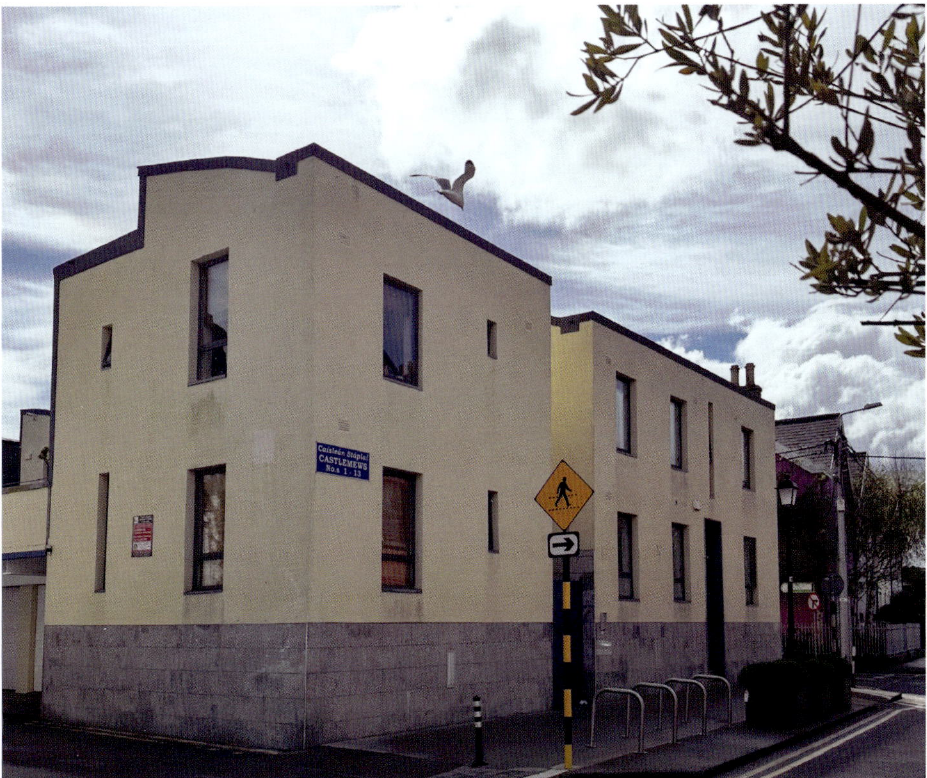

Fig. 4.8—Site of the 'lost' castle at the junction of Castle Street and Dalkey Avenue.

Kavanagh found that the earliest phase of activity on the site was characterised by a series of features associated with a medieval burgage plot and that the pottery assemblage would indicate a date of 1100–1500. The second and most significant phase of activity began with the construction of a substantial stone building directly over the earlier phase. The building occupied the north-west corner of the site and extended out under Dalkey Avenue to the west, fronting onto Castle Street to the north. An almost complete medieval green-glazed floor was recovered beneath the rubble of the east wall. The site was uneven and poorly drained and over the centuries this appears to have destabilised the walls of the building. The evidence suggests that it may have been in ruins by the 1600s.[16] The site was occupied for most of the nineteenth century and into the twentieth century by Connolly's bakery.[17]

5.

Dalkey since 1800

This chapter provides a broad overview of the development of Dalkey since 1800, as a context for the more thematic chapters that follow. It is no exaggeration to say that Dalkey was transformed in the nineteenth century as its population grew rapidly, initially as a result of the opening of the huge quarry at Dalkey Hill and subsequently as a result of an inflow of wealthy developers and residents from Dublin city, boosted by the provision of trams and trains from 1844 onwards.

1800–63

Around 1800, Dalkey was a quiet rural village of a few hundred people with no church or schools. There were a few large houses, but most poorer inhabitants lived in cabins. Five of the seven 'castles' survived in varying states of repair; three of those

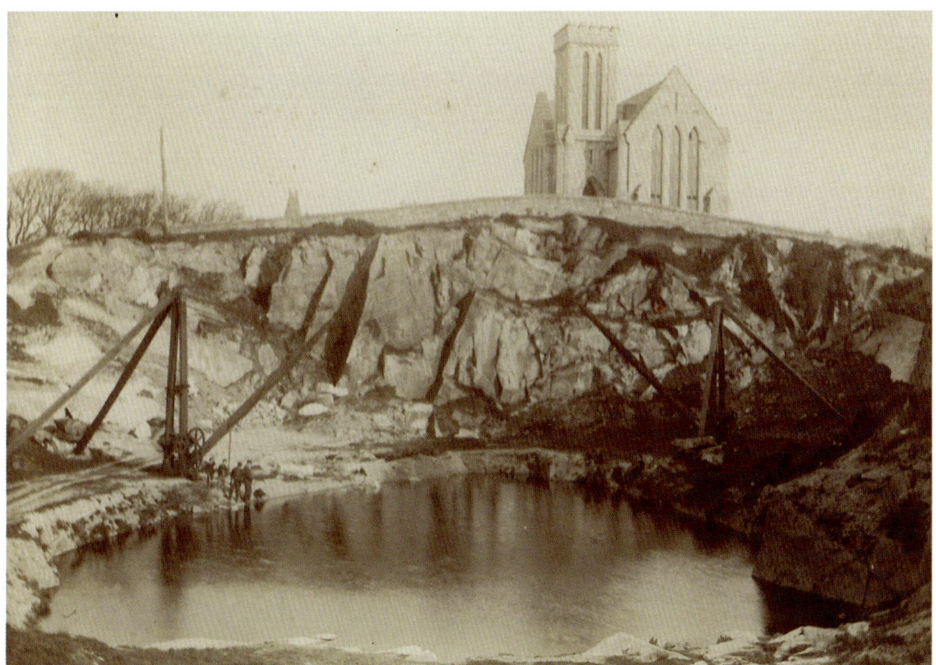

Fig. 5.1—'Meagher's' quarry off Harbour Road, *c.* 1895, with St Patrick's church behind (Harry Blake Knox collection, courtesy of the late Caroline Pritchard).

would be demolished over the next forty years or so. Martello towers were erected on Dalkey Island and on the coastline near Bullock harbour, part of a chain of such fortifications aimed at protecting Dublin from a threatened French invasion which never materialised, rendering the towers redundant within a few years. The Ballast Board quarried granite around Bullock and Sandycove, which it sent across Dublin Bay by barge to be used for harbour works.

The British government, responsible for the administration of Ireland since the Act of Union in 1801, originally intended to develop Howth harbour as the Dublin terminus for passenger and mail traffic with Holyhead in Wales. However, following massive loss of life when two ships were wrecked off Monkstown in 1807, public pressure built up to provide an 'asylum harbour' within the bay, to provide refuge for ships in storms. It was eventually decided to construct such a harbour near the small pier at Dunleary; the design by the engineer John Rennie called for thousands of tons of granite to be used. A Norwegian shipping agent, Richard Toutcher, who had long campaigned for the new harbour, leased land on Dalkey Hill, near Barnhill Road, which gave him the legal right to quarry stone on the land. Other landholders in the vicinity followed suit, and a major quarry began operations in 1817, with the heavy stone being transported to the harbour by means of a truck railway. Within decades, the profile of Dalkey Hill as seen from the village was to be dramatically altered forever. Hundreds of poorly paid workmen were employed, many of them squatting on Dalkey Commons or living in a dense mass of cabins near Ardbrugh Road.

The influx of poor inhabitants created a demand for schools for their children and for rudimentary public health facilities, including a dispensary, particularly to deal with outbreaks of cholera caused by unsanitary living conditions; in general, there was no public water-supply or proper sewerage during the first half of the century. Two Poor Schools were established in the 1820s and 1830s, one at Barnhill Road and one near Sorrento Hill. Many of the wealthier new residents were Protestant, and a church was opened on Harbour Road in 1843. The relatively less affluent Catholic community raised funds for a modest church on Castle Street in 1841; it was extended and improved over the next few decades, although not elevated as a parish church until 1929. Mother Theresa Ball established a Loreto convent and girls' school on grounds purchased from Charles Leslie in 1843 (see Chapter 8 for schools and churches).

Prior to 1800, the neighbourhood had attracted a small number of wealthy Dublin residents, often for the summer months, drawn by its scenic location and proximity to sea bathing. During the 1820s and 1830s, however, several prosperous

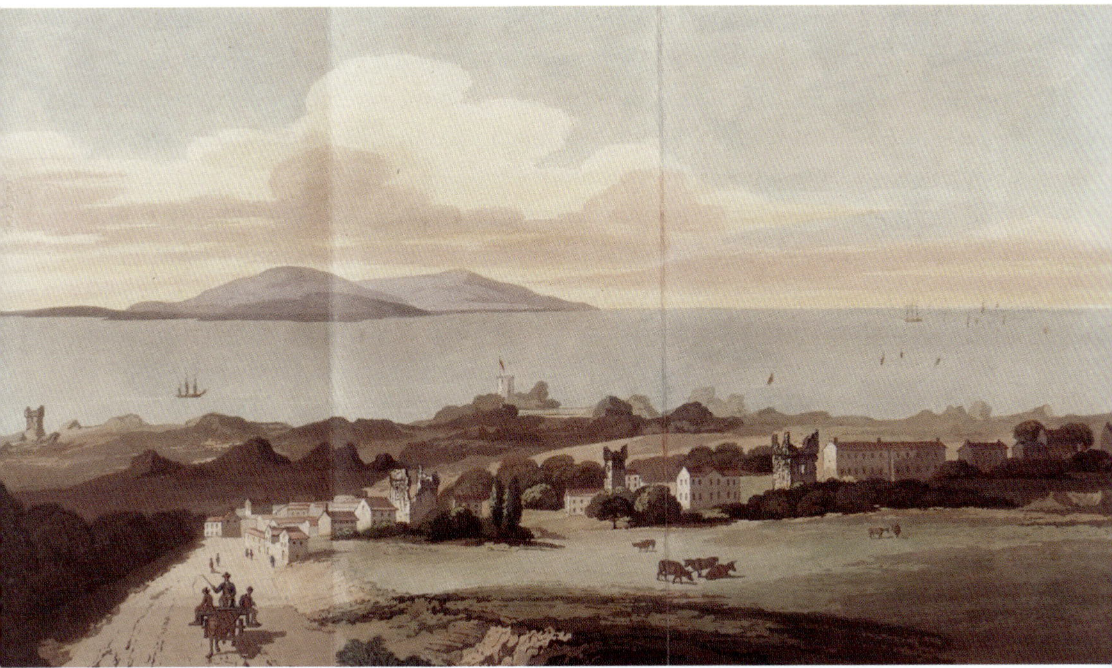

Fig. 5.2—Bay of Dublin, by John Carr, 1806 (courtesy of the National Library of Ireland).

individuals, including Charles Leslie, Richard MacDonnell and Martin Burke (see Chapter 15), began acquiring lands for large villas and terraces, either for themselves or for speculative housing. Most of these lands were on Dalkey Commons, usually with sea views and often purchased relatively cheaply from former squatters. The existing road network needed to be improved and extended, sometimes at the expense of the landowners but sometimes with grants from the County Dublin Grand Jury.

Up to the early nineteenth century Dalkey Commons consisted of rocky grazing lands, interspersed with rough tracks. The remains of an old roadway from Coliemore to the village could be discerned, and another track led from the former lead-mines on the coast overlooking Killiney Bay. Charles Leslie was the first significant land-owner to build villa-type houses at the Dalkey end of Coliemore Road, while the Burke family (Martin, founder of the Shelbourne Hotel, and his son James Milo) were largely responsible for continuing the road beyond the harbour. Hercules Mac-Donnell was responsible for the upgrading of Sorrento Road in the 1840s, to enhance the access to the newly built Sorrento Terrace. Development of the Commons in the 1830s and 1840s was a rough-and-ready process, however: plots acquired from squatters were initially marked out with stone walls, occasional violence broke out among adjoining landowners, and the gunpowder needed to clear large granite boulders was sometimes used to demolish disputed boundaries. When Martin Burke was building a house there in 1845, he was threatened by workmen employed by Patrick Smyth, nephew of Fr Francis Smyth of Mount Alverno, while Burke himself was fined £250 in 1842 when his workmen assaulted Mary Cavanagh, who had bought a site from him on the Commons.[1]

In the absence of local street directories prior to the 1840s, it is difficult to establish what types of shops were available in the early part of the century. More prestigious shops were available in the city centre and in nearby Kingstown. Nonetheless, by 1850 *Thom's Directory* showed that Castle Street could boast two victuallers and one dairy, six grocers/provision dealers, a vintner/tobacconist, a hosiery shop and general mart, a boot-maker, a jaunting car owner and an infant school (see also Chapter 10 on Castle Street).

Two large taverns were opened in 1837, most likely on Castle Street, but both proprietors became insolvent, one within months, the other by 1839. However, in addition to its well-known scenic qualities, Dalkey was developing amenities for summer residents and day-trippers, including boat trips to Dalkey Island and hot and cold seawater baths at Coliemore. Access for visitors was greatly enhanced by the availability of public transport, such as the Atmospheric Railway (1844–54) and steam trains from Bray (1854) and from Dublin city and Kingstown (1856). The Queen's Hotel provided visitor accommodation from 1843, followed by the Albert and Railway hotels in the 1850s (see Chapter 11). There were also several taverns and public houses, such as the Beefsteak Tavern on Castle Street. Samuel Lewis, in his *Topographical Dictionary*, published in 1837, reported that there was a constabulary police station in the village. Its location is unknown, but it probably belonged to the County Constabulary, a uniformed police force established in 1822, which was replaced by the Dublin Metropolitan Police (DMP), set up in 1836. The DMP was initially based in Dublin city; it was not until 1840 that 'F' Division was created to cover the south-east county, including Kingstown and Dalkey. A local landowner, Samuel McComas, leased a plot of land on Sorrento Road to the DMP in 1845 for a police barracks.

In 1844 Ulverton Road was constructed from Bullock to Castle Street. An undated plan for the proposed road in the Porter estate papers[2] indicates that W.E. Porter senior was instrumental in its construction, as much of the land required was in his ownership (Fig. 5.3). The opening of the road led to further housing development in the vicinity, including on Church Road and Carysfort Road, the latter connected with Porter's Road (now St Patrick's Road) in the late 1850s. Ulverton Road also became a tram route from 1879.

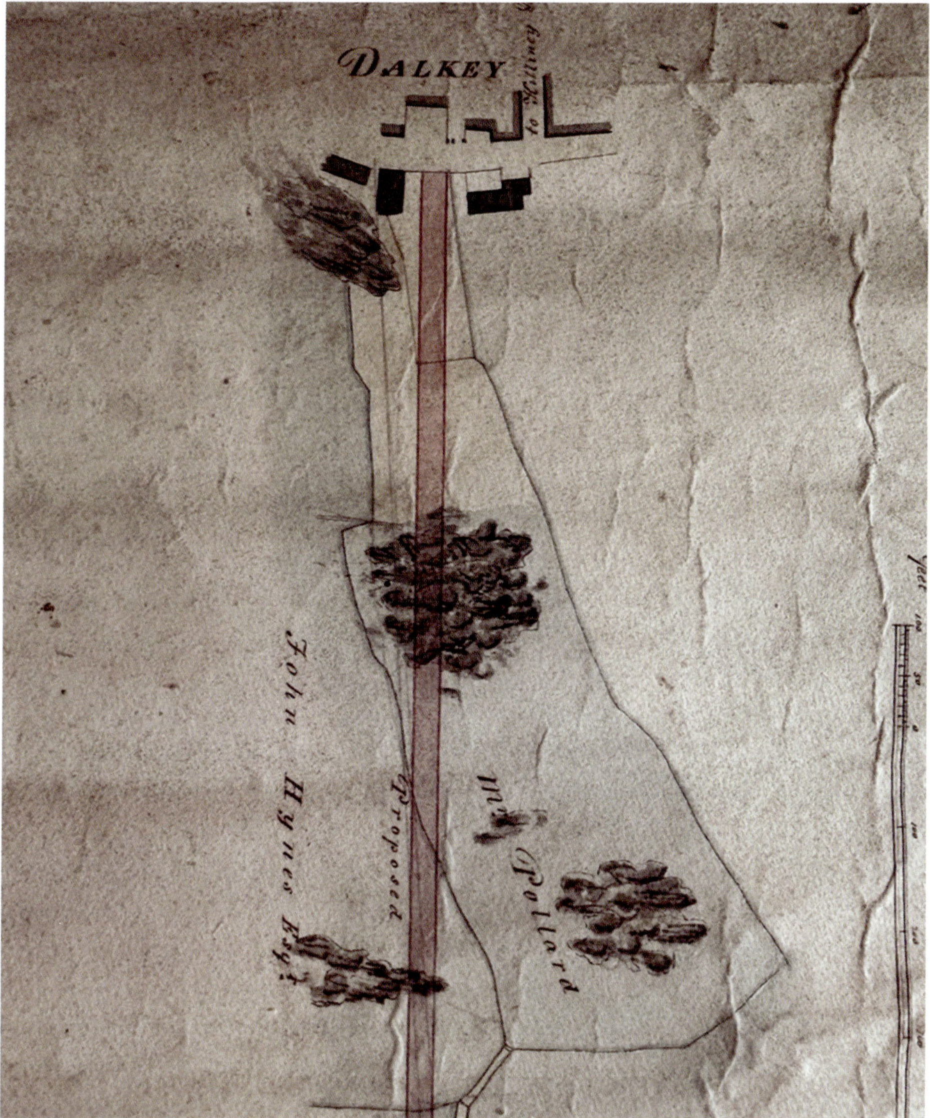

Fig. 5.3—Proposed new [Ulverton] road, *c.* 1840; Castle Street is at the top (courtesy of Brian Porter, Dalkey).

It would appear that the Famine had no major impact on Dalkey, although a relief committee was set up for the wider Kingstown area.[3] The population of Dalkey parish (Bullock was then part of Monkstown parish) increased by 73 per cent between 1841 and 1851, from 1,145 to 1,980, before decreasing slightly to 1,812 in 1861. This may be compared with a 29 per cent fall in the population of the island of Ireland between 1841 and 1861.[4] It is likely that the cholera epidemic in 1832 had a more severe impact, particularly among the quarry workers living in unsanitary conditions.

1863–1945

Property-owning residents in Kingstown established a township there in 1834 under the 1828 Towns Improvement Act. Township status enabled the commissioners to raise local taxes to fund such services as street lighting and paving, sewerage and water-supplies. Glasthule was added to Kingstown in 1855. Significant housing development had taken place around Dalkey since the 1830s, and landowners and merchants began a campaign to create a township under the Towns Improvement (Ireland) Act 1854, culminating in a public meeting in the Queen's Hotel in April 1863 chaired by James Milo Burke. A memorial was sent to the lord lieutenant, together with suggested township boundaries; he consented to the memorial and directed that the public lighting provisions of the 1854 act would apply to Dalkey township. In September 1863 a further meeting of ratepayers was held in the hotel to elect twelve town commissioners, including developers such as J.M. Burke (elected as chairman), Hercules MacDonnell, Gerard Tyrrell, Hugh O'Rorke and John Stewart, together with Castle Street merchants Edward Harrison and Thomas Connolly.

They immediately set about procuring gas lighting for the principal streets, which was switched on in December. The commissioners sponsored the Dalkey Township Act 1867, which extended their powers for the lighting, paving, sewering, draining, cleansing and supplying of the town with water, the erection of two piers at Coliemore harbour, the transfer of the making and construction of roads and footpaths from the grand jury to the commissioners, and the erection of a town hall. Experts such as Dr Cameron, Dublin City Analyst, severely criticised the poor quality of drinking-water from public pumps, and in 1871 the commissioners agreed to obtain a supply of Vartry water from the new Dublin Corporation reservoir. They also re-furbished Goat Castle as their town hall; an assembly room was added in 1892. In 1876 the commissioners were authorised to carry out the main drainage of the township at a cost of £7,000. They facilitated the continuation of Coliemore Road to Sorrento Terrace and supported the opening of Vico Road as a public road. Land at Sorrento Hill was donated as a public park by the MacDonnell family, and land for a park (later known as Dillon's Park) was purchased at Coliemore Road in 1886.

Between 1856 and 1879, the railway company had a monopoly on public transport between Dalkey and the city centre, resulting in relatively high fares for commuters. In the latter year, however, the Dublin Southern District Tram Co. (DSDTC)

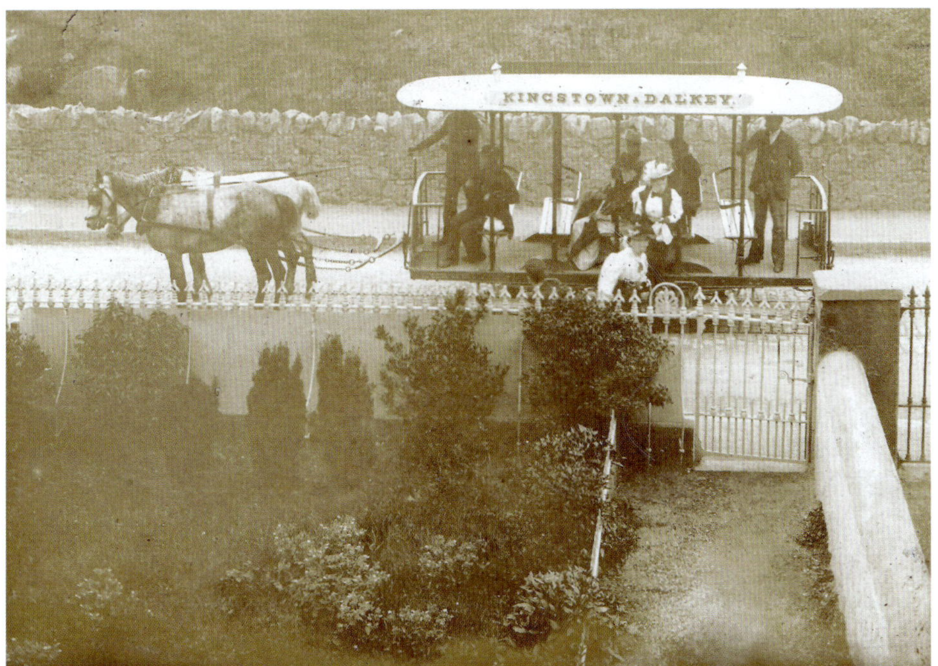

Fig. 5.4—Horse-drawn tram, Dalkey, 1879–96 (Harry Blake Knox collection, courtesy of the late Caroline Pritchard).

opened a 1,220mm-gauge horse-drawn tram line from Royal Marine Road in Kingstown to Castle Street, with a depot behind the former Albert Hotel. Later in 1879, the company built a second line between Blackrock and Haddington Road, but using the standard 1600mm gauge. To further complicate matters, a separate company—the Blackrock & Kingstown Tramways Company—ran trams in the middle section of the route, rendering the journey to Dublin unattractive to Dalkey residents. The issue was resolved years later when the DSDTC acquired the smaller company and electrified the entire route into O'Connell Street, based on the standard gauge. The line opened in May 1896, the first fully electrified tramway in Dublin (Fig. 5.5), with the stables at the Dalkey depot being replaced by an electrical substation. The terminus was at the eastern end of Castle Street, opposite the present Maxwell's pharmacy, while the ticket office was located where the Allcare pharmacy is now. The competition forced the railway company to reduce its fares. The tram company, now called the Dublin United Tramway Co., built twenty-three cottages in 1914 for its workers behind the depot, on and adjoining Carysfort Road.

As both the size and the prosperity of the township's population increased during the late nineteenth century, the range of goods and services was expanded in the

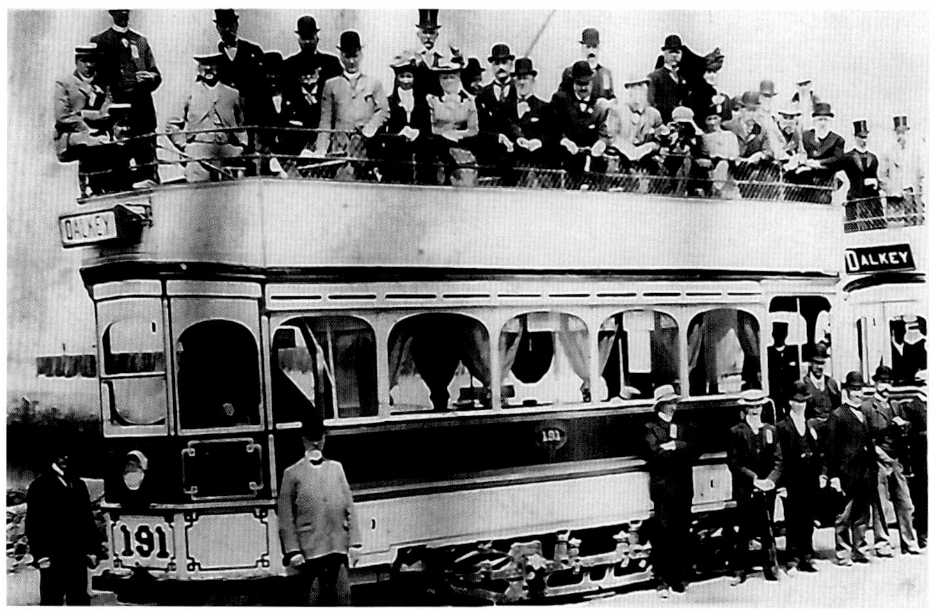

Fig. 5.5—Dalkey's electric tram, *c.* 1896 (courtesy of the National Transport Museum collection).

commercial core based on Castle Street. By 1901 there were seven specialist shops, six shops selling groceries, wines and spirits, three meat/poultry shops, three drapers/dressmakers, two restaurants, a baker and a dispensary. Dalkey received the seal of middle-class respectability in 1898 when Findlater's opened a shop on the south side of the street. Findlater & Co. had been founded in 1823 by Alexander Findlater, a spirit merchant in Burgh Quay. For much of the nineteenth century and well into the twentieth century, Findlater's were Dublin's best-known and most prestigious wine and food merchants, with branches throughout the city and suburbs; their Kingstown shop was one of the earliest, opened in 1830. The Dalkey outlet survived until 1969, when it was taken over initially by H.W. Williams and later by SuperValu. The Royal Bank of Ireland opened a branch office at the entrance to the Tram Yard around the turn of the century; it moved to a new building at the eastern end of Castle Street around 1930, later replaced by the Allied Irish Bank (closed in 2023). The boys' national school on Barnhill Road, first opened in the 1820s, closed in 1901 when it moved to new premises on St Patrick's Road in the heart of Dalkey.

A local government act in 1898 established new county councils, including in County Dublin, and existing townships and sanitary authorities became urban district councils. The new Dalkey Urban District Council was responsible for the former township area and set about building municipal housing schemes such as St Patrick's

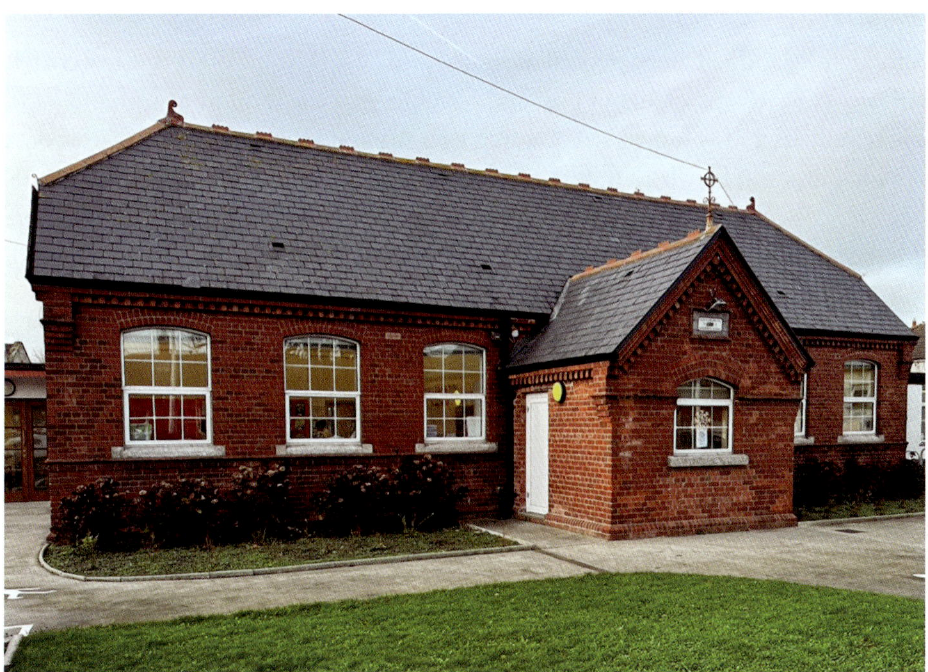

Fig. 5.6—Harold Boys' National School, St Patrick's Road.

Square and Avenue and St Patrick's Road. A public library was opened in Castle Street in 1901, and a new public health dispensary in 1909. Dalkey Island was purchased from the British War Department in 1913, the Martello tower and battery having long since lost any strategic importance. Little development occurred during World War I, the War of Independence and the Civil War. Towards the end of the 1920s, the new Irish government sought to reform local government in Dublin, and in 1930 the four coastal urban districts between Blackrock and Killiney were abolished. Their functions were taken over by Dún Laoghaire Borough Corporation, and the use of Goat Castle as the town hall ceased.

The new corporation built municipal housing schemes at White's Villas and Corrig Road in the 1930s, and radically reshaped the western approach to Dalkey in 1943 when it constructed Hyde Road (named after Ireland's first president, Douglas Hyde), linking Castlepark Road and Ulverton Road. This facilitated the development of a local authority housing scheme at St Begnet's Villas, where the writer Hugh Leonard lived in his late teens, and playing fields at Hyde Park, now the home of Dalkey United Football Club and Cuala GAA. The era of trams came to an end with the closure of the Dalkey route in 1949; the former Tram Yard still awaits redevelopment.

World War II

Although Ireland remained neutral during World War II, some of its effects were felt in Dalkey. There was a lookout post and searchlight at the summit of Sorrento Park, where soldiers and volunteers kept watch over sea and air movements. Nearby, on a sloping hillside at Hawk Cliff, just below the Vico Road, the remains of a huge 'Éire' sign were discovered in 2018. These signs, comprised of white-painted stones, were installed by the Irish Army at over eighty locations around the coast in 1943–4 to warn the pilots of military aircraft that they were entering neutral airspace. Most of the signs—including the one at Dalkey—were covered by vegetation in the decades after the war, and it took a team of Dalkey Tidy Towns volunteers, led by Des Burke-Kennedy, six months to clear this cover and repaint the giant letters (Fig. 5.7). Today there are information panels at the site explaining the historical context and how the sign was refurbished.

In the early hours of 12 March 1946, a wartime sea mine exploded on the rocks below the Cliff Castle Hotel on Coliemore Road, causing damage to the hotel; the blast was felt right along the coast and in Dalkey village. Over 200 houses were damaged to some extent and the State paid about £15,000 in compensation. Fortunately, there were no serious injuries.

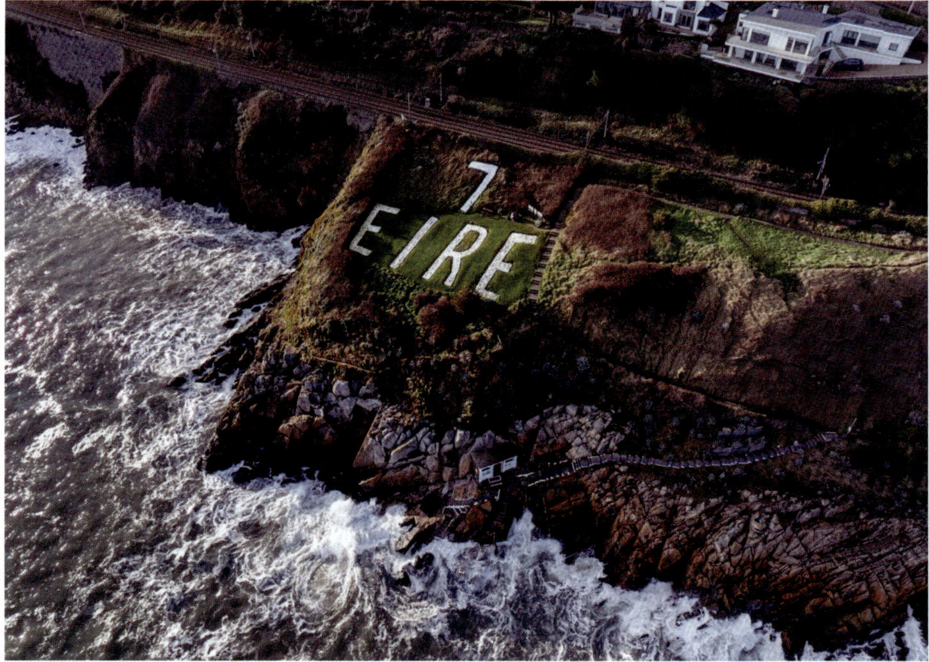

Fig. 5.7—World War II Éire sign at Hawk Cliff, Vico Road (courtesy of Cpl Jonathan Tuft, 105 Squadron, Irish Air Corps).

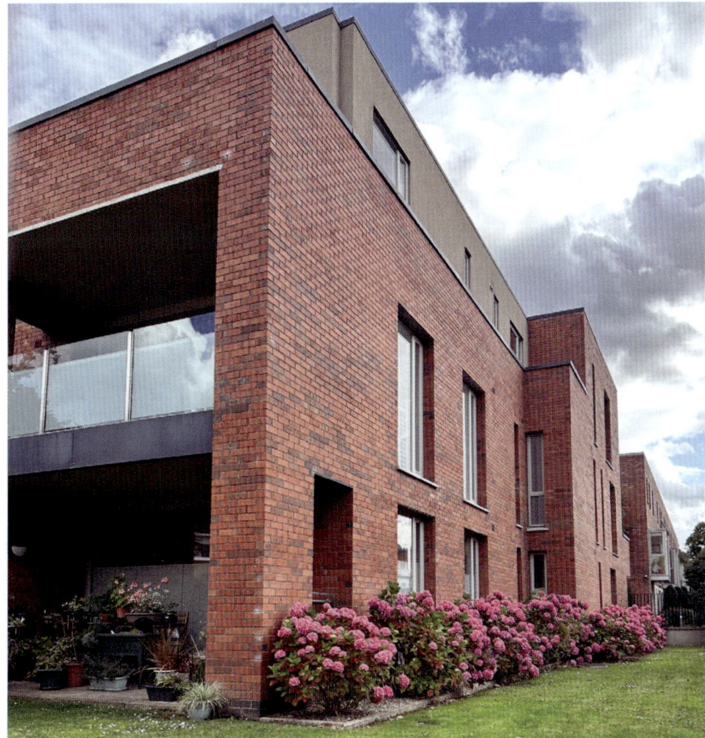

Fig. 5.8—Apartment development on Castlepark Road.

Recent developments

The development of apartments and townhouse schemes gathered pace on infill sites from the 1970s onwards, involving the loss of a number of small hotels which had been a feature around Dalkey since the 1920s and long-established businesses such as Mackey's garden centre on Castlepark Road.

The attraction of the area as a commuter town was enhanced in 1984 when the DART (Dublin Area Rapid Transit) opened, with more frequent rail services to the city centre. Castle Street experienced significant changes in the last quarter of the twentieth century: the presbytery behind the Church of the Assumption was demolished, thus facilitating the development of old persons' dwellings at Kilbegnet Close and a HSE community care facility. The old 1901 public library was replaced by a new building further west on Castle Street in 1989.

Dún Laoghaire–Rathdown County Council superseded the former corporation in 1994, and shortly afterwards the new council developed a heritage centre adjoining Goat Castle and St Begnet's church. The Covid pandemic which began in 2020 resulted in further changes to the streetscape, with the widening of footpaths in Castle Street to facilitate outdoor eating and to slow traffic.

6.

Land ownership in and around Dalkey

From the outset, Dalkey had a complex land ownership pattern, while Bullock had its own distinctive ownership history since the twelfth century (see Chapter 3). At the time of the Anglo-Norman invasion in 1169, the archbishop of Dublin was the dominant landlord in Dalkey, and St Mary's Abbey fulfilled a similar role around Bullock. The king of England acquired hundreds of acres south of Dalkey around Killiney and Rochestown, which were granted to the Talbot family of Malahide as early as 1218.

In 1765 land ownerships in and around Dalkey were mapped by the prolific surveyor of eighteenth-century landed estates Thomas Reading, who identified four major owners: William Bull, Sir William Mayne, the see of Dublin and Christ Church Cathedral. Reading's map also showed that those lands were surrounded by

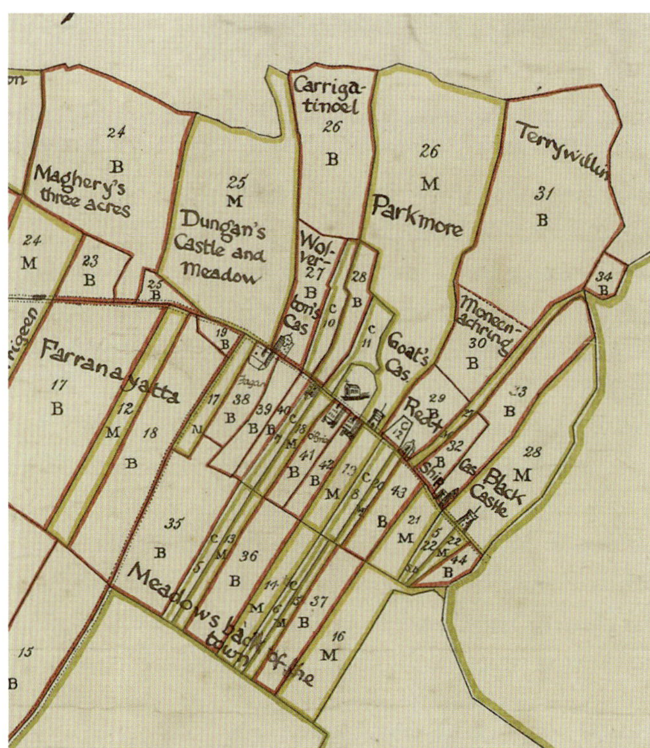

Fig. 6.1—Reading's map of Dalkey, 1765 (courtesy of the Royal Society of Antiquaries of Ireland).

Dalkey Commons to the east and south, and by the 'Lands of Bullock' to the north and west. This chapter looks at how the ownership pattern in 1765 was shaped, and how it evolved and influenced development in the following centuries.

Reading's map

Thomas Reading (*c.* 1704–79) was a professional surveyor who was commissioned by unknown landowner(s) to map property boundaries in and around Dalkey in 1765. A table attached to the map listed the major landowners and their tenants, and the amount of land held by each tenant. The units of acreage were Irish or plantation acres, equivalent to about 1.62 statute acres (0.66ha), used by the Ordnance Survey from the 1820s. Reading's map (Fig. 6.1) shows that many of the individual plots were in the form of long, thin rectangular shapes to the north and south of the main street (later known as Castle Street), almost certainly a relic of medieval burgage plots.[1] These legal boundaries persisted into the nineteenth century, even though they didn't always correspond with the larger field boundaries shown on Ordnance Survey maps of the area from 1837 onwards.

The major landholdings in 1765 identified by Reading were:

	Acres	*Roods*	*Perches*	
William Bull	67	3	26	(45%)
See of Dublin/glebe	49	0	13	(32%)
Sir William Mayne	28	0	4	(18%)
Christ Church	7	0	11	(5%)
Total	**152**	**0**	**34**	

In addition, the Commons of Dalkey amounted to 123 Irish acres and 34 perches, bringing the overall total to about 276 Irish acres (or 447 statute acres). No details about the 'Lands of Bullock' were provided.

The Bull estate

Around 1762 Thomas Archbold of Dalkey mortgaged 60 acres, Wolverton Castle and the House Castle to William Bull.[2] The Archbold family had been settled for centuries on the borders of the Dublin Pale, which they helped defend against the Gaelic Irish tribes who lived in the nearby mountains. Thomas Archbold took an oath in 1750 that he conformed to the Church of Ireland, possibly as a means of overcoming the legal barriers preventing Catholics from owning property under the Penal Laws; he was a churchwarden in Monkstown church in 1752.[3] Virtually nothing is known about William Bull; he may have been a lawyer from Dublin city who died in 1766.[4] His Dalkey estate passed to his son, Revd Richard Bull, who died in 1814; it was then subdivided among Richard's sisters Mary, widow of Robert Graydon, Anne, wife of the barrister William Vavasour, and Sophia, widow of William Pollard of Castlepollard, Co. Westmeath, whose share included the two castles. Sophia died in England in 1835.

Most of Mrs Graydon's share of the Bull estate lay west of Dalkey Avenue and south of Barnhill Road. One of the earliest houses built on the lands was Barn Hill, which was leased to Joseph Sandwith, a Dublin merchant, in the late eighteenth century; following his death, it was leased by Mrs Graydon to Judge Duigenan in 1815.[5] What is shown as 'Bachelors' Walk' on property maps was later developed as Saval Park Road, linking Barnhill Road with Dalkey Avenue. The Graydon estate was purchased by the Porter family in the latter part of the nineteenth century and is now covered with twentieth-century housing such as Barnhill Avenue, Dalkey Park and Hillside.

Anne Vavasour's inheritance included Dalkey Lodge on Barnhill Road, the oldest surviving house in Dalkey, dating from the mid-eighteenth century; it was leased in 1768 by the Dublin bookseller Peter Wilson, who published a description of the village and its surroundings.[6] Perhaps it was no coincidence that the Dunleary Harbour Commissioners commissioned her husband, William Vavasour, to investigate a claim by the dean of Christ Church that, as lord of Dalkey manor, he was entitled to royalties from any proposed quarrying of granite on Dalkey Commons. Vavasour examined title-deeds belonging to the Bull estate and other lands going back to the late seventeenth century and stated that he himself had been familiar with the area for over forty years.[7] Anne died in 1823, leaving her share to her daughter Frances, who three years later granted a lease of land on Barnhill Road near its junction with Dalkey Avenue to Isaac Purcell. Purcell in turn leased the land to William Porter senior, who built Kent Terrace in 1836. William Alexander Porter acquired the Vavasour estate in 1887.[8] Part of former Vavasour lands between Castlepark Road and Barnhill Road were developed for housing in the twentieth century (Wolverton Glen), while the northern part of that plot facilitated first the Atmospheric Railway in 1844 and then the Kingstown to Dalkey line in the next decade.

The third sister, Sophia Pollard, acquired lands adjoining Castle Street, which were important for the physical and economic development of Dalkey during the nineteenth century. Her holding included lands on the north side of the street on which Ulverton Road was constructed around 1844, together with the site of the former Red Cross Inn, replaced around 1792 by Rockview Lodge, which housed the Queen's Hotel after 1842.

Sir William Mayne

In 1750 William Mayne (1722–94) married Frances Allen, younger daughter and co-heir of Joshua Allen of Stillorgan, who inherited a very large estate in counties Dublin and Wicklow. The couple owned 28 plantation acres in the parish of Dalkey in 1765, together with a much larger holding in the Bullock and Sandycove area (see below). The Dalkey holding included Goat Castle, Archbold's Castle and the Black Castle, all of which were standing at the time, together with the sites of Dongan's Castle and the 'seventh castle' (see Chapter 4). In 1776 Mayne was elevated to the peerage of Ireland as Baron Newhaven. He and Frances had one son, who died in infancy. Under a marriage settlement, almost all of Lady Newhaven's estate passed to her elder sister Elizabeth, who had married John Proby; their only son was created Earl of Carysfort in 1789.[9]

Figure 6.2, showing part of the Carysfort estate around 1880, may be compared with the Mayne estate in 1765. The largest single plot (M26—Parkmore and the Goat's Castle garden), comprising over 4 plantation acres, was developed as Rockview

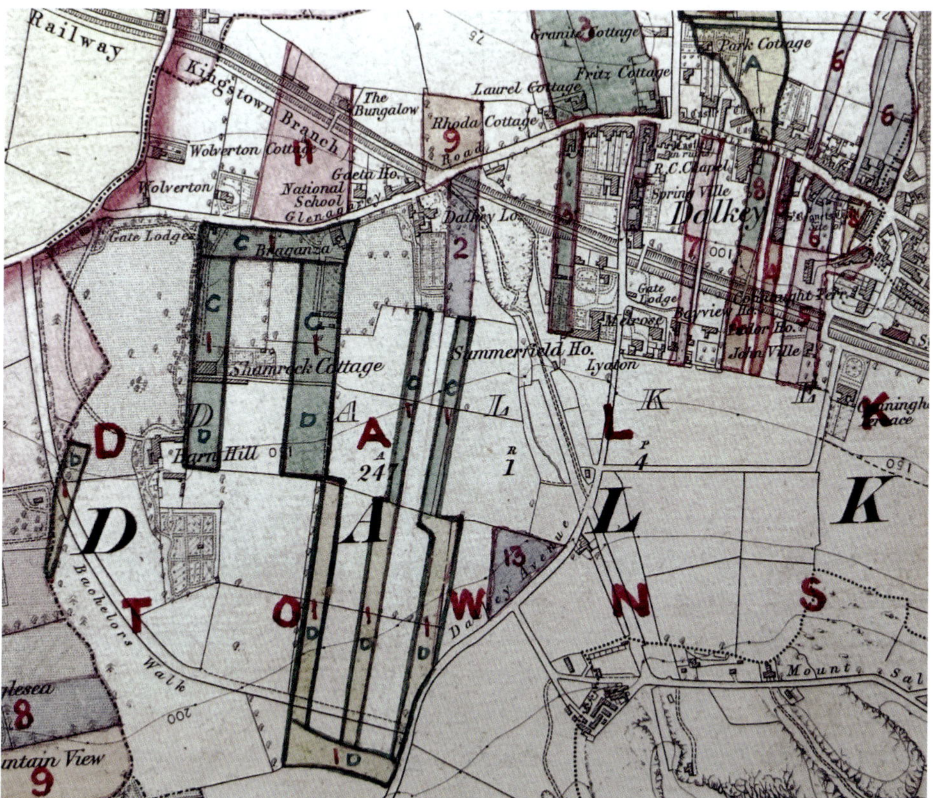

Fig. 6.2—Extract from map of the Dalkey estate of the Earl of Carysfort, *c.* 1880 (courtesy of Local Studies, Dún Laoghaire–Rathdown Lexicon Library).

Lodge/the Queen's Hotel and for mid-nineteenth-century housing on the east side of Ulverton Road. Another large plot (M25—Dungan's Castle, with over 3 plantation acres) is now the site of St Begnet's Villas, while M28 (the Black Castle garden, with about 1.5 plantation acres) forms the western side of Convent Road. All of the holdings on the south side of Castle Street were bisected by the Kingstown to Dalkey railway line in the early 1850s.

The see of Dublin/Dalkey glebe

As shown in Chapter 2, the claim of the archbishop of Dublin, Laurence O'Toole, to lands in and around Dalkey pre-dated the Anglo-Norman invasion, after which Dalkey formed part of the archbishop's manor of Shankill. A survey or 'extent' of the archbishop's lands in 1326 showed that he held 40 acres and thirty-nine burgage holdings in Dalkey. The archbishop's lands were transferred to the Church of Ireland after the Reformation. Forty-eight acres owned by the see in Dalkey were granted to Trinity College Dublin during the Cromwellian period but were given back after the Restoration in 1660.[10] Tormer's map of the see's holding in 1656 (Fig. 6.3) may be compared with the see's lands in 1765, which amounted to over 49 plantation acres (79 statute acres or 32ha), of which 14 plantation acres constituted the glebe for the benefit of the minister of Monkstown. The glebe consisted initially of a series of smallholdings south of Sorrento Road, which were replaced by more substantial houses from the 1840s onwards, although, as shown on Fig. 6.5 below, some of the long back gardens were compulsorily acquired for the Dalkey to Bray railway line in 1849. The opening of Dalkey station in 1854 was followed by the construction nearby of Ardeevin Road and Cunningham Road, and in the twentieth century nearly all of the lands north of Ardbrugh Road/Knocknacree Road were also developed for housing.

Christ Church

The priory of the Holy Trinity in Dublin had held a small amount of land in Dalkey since the medieval era, although the exact date is not known. In particular, the archbishop granted the priory the parish church of St Begnet and adjoining lands.[11] Reading's survey showed that Christ Church Cathedral (as the priory was later known) owned 7 plantation acres in 1765, mainly in the form of long burgage plots on both sides of Castle Street/Barnhill Road, all of which were leased to a Mr Baldwin and sublet to John Watson of Bullock Castle. A tiny plot consisting of only 9 perches (C12 on Reading's map) now forms part of the Queen's Hotel on Castle Street. The other lands, with the exception of the old church and graveyard, have since been de-

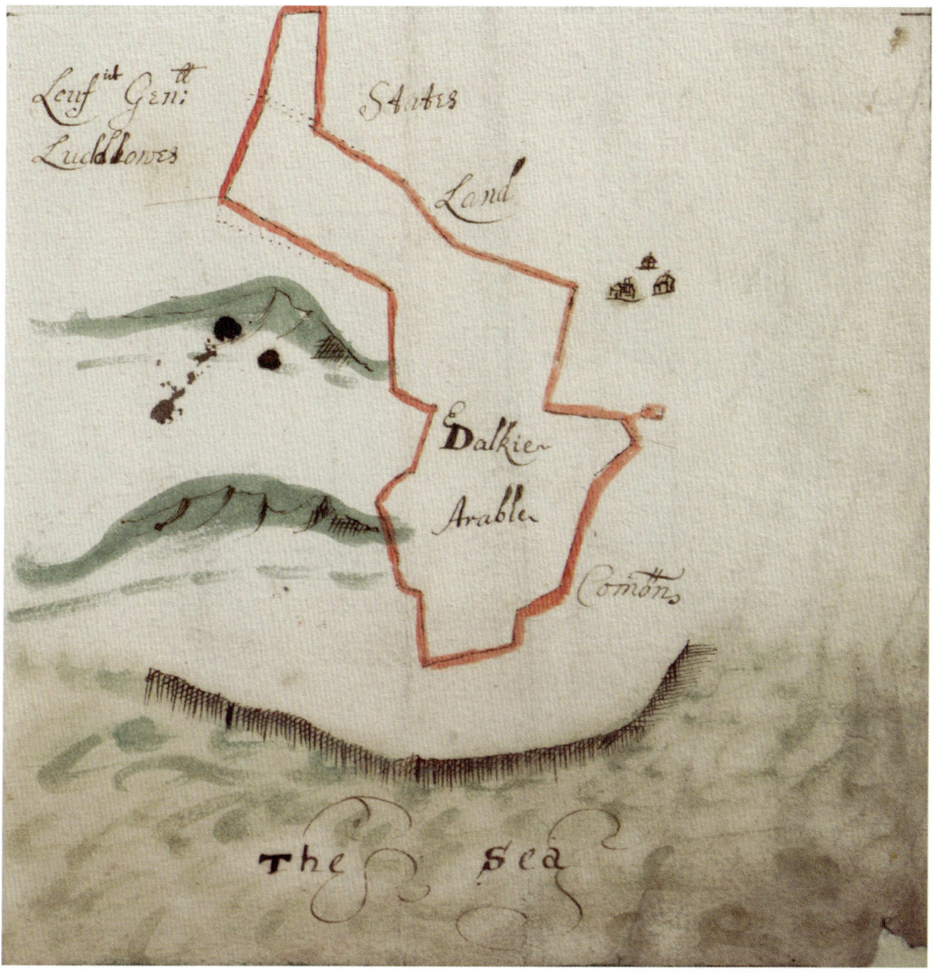

Fig. 6.3—John Tormer's 'Plot of Dalkey in the parish of Dalkey', 1656 (courtesy of the Church Representative Body Library). Note that the top of the map is oriented to the west; north is to the right.

veloped, principally for commercial uses on the main street and for housing on the outskirts of the town.

Lands of Bullock

These were in the parish of Monkstown in 1765 and included lands to the west of the parish of Dalkey. Lord and Lady Newhaven inherited a substantial holding to the north of Dalkey, including between Castlepark and Ulverton Roads and on either side of the western end of Harbour Road.

Lady Newhaven's grandfather, Colonel John Allen (1661–1726), a member of

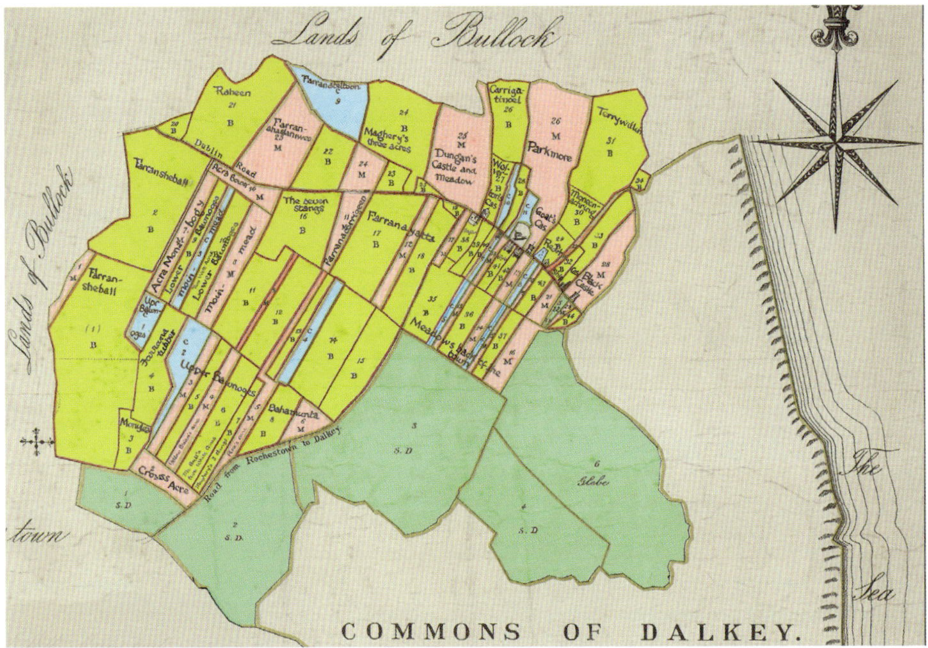

Fig. 6.4—Extract from Reading's survey of 1765, showing lands owned by the see of Dublin (coloured green; the glebe is no. 6) (courtesy of the Royal Society of Antiquaries of Ireland).

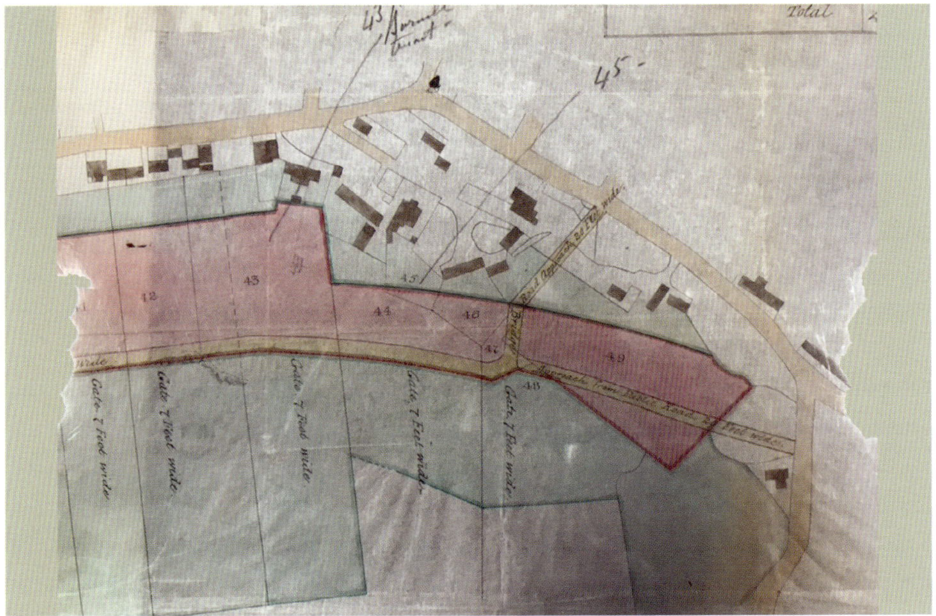

Fig. 6.5—Extract from map showing part of the lands (south of Sorrento Road) to be acquired from the Ecclesiastical Commissioners for the Dalkey to Bray railway line, 1849 (M/6025, reproduced by kind permission of the Director of the National Archives) Note: author's photo taken in the National Archives Reading Room'

the Irish House of Commons for twenty-five years, purchased the former Fagan lands at Bullock from the Crown in 1703. According to the Tithe Applotments,[12] almost 45 acres of those were leased in 1826 to Arthur Perrin, who built Castle Perrin (now called Castle Park), with a further 37 acres leased to the Ballast (Dublin Port) Board for quarrying near Bullock harbour. The latter sublet sites for housing such as Henrietta Place, Bartra, Beulah and Charleville on Harbour Road, together with a site for St Patrick's church, in the 1830s and 1840s. The Carysfort estate included lands on both sides of what became Ulverton Road, east of Castle Park, thus enabling the creation of a new link between Kingstown and Dalkey in 1844. However, many of the fields south of Castle park (which became a school in 1904—see Chapter 8) remained undeveloped until the purchase by Dún Laoghaire Corporation of land for the new Hyde Road in the 1940s; they were known to the young Hugh Leonard as 'the Fields'.

The Commons of Dalkey

The Commons of Dalkey (Fig. 6.1) provided grazing lands for landowners in the village since medieval times, stretching in an arc to the north and east and amounting to 123 plantation acres (almost 200 statute acres) by 1765. In 1773 Robert Barry, who leased the Black Castle at the corner of Castle Street and Convent Road, advertised the sale of his interest in his house and lands: 'There are a few acres of excellent meadow, and an unlimited right of commonage on above 300 acres of good land adjoining the meadow grounds'.[13] The mostly rocky lands, criss-crossed with old tracks, remained largely undeveloped until the early nineteenth century, when wealthy individuals from Dublin such as Charles Leslie, Martin Burke and Dr Richard MacDonnell (see Chapter 15) began buying up plots from squatters living on the Commons after the opening of Dalkey quarry in 1817. In April 1824 a petition was submitted to the lord lieutenant on behalf of some 800 squatters, declaring that 'the said commons are, it seems to be taken in, and [the] petitioners' little cabins are to be thrown down, by which means [the] petitioners and their unhappy and helpless families will be left quite destitute of shelter, in number about 800 people'.[14] A writer in 1840 described the scene as it had been before the enclosure of plots: 'A few cottages stretching from the village along its southern boundary, and a solitary cabin originally built by miners and which still remains, were the only habitations to be seen'.[15]

Many of the sites acquired by speculative developers enjoyed superb coastal settings, overlooking Dublin Bay or Killiney Bay, and expensive villa-style houses were bought or leased by prosperous mercantile and professional individuals, most of whom commuted to their offices in the city. Former rough tracks were transformed into residential roads, such as Sorrento Road and Coliemore Road. According to Hercules MacDonnell, son of Dr Richard, there had at first been only a rugged trackway for a short distance beyond Dalkey village leading toward Sorrento Cottage, and to reach his father's place it was necessary to walk over rough stones and rocks. Mac-Donnell at his own expense had widened the whole Sorrento Road from Dalkey Main Street and had laid the granite kerbing.[16] Nonetheless, the 'privatisation' of the former Commons led to bitter controversy in Dalkey in 1885, with allegations that access to the coastline had been cut off to facilitate the new occupants. At a public meeting held in the Town Hall in October, a Mr Sexton said that he remembered Dalkey since 1825 and a cabin standing where James Milo Burke's castle (probably Queenstown Castle) now stood, and he could walk from where the Loreto convent now stood to White Rock at Killiney Bay. Another said that the town commissioners, with some honourable exceptions, had grabbed land for themselves.[17] Perhaps in an effort to defuse some of the public anger, the commissioners agreed the following year to purchase land on Coliemore Road from J.M. Burke as a public park (now Dillon's Park);[18] it was virtually the last piece of undeveloped land between the road and the coastline.

7.
Housing and roads in nineteenth-century Dalkey

A visitor would have approached Dalkey around 1800 via what was then known as the Dublin road (now Barnhill Road), passing Barn Hill and Dalkey Lodge on the right and fields stretching down to Bullock Castle on the left. Entering the village, the road to Killiney (Dalkey Avenue) would have risen steeply, passing the Mount Mapas estate on Killiney Hill before descending towards Shankill and Bray. The remains of three castles—Wolverton's, Goat and Archbold's—adjoined the main street, lined with a number of large houses up to three storeys high, some incorporating parts of other castles, with gardens and orchards protected by stone walls to the rear. Smaller houses and cabins also faced the street, interspersed with a few taverns and perhaps with some food shops. The ruins of the medieval St Begnet's church lay beside an ancient graveyard, still in use. Ulverton Road had not yet been built; a pedestrian path through the fields and small granite quarries linked Dalkey and Bullock.

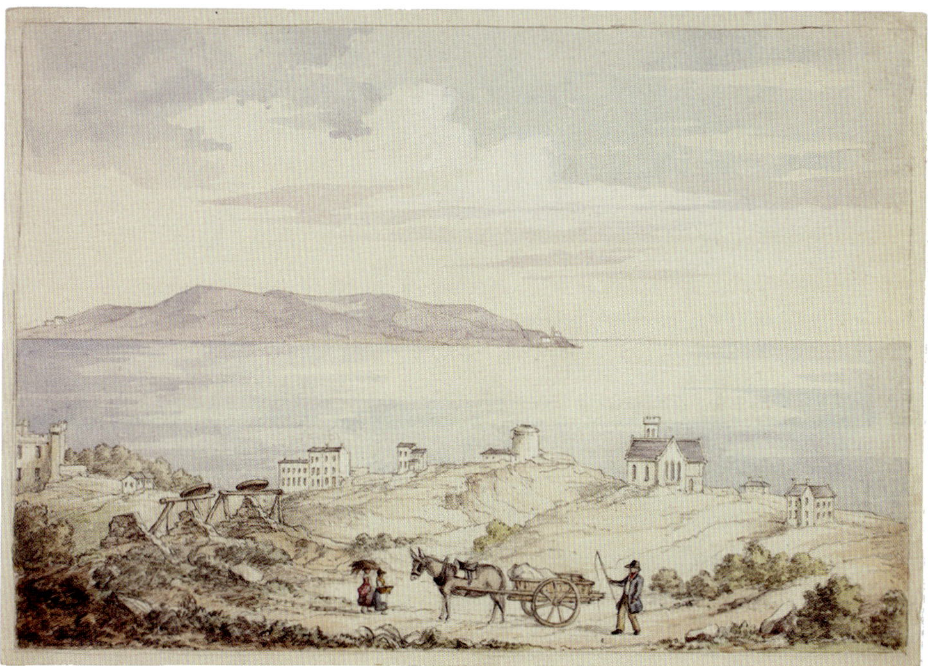

Fig. 7.1—Elizabeth Murray, *Dalkey from the road*, 1843 (courtesy of the Art Institute of Chicago).

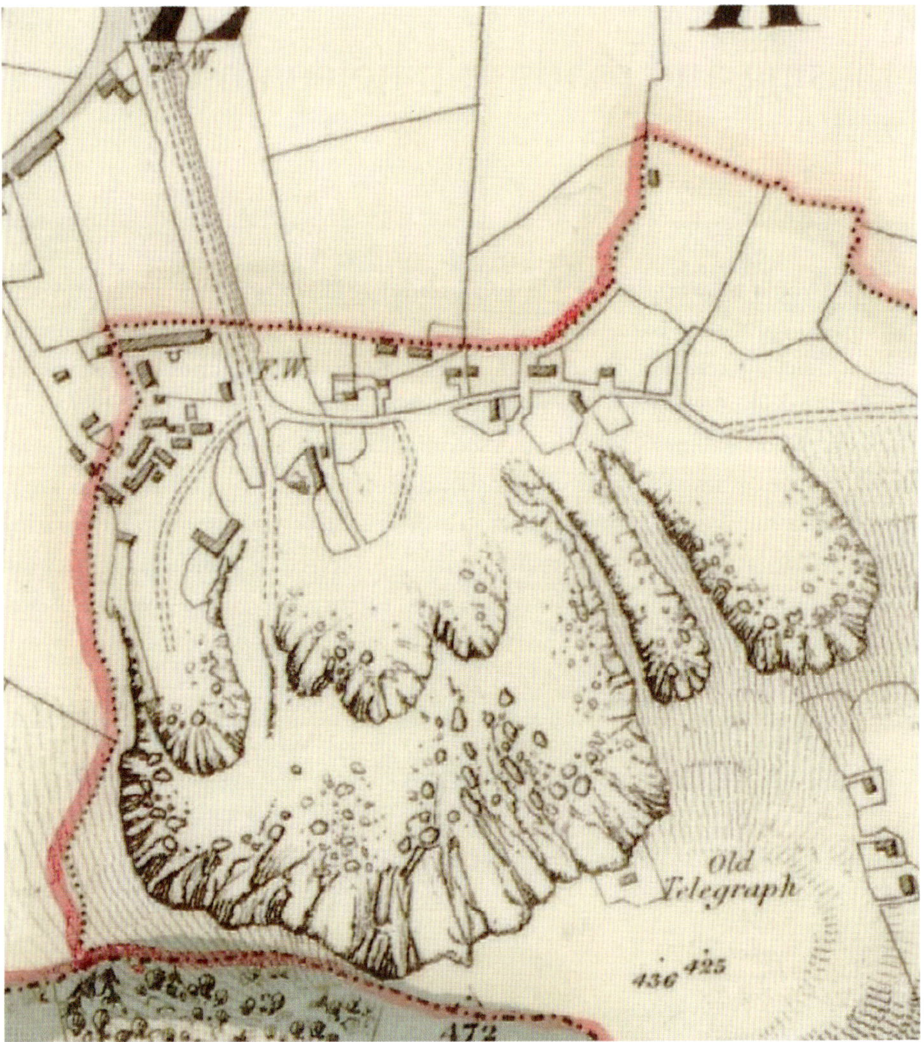

Fig. 7.2—Cluster of cabins near Dalkey quarry, 1843 (Tailte Éireann permit no. 50450108 © Tailte Éireann).

Looking southwards, the visitor would have seen Dalkey Hill looming over the village, surmounted from 1804 by the telegraph tower. At the far end of the main street a rough track led down to Dalkey Sound at Coliemore, where only a few years previously revellers would have boarded boats each summer for the King of Dalkey Island festivities. Another track led to the former lead-mines on the cliffs overlooking Killiney Bay, with a number of small cottages on the glebe lands on the right-hand side of the road. Much of Dalkey Commons between the two tracks consisted of rocky grazing, with few inhabitants.

Stone for the new harbour at Dunleary began to be quarried at Dalkey Hill in 1817, necessitating a workforce of almost 700, many of whom squatted on the Commons and near the quarry. A cluster of cabins near Ardbrugh Road was shown on the first Ordnance Survey six-inch map (Fig. 7.2).

From the 1820s onwards, a number of wealthy individuals from Dublin who had become acquainted with the scenic views around Dalkey began buying plots of land on the Commons east of the village and extending as far as the coast at Killiney Bay. One of the earliest developers was Charles Leslie, a wholesale chemist, who acquired about 8 hectares (20 acres) between the road to Coliemore and the coast, adjoining the village. In order to build his mansion at Carraig-na-Gréine, he had to rehouse some of the former squatters on a nearby lane, later known as Leslie Avenue. His in-laws, the Peacocke family, later built Villaggio on lands east of Carraig-na-Gréine.

Martin Burke, owner of the Seapoint and Shelbourne hotels, also bought land between Dalkey Sound at Coliemore and Sorrento Road; both he and his son James Milo Burke developed several large houses in the area, including Queenstown Castle, Victoria House, Springfield House and Khyber Pass House. One such house, Inniscorrig on Coliemore Road, was the Dalkey residence of the eminent heart surgeon Sir Dominic Corrigan. The grand jury awarded funding in 1848[1] to improve the road from Dalkey to the new baths at Coliemore, but it was to be several decades before the road was extended to connect with Sorrento Terrace. James Burke later claimed[2] that his father had constructed Nerano Road and the other roads adjoining his land at a cost of over £1,000 in 1844 and had kept them in repair for several years until they were handed over to the town commissioners.

Two other Dublin merchants—Gerrard Tyrrell, a bookseller in Lower Sackville Street (now O'Connell Street), and Samuel McComas, a tailor—were active in buying sites around Coliemore Road in the 1840s; Tyrrell built Tempe Terrace, while McComas built Rockfort Terrace. Two of the houses on Rockfort Terrace were put up for sale in 1854, and the sale particulars illustrate how the rental market for that kind of property operated:

'Rockfort Terrace was built under the immediate superintendence of the present owners, of the best materials and without any view to sale. It has been kept in perfect repair and is well suited to permanent residences … The houses are well furnished, and have been constantly let to the most respectable families for the summer months at £15 to £20 per month for each house, and for the last 2 or 3 years the demand for houses in this most cheerful and healthy neighbourhood has far exceeded the supply.'[3]

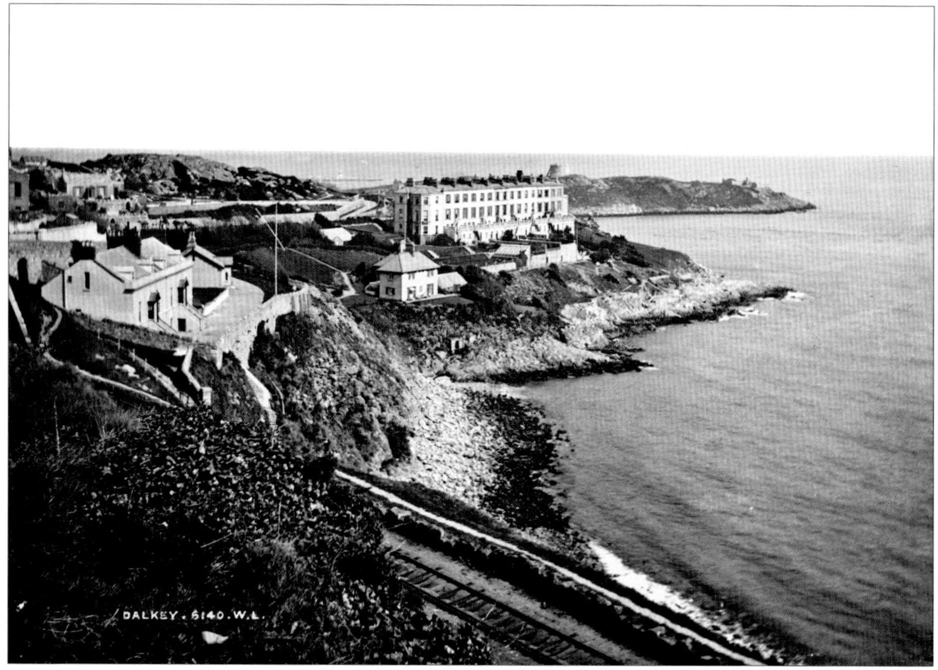

Fig. 7.3—Sorrento Terrace and Sorrento Cottage (courtesy of the National Library of Ireland).

Revd Dr Richard MacDonnell, a future provost of TCD, bought an extensive tract of land overlooking Dalkey Island and Killiney Bay, and built a modest cottage, which he named Sorrento Cottage, on a steeply sloping site near the former lead-mines around 1835. A Franciscan priest named Revd Francis Smyth also purchased land at that time, on higher ground above MacDonnell's; he built a house which he called Mount Alverno in honour of St Francis, founder of the order. Smyth opened a small oratory there, and also a school for children of the poor (see Chapter 8).

MacDonnell and his son Hercules were instrumental in developing Sorrento Terrace (Fig. 7.3) in the mid-1840s, and thus the road from Dalkey became known as Sorrento Road. Hercules succeeded in obtaining funding from the County Dublin Grand Jury to improve the road, which up to then would have been little more than a rough track. In 1845 funding was approved for widening 164 perches (approximately 820m) of road from Dalkey to Sorrento Terrace to a width of 24ft.[4] While William Porter had built four terraced houses at Kent Terrace in Dalkey in 1836, Sorrento Terrace was a much grander project, on a superb site overlooking Killiney Bay and with extensive private open space for the tenants. The original plans showed a terrace of 22 houses, but this was scaled back by around 1845 to eight. Strict lease terms drawn up by Hercules MacDonnell required the lessees to spend at least £1000

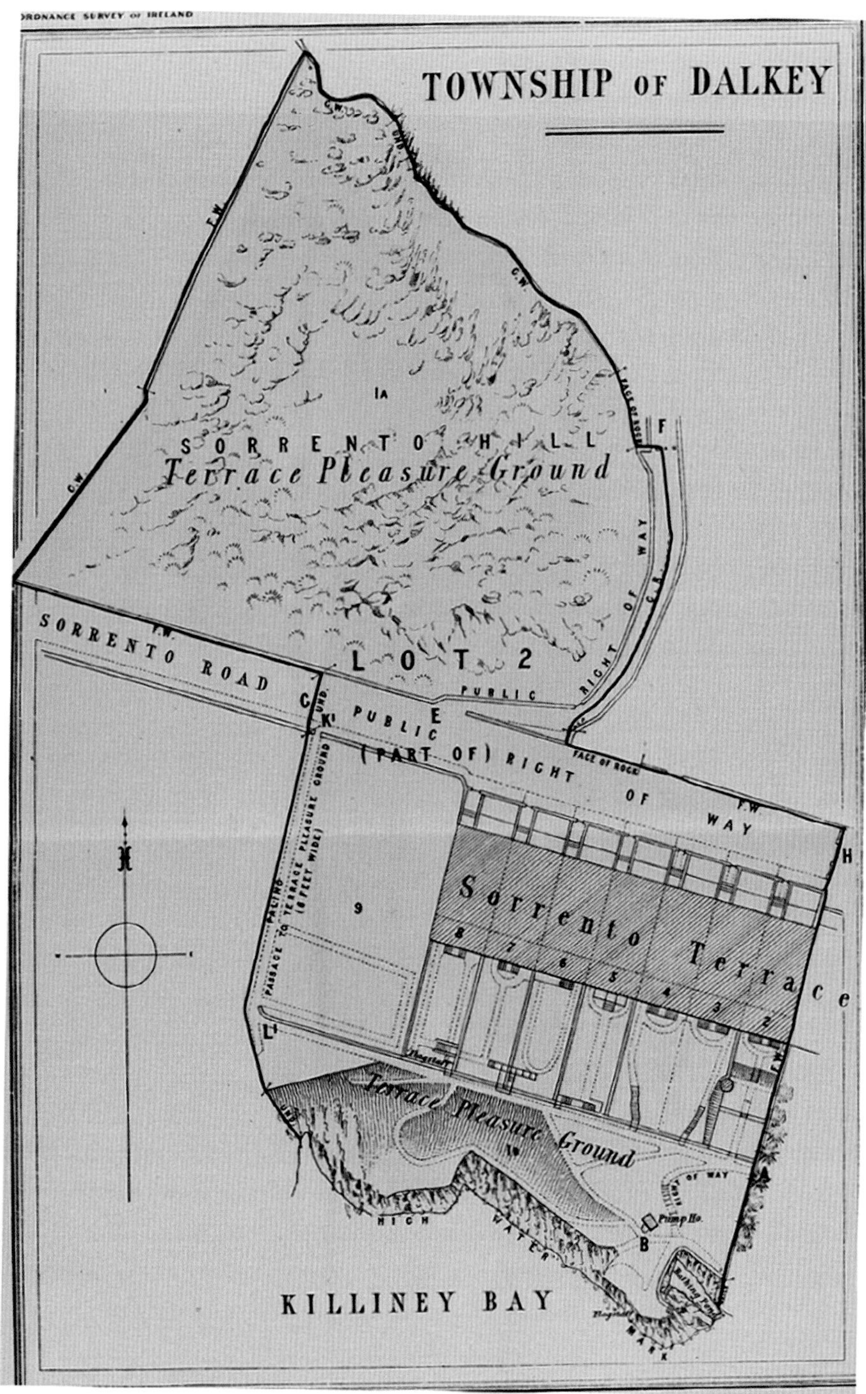

Fig. 7.4—Sale of MacDonnell estate, Landed Estates Court, July 1873 (reproduced by kind permission of the Director of the National Archives).

sterling on building a substantial house with good and sufficient materials and of the shape, elevation, proportions and colours drawn or described in the working plans designed by Messrs. Darley and Montgomery Architects.[5] The houses were constructed by Edward Masterson, a highly reputable local builder.

The MacDonnells also leased building land to other developers: Henry Gonne, the first town clerk in Dalkey, built several houses in the early 1860s near the junction of Sorrento Road and Vico Road. The latter was a cul-de-sac at that time, as Robert Warren, owner of the Mount Mapas estate at Killiney Hill, had erected a wall preventing a through road to Killiney village; it was not until 1889 that the private rights were bought out and the Vico Road was opened to the public. Grand jury records would suggest that Mount Salus Road and Knocknacree Road were constructed in the 1840s and 1850s.

Many of the larger houses built in the 1830s and 1840s were advertised for letting — often on a seasonal basis — in the Dublin newspapers, which provide interesting details not only about the houses but aspects of life at the time. For example, it was usual to specify that such houses included servants' bedrooms in addition to family rooms; stables and coach houses were also a common feature, as were on-site water supplies. The ads often mentioned well-stocked gardens – an important attraction for large households. Other selling points included sea views and/or proximity to the Atmospheric Railway (from 1844 to 1854).

Small terraces, such as Edward Terrace and Eagle Terrace, and houses were built on infill sites on Sorrento Road from the 1850s. Samuel McComas owned a site on Sorrento Road which he leased to the Metropolitan Police in 1845; the police station was later enlarged and had an access from Tubbermore Road, which was known as Barrack Street and Ben Eder Road in the 1860s. The opening of Dalkey railway station in 1854 led to the construction of what is now known as Railway Road and the development of residential properties such as Leinster Terrace and Connaught Terrace in the vicinity. Up to then Sorrento Road had merged with Castle Street; now its western end was clearly defined, with the building which now houses Finnegan's pub being built in 1862.

In general we know little about the contractors who built the houses and terraces around Dalkey in the nineteenth century, but John Cunningham is an exception. Cunningham lived at Johnville, a small house south of Castle Street which he later enlarged. When the railway company built Railway road and the railway bridge just west of the station, Cunningham bought glebe land on the south side of the railway line. He built large five-bedroom houses on Ardeevin Road in 1863 and laid out the road that bears his name. As a public works contractor, his firm was responsible for major works at Coliemore harbour in 1868.

Castle Street accommodated both residential and commercial properties; shops and pubs often included living quarters. Gerrard Tyrrell owned several properties on the street, including eleven cottages. William Porter of Kent Terrace appears to have developed Porter's Road (now St Patrick's Road) and Carysfort Road in the late 1850s, as shown on the survey map prepared by Mr Carmody for the town commissioners in 1863, but it was not until the early twentieth century that two major housing schemes were commenced on these roads: local authority cottages on St Patrick's Road and Tramway Cottages on Carysfort Road.

Ulverton Road was built about 1844 (Fig. 7.5); before that time the main route from Kingstown to Dalkey was via Glasthule, Castlepark Road and Barnhill Road, with a foot path linking Bullock and Dalkey Castle (shown as a dotted line on Taylor's map in 1816 — see Fig. 3.4). Once more Gerrard Tyrrell seems to have been one of the key landowners; in 1845 he advertised the letting, in one or more lots, of 600ft of building ground 'fronting the new street' in the town of Dalkey.[6] Some years later, he was instrumental in requesting the grand jury for the county of Dublin

'to make Presentments to repair 168 perches [approx. 840m] of the road from Dublin to Dalkey, between the turn to Bullock harbour and Dalkey Street, at an expense of £200, to be defrayed by the Barony of Rathdown; and also to build 626 perches [approx. 3,130m] of the parapets and fence walls on said road, between the steep hill at Bullock and Dalkey Street, as a protection to said road, at an expense of £150, to be defrayed by said Barony'.[7]

Terraced houses were built in the 1860s, when the street was one of the first in Dalkey to be lit by gas lights. The opening of Ulverton Road facilitated the construction of Church Road and Carysfort Road, both housing streets, and in 1879 it formed part of the first tram route into Dalkey (see Chapter 9).

For centuries the area around Bullock harbour had developed separately from Dalkey, and it had its own fishing community. The Ballast Board built pilots' cottages beside the quay in 1806, and initially the road leading uphill to local granite quarries was a private road owned by the Board. According to O'Flanagan,

'On the extreme end of the right wall of Harbour Road stands the cottage which, formerly kept by "Crow" Cullen, was owned by the Ballast Office; the tenant operated a gate, barring passage to all but persons with genuine business on Harbour Road'.[8]

However, the Ballast Board donated a site on the road for St Patrick's church, opened in 1843, and a succession of substantial houses were built in the 1830s and 1840s,

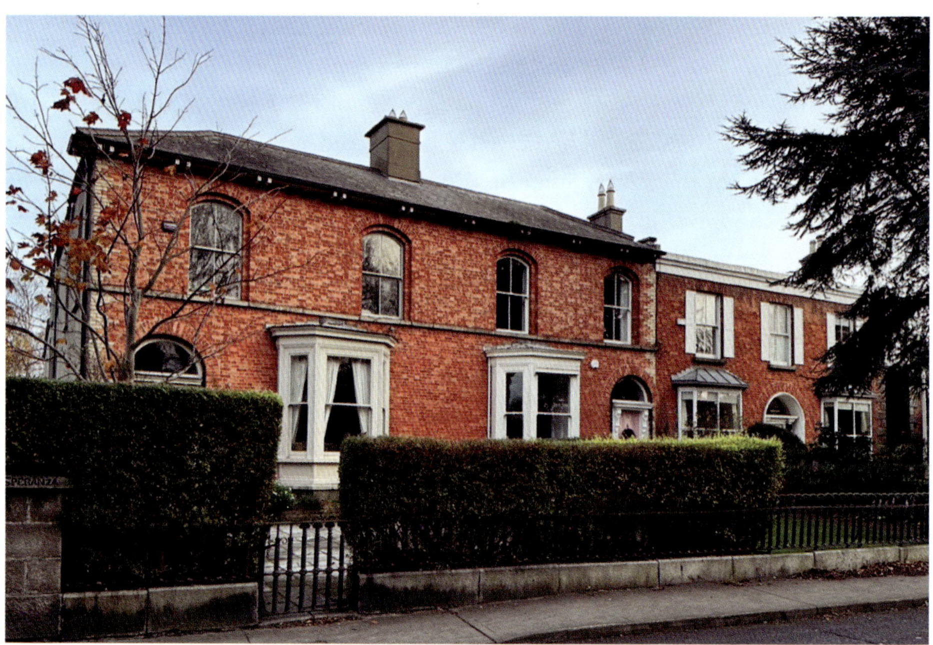

Fig. 7.5—Ulverton Road.

so that Harbour Road became a public road connecting with Convent Road. The latter may have had a previous existence as a lane leading from the village to the shoreline, but it acquired a new function—and a new name—following the opening of Loreto Abbey convent and school in 1843. An advertisement in 1844 for the recently built Beulah testified to the quality of houses being provided on Harbour Road:

> 'First-class country residence, opposite Dalkey Church, to be let for the remainder of the season. On 2 acres, large coach house and stabling. Plentiful supply of water. 3 reception rooms, 5 bed chambers, servants' hall and apartments. Dressing rooms, water closet.'[9]

It is worth noting the references to both water-supply and sanitation in the advertisement. Dalkey had no piped water-supply until the arrival of Vartry water from Dublin Corporation's reservoir in County Wicklow around 1870; wealthier residents had private pumps, while the poor relied on a limited number of pumps on public streets, such as the one on Tubbermore Road. Similarly, there was no comprehensive sewerage system until one was developed by the town commissioners in the mid-1870s (see Chapter 12).

8.
Dalkey schools and churches

As Dalkey's population expanded from the 1820s onwards, there was a need to provide new schools and churches. The schools were mostly founded by the two main religious denominations—Catholic and Church of Ireland—but from the outset there was also a tradition of small private schools, often located in larger houses. The Catholics in early nineteenth-century Dalkey tended to be poorer than their Protestant neighbours, and their new parish church on Castle Street, opened in 1841, was a much less elaborate building initially than St Patrick's church on Harbour Road, opened two years later; both had to be enlarged later in the century as new residents continued to settle in the area.

Schools

Dalkey is well provided with schools—four primary and one secondary, all of which were established over a century ago. This chapter sets out the history of those schools and also describes a wide range of small private schools that existed at different times during the nineteenth and early twentieth centuries.

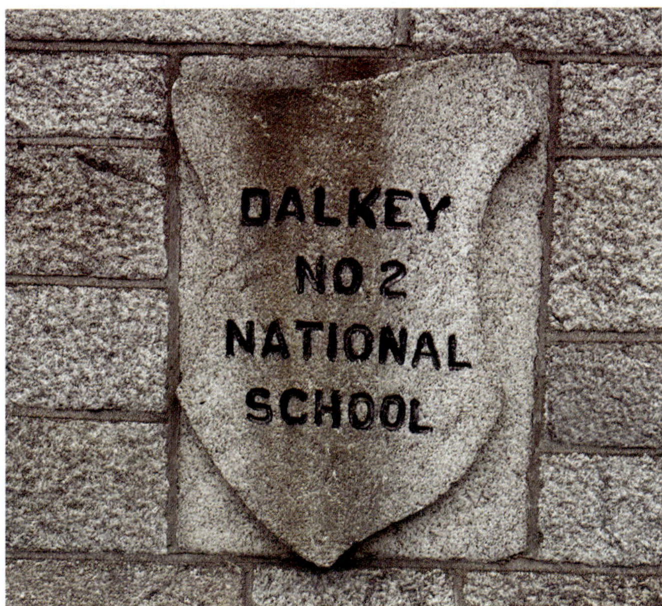

Fig. 8.1—Plaque attached to St Patrick's NS, Harbour Road. (The first national school in Dalkey was at Barnhill Road.)

Charity school, Dalkey Commons

Dalkey and Bullock were relatively small settlements during the eighteenth century. It is possible that the children of tenant farmers and fishermen were educated in hedge schools, but it is in the nature of such shadowy schools that no evidence of their existence in the area survives. The sudden arrival of hundreds of migrant quarry-workers after the opening of Dalkey quarry in 1817 created an immediate need to provide some form of education for their children. The workers were poorly paid; many families lived in makeshift accommodation near the quarry, including squatters on rocky grazing land on Dalkey Commons.

The earliest school that we know about was a charity or 'poor' school founded around 1820 on Sorrento Hill, although its precise origins are somewhat opaque. According to the history of the Irish Franciscans,[1] a number of laymen in the Third Order of St Francis had established a residence and school in Milltown, a suburb of Dublin, in May 1820 for poor children and illiterate adults. They named it Mount Alverna, in memory of the mountain in Tuscany where St Francis saw a divine apparition in 1224. A second foundation, also called Mount Alverna (later changed to Mount Alverno), was established on Sorrento Hill in November 1820 under the direction of Fr Francis Smyth, a Franciscan from Merchants' Quay friary. However, Fr Smyth himself claimed that he had bought land there in the 1820s and had built a small house and chapel.[2] Ownership of the land led to later conflict between Fr Smyth and his religious superiors.

D'Alton, writing in 1838, described the school as being 'on the ascent of the hill above Dr MacDonnell's cottage [Sorrento Cottage] … maintained by contributions of the gentry and attended by 90 children of both sexes'.[3] A school is clearly identified at Mount Alverno on a draft Ordnance Survey map produced in 1837 (known as a fair plan),[4] but was not shown on a further draft in 1837. It may be that most of the original squatters nearby had either been bought out by developers or had left the area, since stone production at Dalkey quarry was reduced as Kingstown harbour neared completion.

National school, Barnhill Road, and Harold Boys' National School, St Patrick's Road

The school on Barnhill Road, although it no longer exists as such, was the predecessor of Harold Boys' National School on St Patrick's Road between 1824 and 1901, and thus the two schools have a combined history of almost two centuries.

The second 'poor school' was developed in the 1820s on Barnhill Road, on the site of the former Walshe garage (Fig. 8.2); this school was also intended to serve the children of poor quarrymen, some of whom lived in a cluster of small houses on

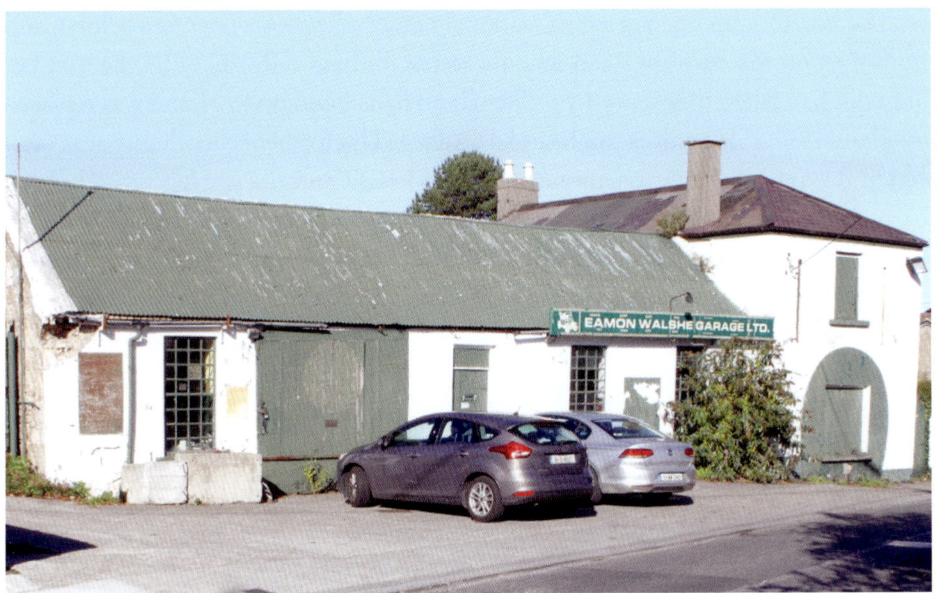

Fig. 8.2—Location of the former national school, Barnhill Road (prior to redevelopment of the site).

Ardbrugh Road. Although over 90 per cent of the 1,400 people living in Dalkey parish in 1824 were Catholic, there was as yet no Catholic church, and so it fell to Fr Doyle, parish priest of Loughlinstown, to advertise for a schoolmaster and mistress, and the school was built that year, funded by public subscriptions.[5] The first schoolmaster was Laurence O'Brien, who only stayed a few years.

By 1828 Dalkey had come within the remit of the Catholic parish of Cabinteely, and in that year Frs McKenna and Sheridan re-advertised for a master and mistress for the school (Fr Sheridan became parish priest of Kingstown in 1829 and was instrumental in building a church in Dalkey in 1841—see below). James Hunt and his wife Margaret were appointed, assisted by their daughter Frances. Two years later, however, Hunt appealed to the lord lieutenant for financial assistance, saying that since the stoppage of works at Kingstown harbour the poor parents were unable to pay school fees; his nominal salary of £6.10.0 per annum was insufficient, and he and his wife were providing free education.[6] The poor school became a national school in 1832, enabling a grant of £28 to be paid annually. According to an official report in 1835, 143 boys and 114 girls attended the school, some of whom paid one penny a week; all were taught reading, writing and arithmetic, plus needlework for the girls.[7] At a meeting of the school governors in 1836 in the schoolhouse, presided over by Fr Sheridan, it was resolved that two tons of coal be given for the use of the boys' and girls' schoolrooms.[8]

The Loreto nuns opened a girls' national school a few years later (see below), and from then on the Barnhill Road school catered for boys only. By 1868 the number of pupils had fallen to seventy-five. The school had closed by 1901 and was replaced by Harold Boys' School in the heart of Dalkey. The former schoolhouse was converted for use as a motor repair garage in the 1960s, and the site has recently been redeveloped for housing. The blessing of the new boys' school on St Patrick's Road, erected as a memorial to the late Canon George Harold (parish priest of Glasthule and Dalkey), took place in January 1901. The original school buildings have been expanded in recent years.

Loreto girls' secondary and primary schools
Mother Mary Teresa Ball purchased a three-acre site around 1840 from Charles Leslie, the wealthy merchant who owned Carraig-na-Gréine, off Coliemore Road (see Chapter 15). While Loreto Abbey was being built, she rented Bullock Castle and its adjoining house, where she established a temporary convent, a boarding-school and day-school. Following completion of the abbey convent in 1843 (Fig. 8.3), she opened a girls' school for boarders and day pupils along with a free school, the fourth Loreto foundation in Ireland in addition to Rathfarnham, St Stephen's Green and Navan. The road linking the abbey to Dalkey village became known as Convent Road. The primary school off Harbour Road/Convent Road joined the National School system, and 129 girls were enrolled by 1868.

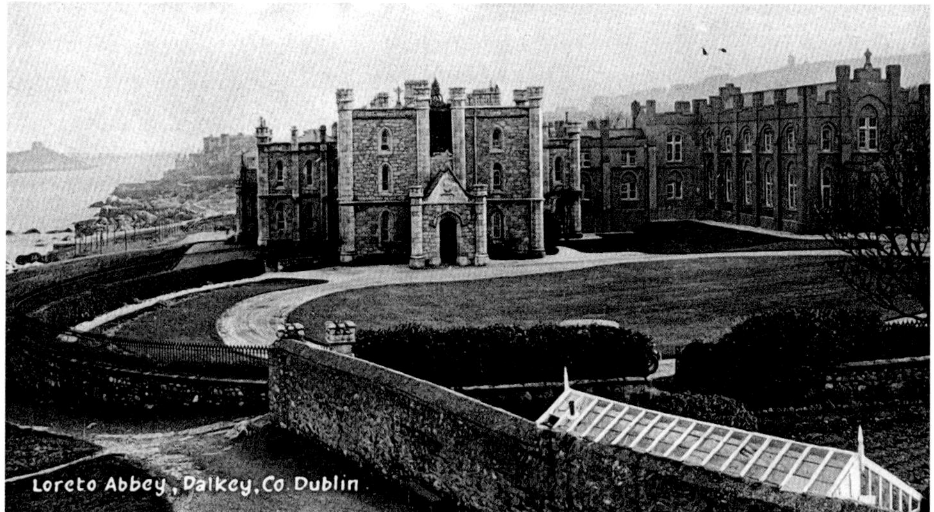

Fig. 8.3—Loreto Abbey, Dalkey (courtesy of the Irish Province IBVM (Loreto) Archives).

In the 1890s a co-operative group was set up in an old residence within the convent grounds to develop the general needlework and art of embroidery of girls leaving the school. Their work, particularly in the making of religious vestments and banners, was highly regarded.[9] The Loreto Sisters purchased Carraig-na-Gréine and its grounds from the Weir family (who took over from the original Leslie family) in 1934 and set up a private junior school, which remained in operation until its closure in 1987. The abbey secondary school has been continuously developed since 1843, the first major extension being the addition of a concert hall, large dormitory and music rooms in 1920. In 1982 the boarding-school was closed. More recently a large sports hall was constructed.

The primary school, which caters mainly for girls (with some boys in the junior classes), also built new classrooms and a school hall in the second half of the twentieth century.

St Patrick's National School, Harbour Road
While Charles Leslie contributed indirectly to the foundation of the Loreto secondary and primary schools through the sale of land to Mother Teresa Ball, he was directly responsible for the construction in 1868 of a primary school attached to St Patrick's church by donating £1,000 towards the construction of the sexton's lodge and par-

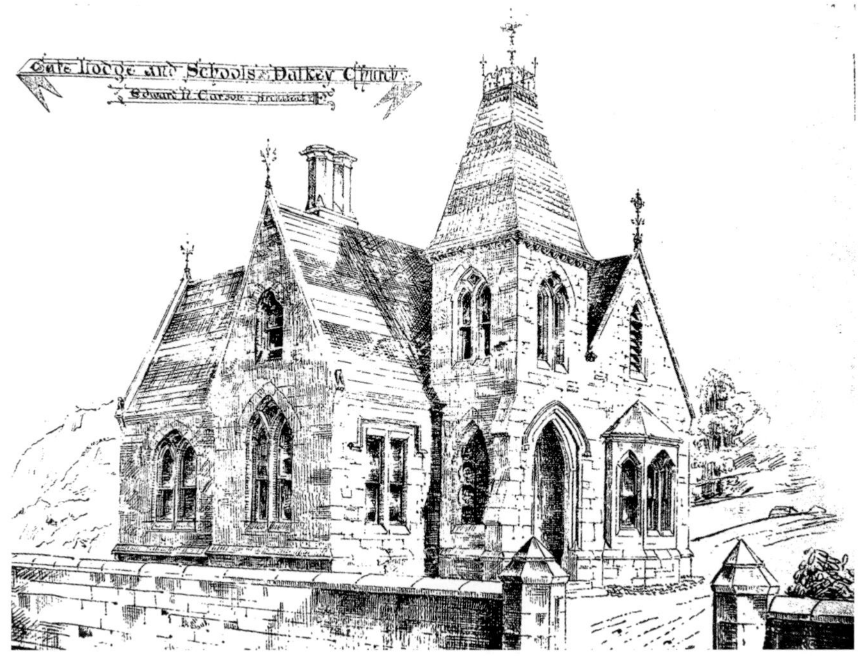

Fig. 8.4—St Patrick's school, Harbour Road, as depicted in *The Irish Builder*, 1 September 1870 (courtesy of the Irish Architectural Archive).

ochial hall, which was designed by Edward Carson, father of the famous politician (Fig. 8.4). An official report in 1868[10] recorded that Dalkey National School was located on Ulverton Road; this is likely to refer to the Dalkey Infant School which had moved from its previous location at no. 4 Castle Street in the late 1860s (see below).

Up to the 1950s there was one large classroom in what is now the Northover Hall building. Increased numbers in the early 1960s resulted in the provision of a new entrance hallway, kitchen and toilets, with a parish room and office upstairs.

Castle Park School

On 29 March 1904 the *Irish Times* announced that the castellated house known as Castle Park, set in 34 acres, had been sold for just over £4,000. In September that year an Englishman, Mr Wilfred Toone, founded a private school for boys, with an initial enrolment of twenty pupils. He handed over the school to Donald Pringle in 1938 and, after the latter's death, ownership passed to a limited company with charitable status in 1965. Castle Park is now a private independent primary school, educating boys and girls from age 3 to 12 years (Fig. 8.5).

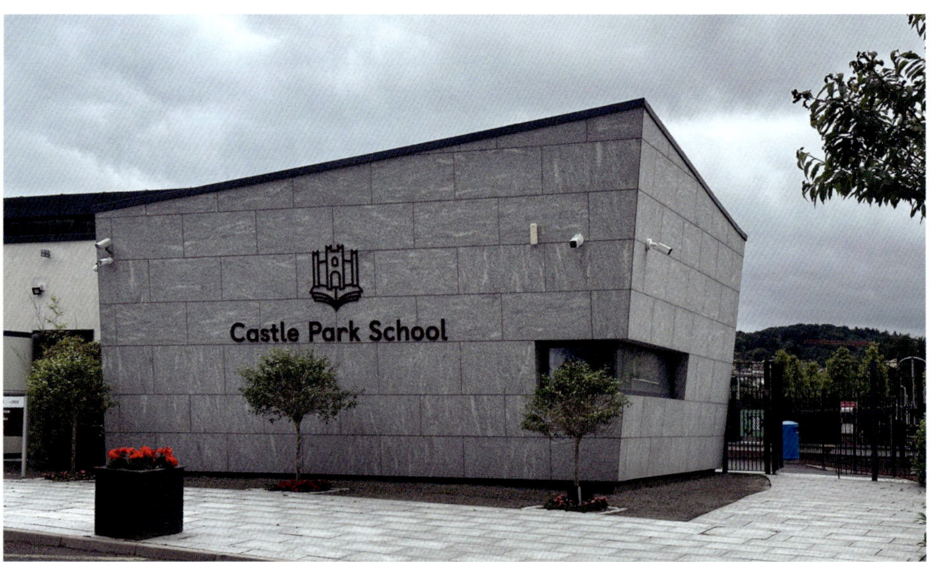

Fig. 8.5—Castle Park School.

Other private schools in the nineteenth and early twentieth centuries
Many small private schools operated in Dalkey at different times during the nineteenth and early twentieth centuries, but none still exists today.

A government report in 1826 recorded a school for twenty Catholic children in a thatched house run by an Esther Smith in the Dalkey area.[11] The exact location of the Dalkey Infantine Boarding School, run by the Misses Stephens in 1825, was not specified, but when they let their house in 1827 its description matched that of Rockview Lodge, which later became the Queen's Hotel.[12] According to *Thom's Directory*, there was another infant school, this time on the opposite side of Castle Street, in the 1840s and 1850s, initially operated by Catherine Ellis. This was linked to St Patrick's church, with religious meetings being held in the evenings; the school moved in 1867 to Ulverton Road, most likely to the meeting hall near the junction with Carysfort Road. It was replaced by the new school beside the church in 1870. The Dalkey Collegiate School was based in Dalkey House, behind the current Masonic Lodge, from 1861 to 1866.[13] A Mrs Madden ran a private school at Kent Terrace which had twenty pupils in 1868, but it was closed by 1881.[14] Madame A. Pouteney taught French at Hillview Cottage, Castle Street, in 1892 (*Thom's Directory*). Almost directly opposite, Tudor House (now off Kilbegnet Close) was leased to the Portsmouth Naval Academy and used as a preparatory school for boys around 1900; S.A. Rootham was listed as the schoolmaster between 1912 and 1921.[15]

Clifton School

One of Dalkey's private schools, Clifton School, was immortalised in James Joyce's *Ulysses*, although not named as such. The school began life in 1893 at Clifton House, Coliemore Road, offering classes in classics, mathematics and modern languages, but it had moved to Summerfield House, Dalkey Avenue, by 1895. Joyce taught there briefly in August 1904 and reimagined his experience in the second chapter of *Ulysses*, which was not published until 1922. Long before that, in the autumn of 1904, the school had made its final move to Cintra on the Vico Road, where it only lasted a few years.[16]

Dalkey churches

At the beginning of the nineteenth century neither Dalkey nor Bullock had any functioning churches, as the medieval parish church of St Begnet in Castle Street had been in ruins since 1630. By 1900, however, there were three churches open for public worship (as well as a chapel in Loreto Abbey). During the century the total population increased significantly, but the proportion of Roman Catholics declined from 88 per cent in 1834 to 69 per cent by 1901.[17] This was largely due to an increase in the share of the Church of Ireland from 11 per cent to 25 per cent over the same period, reflecting an influx of wealthier Protestants.

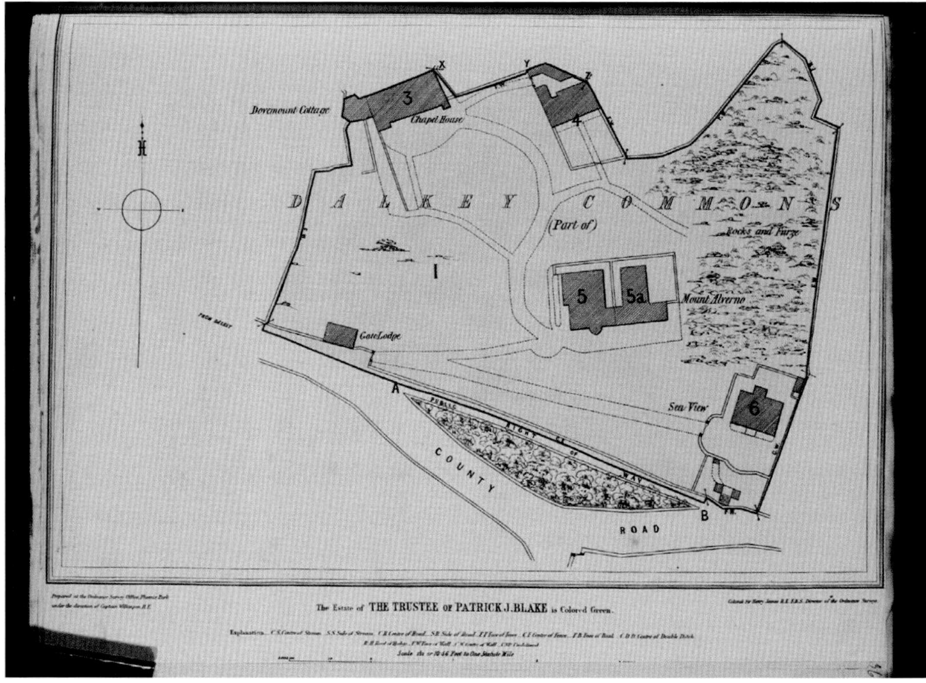

Fig. 8.6—Landed Estates Court map showing the Chapel House at Mount Alverno, 1868 (reproduced by kind permission of the Director of the National Archives).

Oratory at Mount Alverno, Sorrento Road

In the 1820s Fr Smyth, the Franciscan priest who developed the first 'poor school' in Dalkey, acquired some acres of land near Sorrento Hill, overlooking Killiney Bay. He built a house named Mount Alverno, and within the grounds erected a smaller structure known as the Dove House (adjoining the later Kilross House), which accommodated an oratory. As there was no Catholic church in Dalkey until 1841, he allowed local people to attend Mass in the oratory. After his death in 1853, when use of the oratory had ceased, some of the Mount Alverno property passed to the Franciscan order, with the remainder being inherited by his nephew, Patrick Smyth. The latter sold the Dove House in 1857, and the overall site was redeveloped in the 1860s (Fig. 8.6).

Church of the Assumption, Castle Street

In 1840 Canon Sheridan, parish priest of Kingstown, convened a public meeting in Dalkey with a view to building a Catholic church to serve the growing population; £400 was raised, and a site attached to Bay View House on the south side of Castle Street, opposite the former parish church of St Begnet, was leased by Thomas Con-

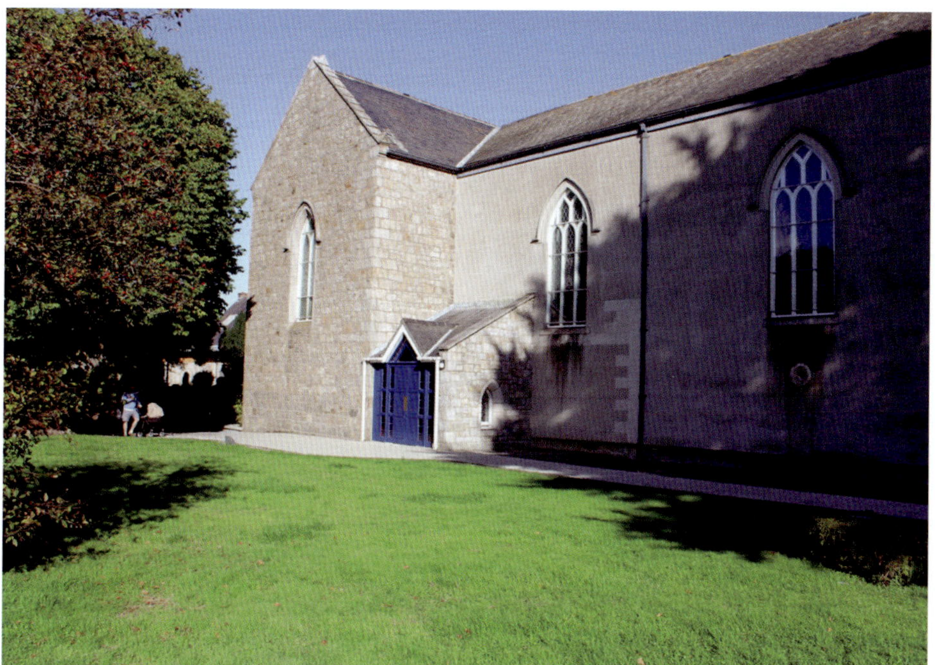

Fig. 8.7—Church of the Assumption, Dalkey.

nolly, who owned a thriving bakery business nearby. At first the structure, built of rubble and clad with plaster, was set back about 10m from the street. The new church was consecrated by Archbishop Murray in 1841. As Dalkey was part of the parish of Kingstown, a curate was appointed, but it was not until around 1884 that curates were housed in a presbytery at the rear of the church. Dalkey became a separate parish in 1927, with the parish priest living on Ulverton Road.

The church was rebuilt by Fr George Harold in 1872. This time, cut granite was used to build the extended church, which included a gallery and bell-tower; the sanctuary was brought forward so that the end wall of the church was at the back of the footpath on Castle Street (Fig. 8.7). The entire site was donated by Canon James Connolly, parish priest of Harrington Street and a son of Thomas Connolly.

The church was renovated for its 150th anniversary in 1991. The presbytery was demolished, and the site was used to provide old persons' houses at Kilbegnet Close and new houses for the priests to the rear of the church.

St Patrick's church, Harbour Road

By the early 1830s the Protestant population of the area from Kingstown to Killiney had grown substantially owing to the influx of new housing, but the only church

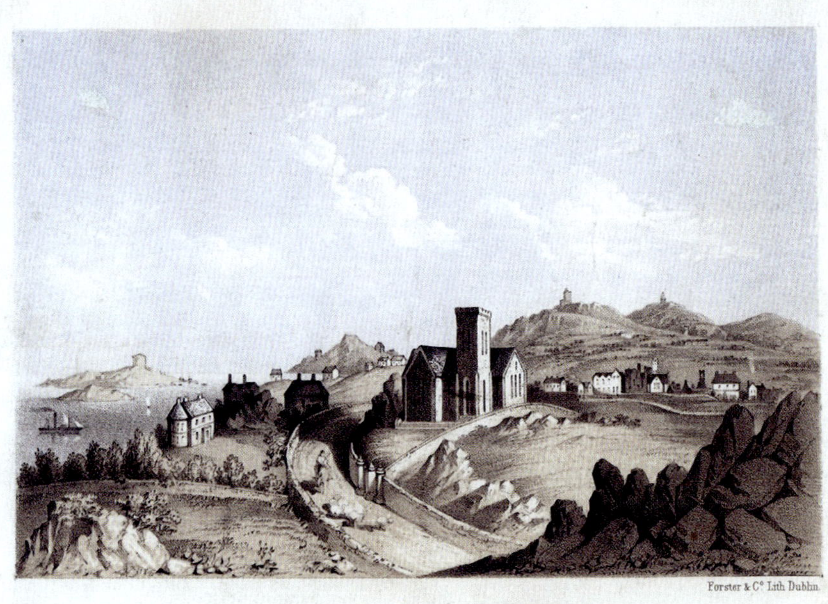

Fig. 8.8—St Patrick's church, Harbour Road (courtesy of Brian Meyer, Dalkey).

was in Monkstown, where the old building was replaced by a larger one in 1831. The Dalkey/Bullock area was served by St Matthias's church in Ballybrack from 1835, and also by a temporary church on Killiney Hill Road. The need for a permanent church to meet the needs of the residents had been identified and various sites had been examined by a building committee established in 1836. One of those sites was close to Castle Street; the site map indicated the future line of Ulverton Road,[18] which was not built until about 1844 (see Chapter 7).

Lieutenant William Hutchison, who had served as Inspector of Quarries for the Ballast Board (now the Port and Docks Board) at Bullock, was instrumental in persuading the board to sublet a one-acre site on Harbour Road for the proposed church at a peppercorn rent in 1837. Tenders for a church to accommodate 700 persons were advertised in April 1839, and a design prepared by Jacob Owen was accepted in July. A building cost of £1,600 was agreed with the contractor in April 1840, with stone from an adjacent quarry being used. The church (Fig. 8.8), originally a chapel of ease within Monkstown parish, was opened by Archbishop Whately in 1843 on a landmark site overlooking Bullock but was not consecrated as a parish church—St

Patrick's—until 1868.[19]

A meeting of the church trustees in 1861 recommended that a residence for the minister be built, as Revd Edward Leet and his family had been living in rented accommodation in Sandycove for over twenty years. It took a further five years before the rectory was completed, however, in a former quarry south of the church. The church itself was improved in 1879 through the addition of a new chancel, vestry and organ chamber.

Wesleyan chapel, Rockfort Avenue

A small Wesleyan chapel and preaching-house was opened on Rockfort Avenue in 1861. Its main sponsor was a merchant tailor, Samuel McComas, who had developed

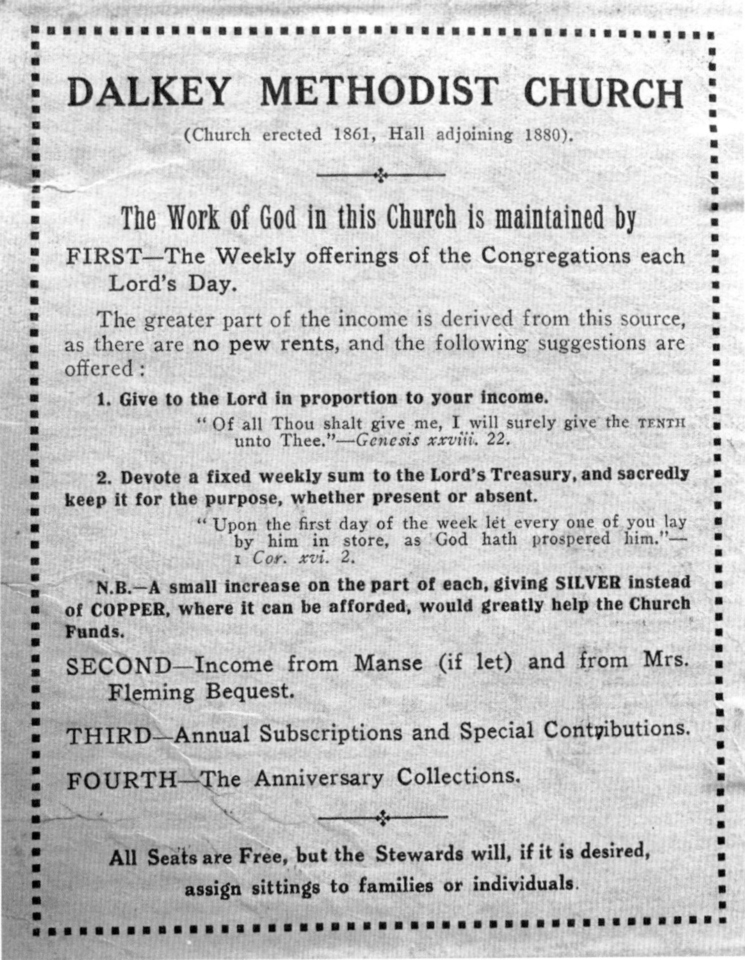

Fig. 8.9—Dalkey Methodist Church notice (courtesy of Peter Pearson).

Rockfort Terrace; the manse at Epworth on Rockfort Avenue and Rockfort House had been designed for McComas by the architect Alfred Jones.

The Methodist community in Dalkey numbered only seventy-seven in 1901 (compared with 831 Anglicans). The chapel was closed in 1973, and the manse was sold the following year.

9.
Trains, omnibuses and trams

At the time of the Act of Union in 1801 the built-up area of Dublin city was largely confined within the canal ring. By the end of the nineteenth century significant suburban expansion had resulted in the creation of nine townships outside the city boundary, stretching from Drumcondra and Clontarf on the north side to Dalkey and Killiney on the south.[1] It was no coincidence that all of the townships were served by train or tram lines, or a combination of both, enabling people to live in the suburbs and commute to work in the city. Dalkey's trains, and later its trams, also brought city residents to enjoy its scenic and coastal amenities at weekends and during the summer.

Railways
In the space of less than forty years (1817–56) Dalkey experienced three different railway systems: the truck railway that brought granite from Dalkey Hill to the new harbour at Kingstown, the Atmospheric Railway, whose cutting-edge technology attracted widespread publicity, and the steam locomotive trains that linked Dalkey to Dublin city and southwards to Wicklow and Wexford (from 1854–6 onwards). Diesel replaced steam power in the twentieth century, and the Dublin to Greystones section was electrified in 1984.

(i) The truck railway (1817– c. 1860)
Thanks mainly to the efforts of the Norwegian shipbroker Richard Toutcher (see Chapter 15), who not only campaigned for the establishment of an asylum harbour at Dunleary but also leased land near Dalkey Hill which gave him the right to quarry the underlying granite, an act of the Westminster parliament in 1815 established harbour commissioners. Other landowners on Dalkey Hill also gave their consent for the quarrying of the stone needed for the new harbour, whose design was extended to include a West Pier as well as the originally proposed East Pier. The new commissioners lost no time in issuing a specification to stone contractors: over 1,000 tonnes of stone would be required each working day.

Also in 1815, John Rennie, the harbour engineer, commissioned Netlam Giles

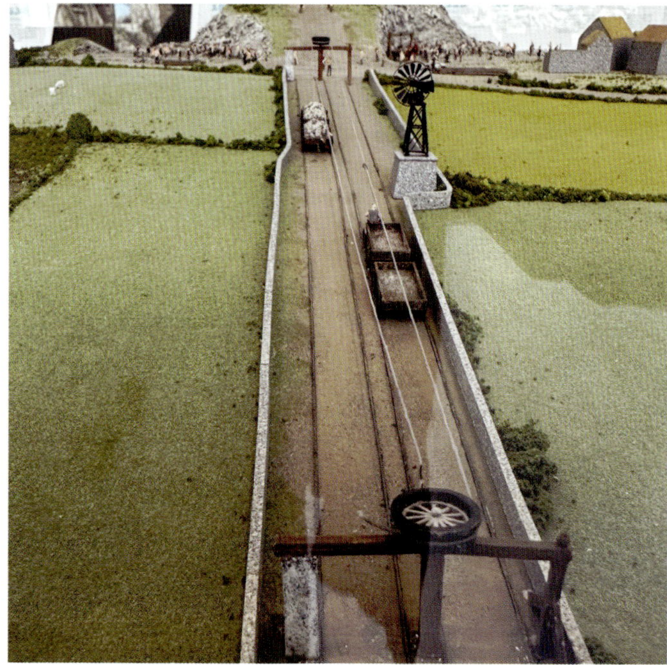

Fig. 9.1—Scale model of the Dalkey quarry truck railway. The model, by Gerard Crowley, is on view at Dalkey Castle Heritage Centre.

to survey potential routes for a truckway to transport the granite between Dalkey quarry and Dunleary, a distance of about 3km (Fig. 9.1). Giles identified four possible routes;[2] the route that involved the lowest gradient and least cost was selected, and we know it today as the Metals.

Horses pulled the laden wagons downhill and the empty wagons uphill; a system of pulleys and chains was used within the quarry itself—the location of the 'friction wheels' was noted on the earliest Ordnance Survey maps.[3] Over 200 men were employed in driving the wagons at peak production in the 1820s. The amount of stone required diminished after substantial completion of both piers in the 1840s, and use of the truck railway ceased completely around 1860. As will be seen in the following sections, however, part of the route of the Metals was used initially for the Atmospheric Railway from 1844, and subsequently for steam-driven locomotive trains from 1856 (and now the DART line).

(ii) The Atmospheric Railway (1844–54)

The Dublin to Kingstown railway, the first passenger railway in Ireland, opened in 1834, and even before then the railway company had in mind extending it southwards, initially to Dalkey, although it was to be some years before their plans could be implemented. In 1839 the directors, and James Pim in particular, became enthusiastic about an experimental atmospheric railway which Samuel Clegg and the Samuda brothers had demonstrated in London, and decided to adopt it for the proposed Kingstown to Dalkey line. Three years later, the Office of Public Works (which had taken over responsibility for Kingstown harbour from the commissioners) offered a loan of £25,000 to the railway company along with consent to use part of the truck railway route from Dalkey quarry. The company signed contracts with the Samudas to build the rolling-stock and with the foremost railway engineer, William Dargan, to carry out the earthworks. This involved excavating a 2.5m-deep cutting which would pass under any public roads along the 2.8km route; the company did not have any powers to acquire property compulsorily. Hundreds of workers were employed in 1842–3 in excavating the line and laying the tracks; extra costs were involved when granite was encountered *en route*. As surface water might have accumulated in the cutting, drainage pipes to the sea had to be laid.

The technology involved laying a vacuum pipe along the entire route, with a steam engine located at the Dalkey terminus just west of Barnhill Road, on the north side of the Metals (Fig. 9.2).[4] The steam engine and air pump created the vacuum that pulled the train uphill from Kingstown; the return journey was powered by gravity. A seven-carriage train could accommodate 200 people on the three-minute journey, but on average each train only carried fourteen passengers. There was a reservoir fed by a small stream to supply the steam engine and a shed at the terminus, which was about a three-minute walk from Castle Street.

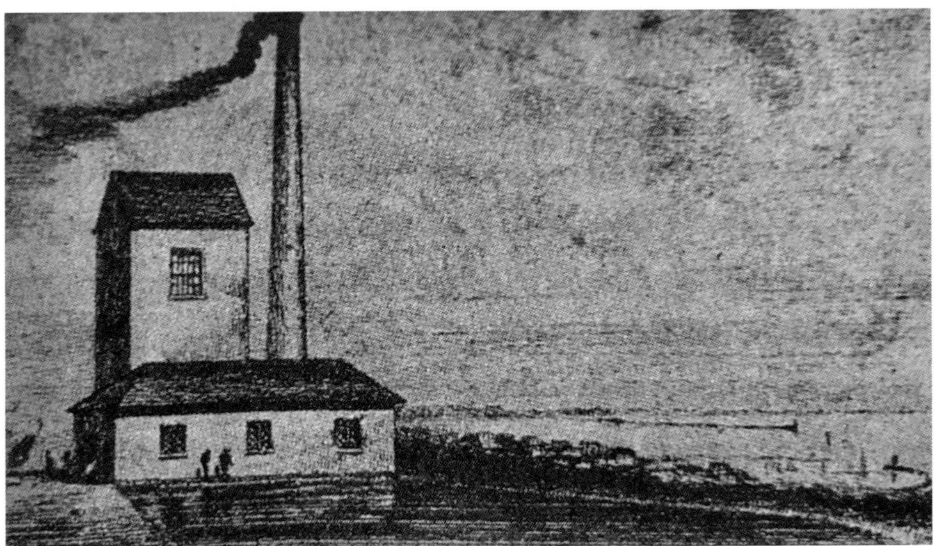

Fig. 9.2—The Atmospheric Railway engine house near Barnhill Road from John Kirkwood's 'View of a map of the railway from Westland Row to Killiney', c. 1844 (courtesy of the National Library of Ireland).

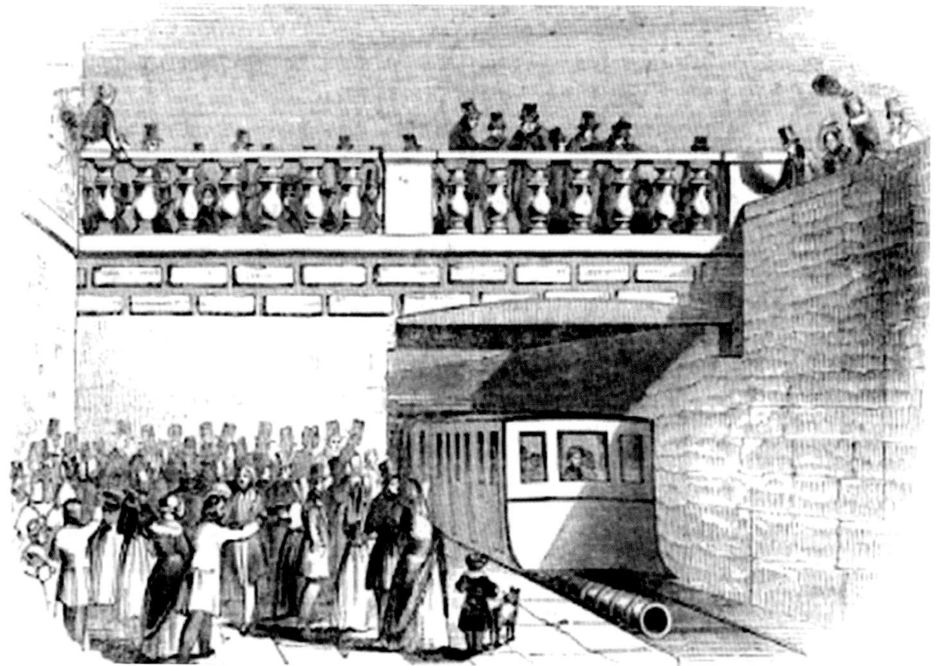

Fig. 9.3—The Atmospheric Railway station at Kingstown, 1844 (*The Illustrated London News,* courtesy of Alamy).

Work on the line progressed rapidly in 1843, with a successful experimental trip taking place in August. The Queen's Hotel in Castle Street, which appears to have opened in 1842 (see Chapter 11), began to advertise its proximity to the Dalkey terminus, even in advance of the official opening of the line in March 1844. Trains ran every thirty minutes in each direction between 8 a.m. and 9 p.m. (Fig. 9.3).

The route initially proved immensely popular; over 148,000 passengers were carried during the first six months of operation. As it was the only commercial atmospheric railway at the time, it attracted enormous attention throughout the UK and Europe. The King of Bavaria sent Dr Pauli, an eminent engineer, to inspect the system, and C.F. Mallet prepared a detailed technical report for the French government. Newspaper advertisements for houses for sale or rent around Dalkey mentioned the railway, and a public house at the bottom of Barnhill Road was named the Atmospheric Tavern.

As early as 1844 the railway company mooted the possibility of extending the railway from Dalkey to Bray using the atmospheric system, but the limitations of the technology became more apparent as time passed. In particular, it proved difficult to maintain an adequate vacuum in the leather pipe, and commuters from Dalkey to the city centre were obliged to change to a locomotive train at Kingstown. It was decided, therefore, that the entire route from Kingstown to Bray and onwards to Wexford would use steam engines, although this would entail adapting the route from Kingstown to Dalkey, making it wider and deeper to accommodate locomotive trains. The last atmospheric train ran on 12 April 1854 after ten years of operation, and the line was handed over for adaptation. The engine house and other facilities at the Dalkey terminus were dismantled, but the location of the terminus between Barnhill Lawn and the present DART line can still be discerned.

(iii) Locomotive trains (from 1854)

In August 1844 a delegation from the British Great Western Railway Company, including their chief engineer Isambard Kingdom Brunel, came over to see the atmospheric railway in operation. The company was planning to build a railway into south Wales to connect with a new sea route from Fishguard to Rosslare, and they suggested a joint venture with the Dublin & Kingstown Railway Company to develop a line from Dublin to Wexford. A new company—the Waterford, Wexford, Wicklow & Dublin Railway—was incorporated by act of parliament in 1846, and work started on the section from Dublin to Wicklow the following year, notices having been served on affected landowners along the route.

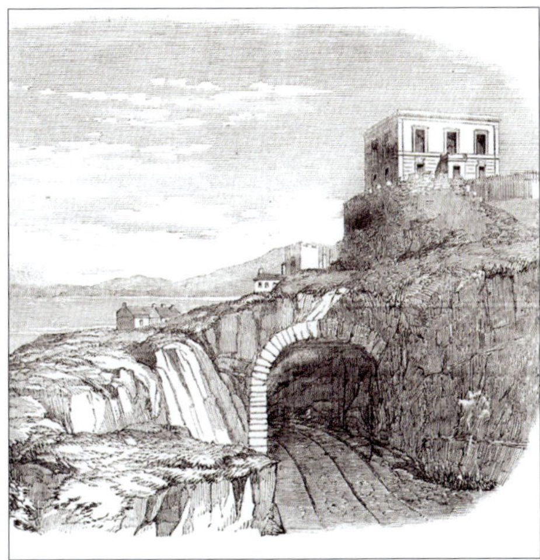

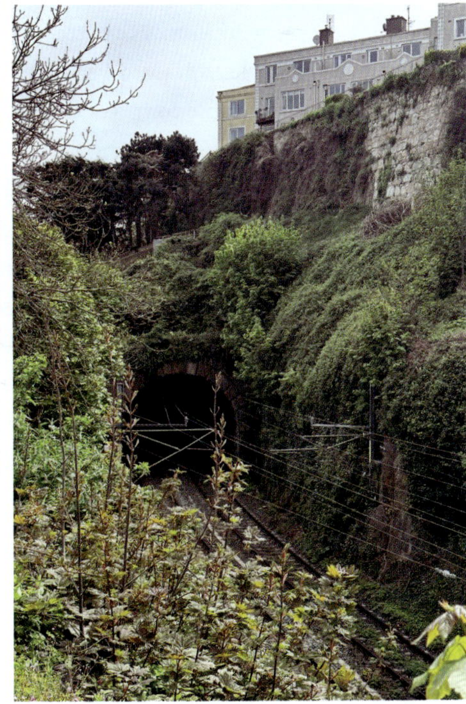

Fig. 9.4—Left: Railway tunnel between Dalkey and Killiney, with Khyber Pass House on the right (*Illustrated London News*, 3 November 1855, courtesy of Alamy). Right: The same view today, with apartments on the site of Khyber Pass House.

Construction work involved creating a deep cutting into the granite between Barnhill Road and the proposed new railway station at the eastern end of Dalkey village, to ensure that the gradient would not be too steep for trains. The next stage was to excavate a tunnel near Martin Burke's house, Khyber Pass, overlooking the Vico Road (Fig. 9.4), followed by the building of retaining walls to protect the railway above the cliffs at Killiney Bay. William Dargan once more supervised the engineering challenges involved, which were particularly significant around Bray Head, where hundreds of pounds of gunpowder were required for blasting each day.[5] It was decided in 1851 that the company would focus initially on the line to Wicklow, as the original plan for the 245km route to Waterford was deemed too ambitious.

An inland railway from Harcourt Street to Bray was also constructed; the first steam trains ran from Bray to Harcourt Street and from Bray to the new station in Dalkey in July 1854. However, work could not start on the Kingstown to Barnhill Road section until the route was handed over after closure of the atmospheric railway in 1854. The line had to be widened to accommodate the standard railway gauge, 1,600mm, compared to the 1,435mm gauge of the atmospheric trains; curves had to be eased and the ground deepened to allow the chimneys of the steam engines to pass under the bridges *en route*. An omnibus service operated between Kingstown and Dalkey during the construction works.

The first trains between Kingstown and the new Dalkey station commenced in July 1856; the new station was better located to serve the extensive housing development that had taken place on Dalkey Commons during the preceding decades, and commuters were able to travel the entire route to Westland Row station without having to change trains at Kingstown. Excursion trains for events such as boat races proved popular and boosted Dalkey's popularity as a recreational resort, including its hot baths near Coliemore harbour and day-trips to Dalkey Island. As had happened with the atmospheric railway, advertisements for houses mentioned walking distances to the new station; the access road was called Railway Road, with a small hotel of the same name being located near the junction with Castle Street.

Between 1878 and 1881 the volume of rail traffic required the laying of a second track, which in turn necessitated the widening of cuttings and tunnels. The line from the city centre to Greystones was electrified as part of the DART project in 1984.

Omnibuses

Pending the arrival of the first tram from Kingstown to Dalkey in March 1879, Dalkey was served by a variety of horse-drawn cars and omnibuses, operating on public roads. As early as 1828 an advertisement for the letting of two houses on Dalkey Avenue mentioned that 'public cars' left Dalkey for Dublin at 8 a.m., 9 a.m. and 10 a.m. and returned in the evening.[6] These were the precursors of omnibuses, which were introduced in London in 1829, whereby horse-drawn coaches ran on commuter routes to a published timetable. In 1838 Thomas Cane, proprietor of probably the first hotel on Castle Street, thanked the directors of the Dublin & Kingstown Railway (DKR) Company for arranging an omnibus service from Kingstown station to his hotel.[7]

The arrival of trains in Dalkey from 1844 onwards spurred the development of the hospitality trade, including jaunting cars to bring visitors to scenic locations and to the baths at Coliemore harbour; Daniel Carr operated such a service from Castle Street throughout the 1850s.[8] According to the noted local historian F.M. O'Flanagan, Dockery's bus service ran a horse-drawn omnibus from Pat Byrne's tavern on Castle Street to Kingstown between 1850 and 1880.[9] Following the closure of the Atmospheric Railway in April 1854, the DKR brought in an omnibus service between Kingstown and Dalkey stations which lasted until November that year. In 1861 the Dublin & Kingstown Omnibus Company began a service between the city centre and Kingstown, with twelve return trips each day. The following year P.W. Bryan, a director of the company, developed a connecting service from Kingstown to Castle Street.

Horse trams

The omnibus was not without its drawbacks, however, particularly in terms of passenger comfort, as its solid wheels rode over cobblestone roads. A new system was devised in New York in 1832 whereby horse-drawn coaches ran on metal tracks set into the road, but it took decades before such 'trams' were adopted on this side of the Atlantic. The first Dublin horse tram began in 1872, operating between College Green and Rathgar. The trams were double-deckers, with the upper deck being open, and quickly proved popular with the public. Within a few years an act of parliament allowed the Dublin Southern District Tramways Company (DSDTC) to build two tramways, one of which ran from Marine Road in Kingstown (Fig. 9.5) to the junction of Castle Street and Convent Road, via George's Street, Glasthule and Ulverton Road, with a depot on the north side of Castle Street. For various reasons, including opposition from the railway company, the tram route was constructed using a narrow 1,220mm gauge rather than the standard 1,600mm gauge.[10] The line opened in 1879.

Electric trams

The DSDTC's second line, built to a standard gauge between Blackrock and Haddington Road (where it joined the Sandymount–city centre route), also opened

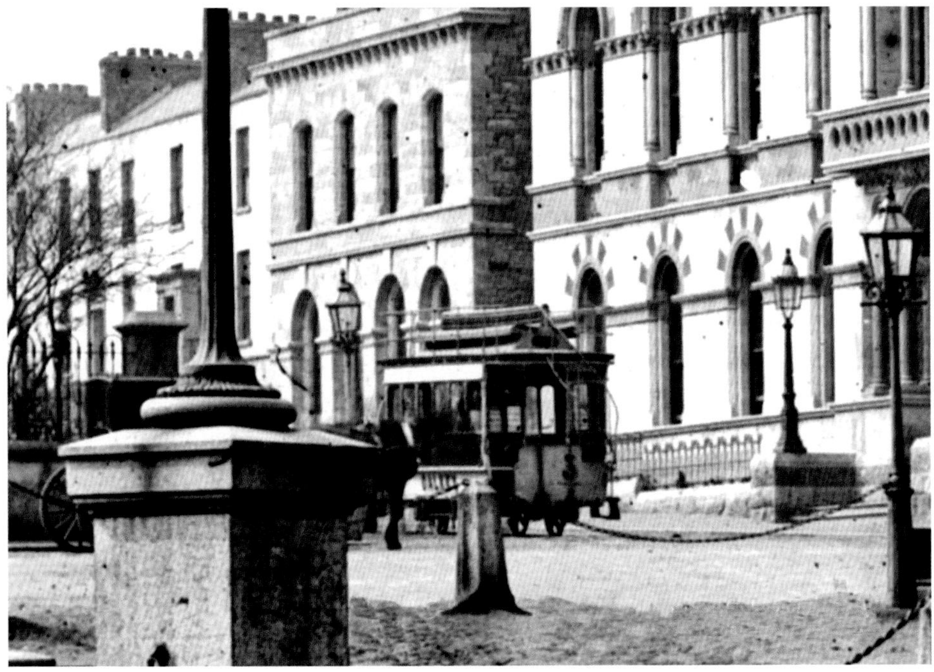

Fig. 9.5—Horse-drawn tram on Marine Road, Kingstown (1879–96) (courtesy of the National Transport Museum collection).

in the same year, but this left a gap between Kingstown and Blackrock for Dalkey passengers which was not filled until 1885, when it was operated by a different tram company. The journey to the city centre took much longer than the train trip and necessitated changing trams at Kingstown because of the different gauges. The DSDTC bought out the company running the Kingstown to Blackrock section and proposed the electrification of the entire line from Dalkey to Haddington Road. The acquisition and new technology were permitted by an act of parliament in 1893; electric trams had been successfully trialled in England since 1885.

The project involved reconstruction of the entire route, including the widening of the track from Dalkey to Kingstown. Electric power was supplied from the generating station at Shelbourne Road via underground cables to a substation at the Tramyard in Dalkey. The inaugural trip of the electric tram—the first in Dublin—took place in February 1896, with company officials and councillors celebrating the occasion at a function in the Queen's Hotel; the line opened to the public on 16 May (Fig. 9.6), with an extension to O'Connell Street in 1898.

From Dalkey the trams took about 45 minutes to reach Nelson's Pillar, and the competition forced the railway company to reduce its fares. Later in 1896 the

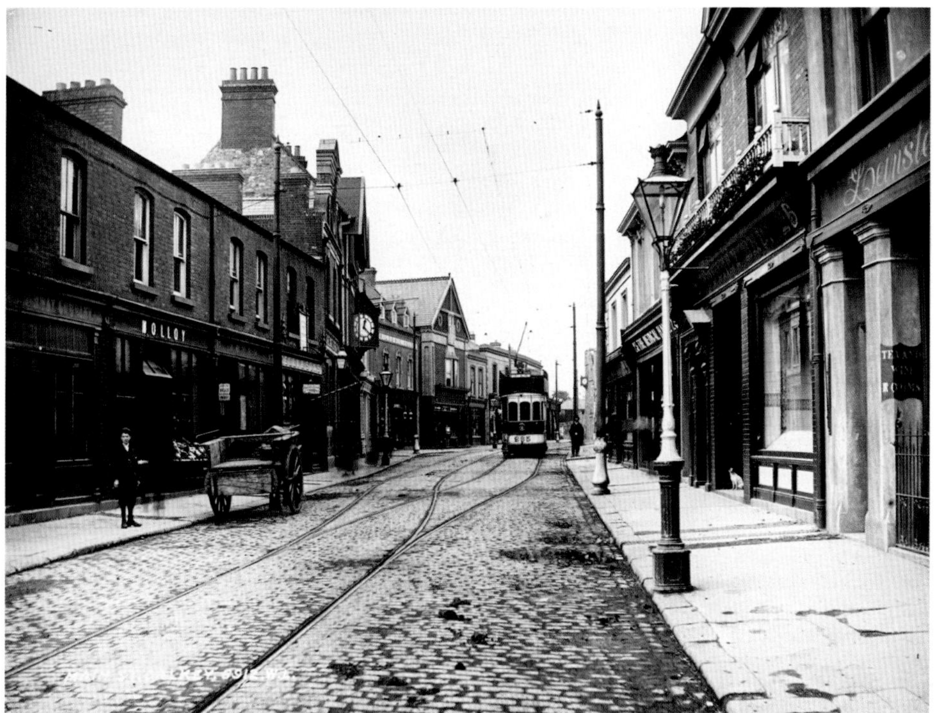

Fig. 9.6—No. 8 tram approaching its terminus at the eastern end of Castle Street, *c.* 1900 (courtesy of the National Library of Ireland).

DSDTC merged with the Dublin United Tramways Company (DUTC), which continued to operate the Dalkey trams until it was replaced by CIÉ in 1945. In 1918 the Dalkey trams were assigned the No. 8 route number, replacing the previous green shamrock symbol introduced in 1903; the number was carried forward to the bus route that replaced the trams after 1949.

In the closing decades of the nineteenth century the DUTC began to build cottages for its employees near its depots, including twenty-three cottages on Carysfort Road, just behind the Tramyard on Castle Street, which were constructed in 1914 (Fig. 9.7). These single-storey cottages were similar to other DUTC schemes, including that at Newtown Villas in Blackrock, which were built to a standard plan at a cost of around £150 per cottage. The tram cottages were typically of red brick, with a central porch flanked by a window on either side.[11]

In the late 1920s the availability of diesel-engine buses threatened the future of the trams, since the buses were not confined to fixed routes, and by 1935 the DUTC took the decision to phase out trams. The process was delayed somewhat by World War II; the last tram from Dalkey to Blackrock ran on the evening of 9 July 1949,

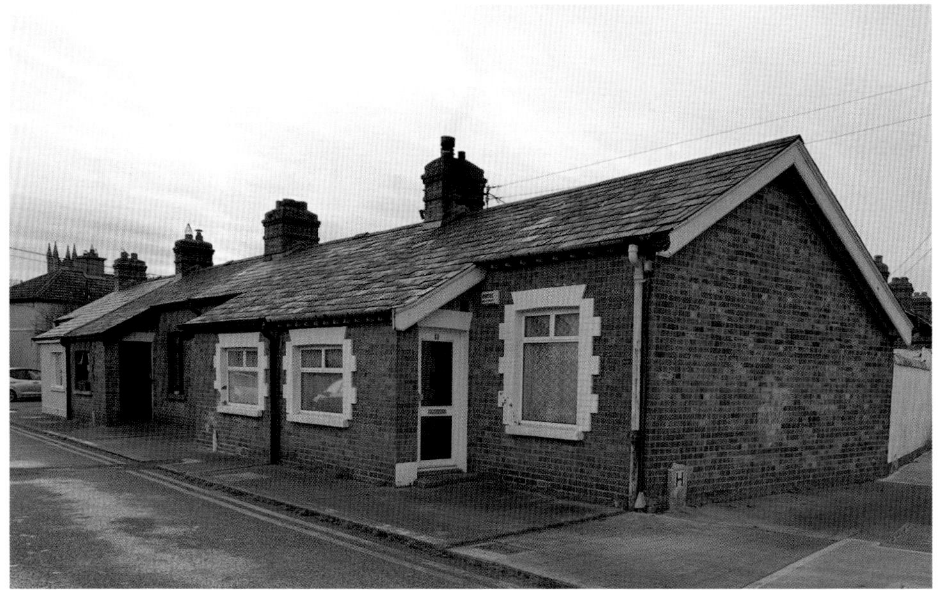

Fig. 9.7—Tram cottages, Carysfort Road, Dalkey.

but it was virtually destroyed by souvenir-hunters and vandals. One of the trams that operated on the Dalkey line was restored (DUTC 253) and is on display in the National Transport Museum in Howth, Co. Dublin. The Tramyard in Castle Street was used for a variety of purposes after its closure in 1949 and is currently awaiting redevelopment. The tracks set in cobblestones are still visible.

10.

Castle Street

1600 to 1800

Castle Street has been the commercial core of the wider Dalkey area for over 500 years since the castles were first built in the fourteenth or fifteenth century as merchants' storehouses. Between about 1600 and 1800, however, Dalkey reverted to being a quiet rural village on the fringes of the capital city, most of its inhabitants being farmers or fishermen. From about 1750 onwards it began to attract a handful of wealthier residents during the summer season, and it is possible that some small food shops would have opened on the main street. It is also likely that, as was the case in Dublin city centre, street traders would have supplied daily necessities such as bread, milk, fish and vegetables, and even clothes and shoes.[1] Two public houses were shown on the north side of the street on Reading's map of 1765, one on the site of the later Queen's Hotel.

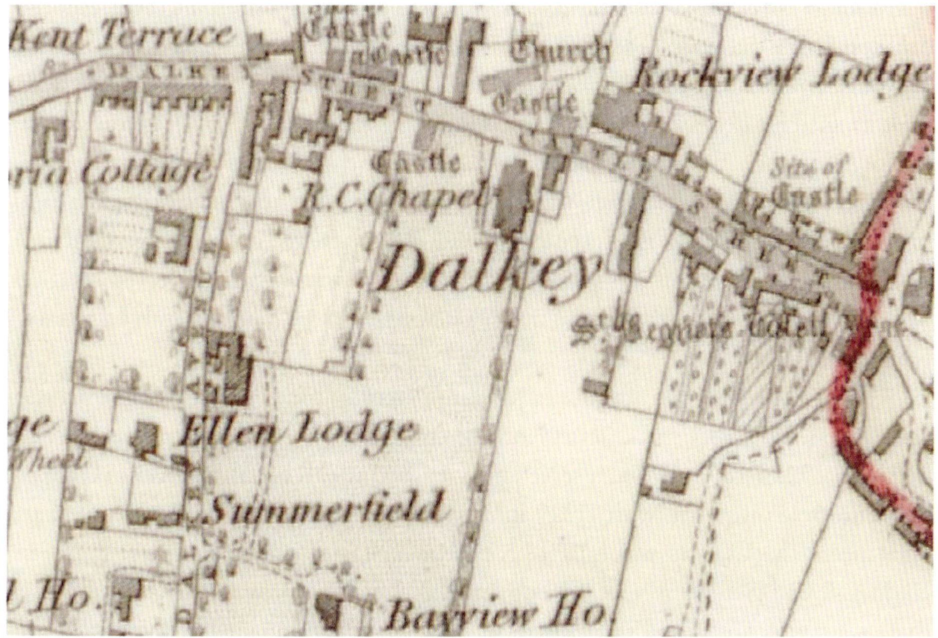

Fig. 10.1—Castle Street, 1843 (Tailte Éireann permit no. 50450108 © Tailte Éireann).

Name of the street

The name 'Castle Street' only came into use in the early nineteenth century; up to then it was generally referred to as 'the street of Dalkey', which was understandable given the size of the village prior to the beginning of housing development in the vicinity in the 1830s. The first 6in. Ordnance Survey map in 1843 (Fig. 10.1) shows that 'Dalkey Street' extended from Kent Terrace as far as Archbold's Castle, while Castle Street continued eastwards towards Sorrento Road, before the latter name was more widely used in the 1840s. There is very little information about commercial activity before then, except that a Mr Shannon operated a tavern in a substantial premises on the south side of the street prior to 1829. Two further taverns/hotels were opened in 1837 by George Sterling and Thomas Cane; the first lasted only a few months and the other closed after two years (see Chapter 11).

1840 to 1860

The first of Thom's street directories to list individual businesses on Castle Street appeared in 1846. Thomas Connolly, a prominent Catholic businessman (see Chapter 15), founded a grocery and bakery at the corner of Castle Street and Dalkey Avenue in the 1830s, a business which survived for over a century. He also operated the post office in the late 1840s in an adjoining premises, but this franchise was held by different traders over the years and hence in different locations within the town. Another business from that era—the Queen's, founded in 1843—is the longest-surviving business in Dalkey. The neighbouring Dalkey Hotel and Tavern, owned by John Helton until his death in 1847, became the Albert Hotel in the 1850s before closing its doors in 1862. Edward Harrison was a grocer and spirit dealer on the south side of the street in 1843; in the following decade he moved to new premises at the junction of Castle Street and the recently opened Porter's Road (now St Patrick's Road). Like Connolly, Harrison was one of the first town commissioners elected in 1863. There were two victuallers on the north side of the street, James Lamb and Garret Kindellan.

There were numerous business failures in Dalkey in the 1840s and following decades. It was still a very small settlement; the town had only 304 inhabitants in 1841, falling to 252 in 1852. While it served a wider catchment, businesses had to compete with nearby Kingstown, with 7,229 inhabitants in 1841 and 10,453 a decade later. This meant that as early as the 1830s Kingstown boasted a wide variety of shops, including several victuallers, taverns, boot- and shoemakers, grocers, a chandler, a linen draper, a confectioner and three chemists.[2] Alex Findlater opened his high-class grocery outlet in Kingstown in 1834; it was to be more than sixty years before the Dalkey branch was established. Three major hotels, including Hayes's Royal Hotel, were opened in Kingstown in the late 1820s;[3] in size and quality they were far superior to their more modest rivals in Dalkey in 1837. It should also be remembered that residents of Dublin city could access Kingstown by train from 1834, whereas the Atmospheric Railway between Kingstown and Dalkey did not commence services until 1844.

1860 to 1880

The sale of Michael Knee's property on the south side of Castle Street in 1862,[4] and particularly the descriptive details provided for the information of potential purchasers, provides a fascinating glimpse into the commercial life of Dalkey at that time. It is interesting that the location was described as the best business part of the town. Knee had been a shopkeeper in Dalkey since the 1840s, first as a provision dealer and later as a haberdasher. He became insolvent in 1862 and his property at 10–13 Castle Street was put up for sale at the Landed Estates Court. His title to those premises, together with a linear plot beside what is now the church car park, dated back to 1806. He leased No. 13 to Patrick Byrne, a vintner, for the modest rent of £3 a year; the house was probably the original from 1806 and the rear garden stretched back about 230ft, perhaps reflecting the medieval burgage plots. Knee built No. 12, which he leased to Robert Davis for £36 a year; Davis ran a successful Italian warehouse and grocery business. Knee also built No. 11, which was let to Samuel Baker at a yearly rent of £60; Baker had several other prosperous grocery shops in Dublin city. In the same year the annual rent for the Queen's Hotel was only £30. Baker's was probably the most prestigious grocery shop in Dalkey prior to the arrival of Findlater's at the end of the century. Knee himself lived in No. 10, which he had substantially rebuilt. He had leased land in 1828 to John Hynes, who also leased Rockview Lodge across the street; three cottages were shown on the plot in 1843. It may be that Knee overstretched his resources in the amount of construction he undertook, notwithstanding the substantial rental income from two of his tenants.

The first town commissioners elected in 1863 had very few powers, but one they did possess was public lighting, and by December that year street lighting was switched on in Castle Street, Ulverton Road and Dalkey Avenue. In November they appointed Mr C. Carmody CE to make a survey and enlarged map of the township; his map (Fig. 10.2), which is now on display in the Heritage Centre, shows:

- development on what would be called Greenmount Avenue by 1870;
- Railway Road leading to the station and the bridge leading to Ardeevin Road;
- what was called Barrack Street (now Tubbermore Road);

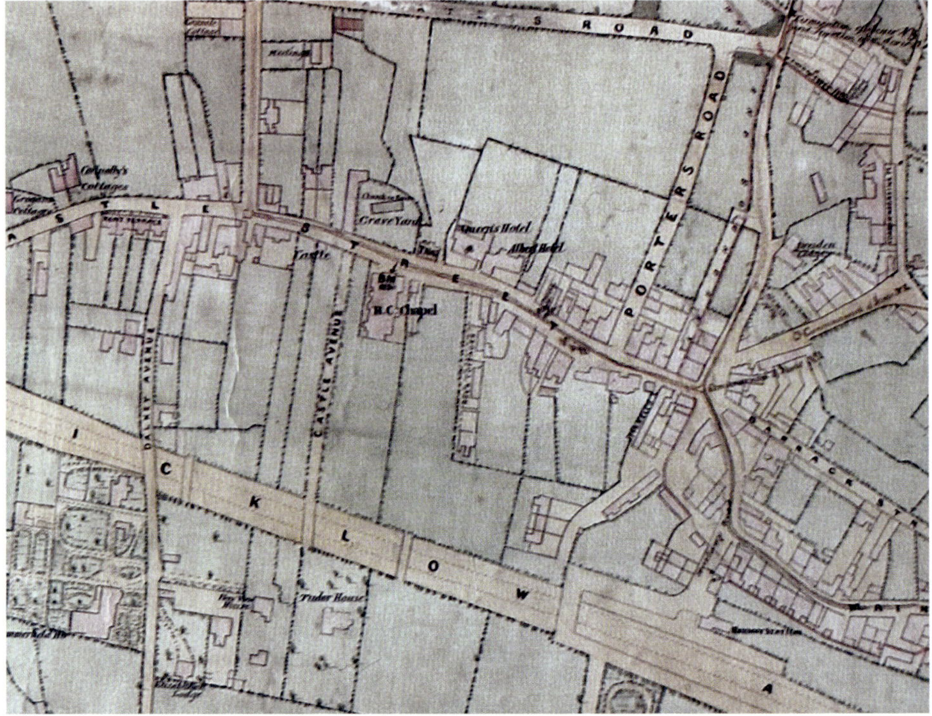

Fig. 10.2—Extract from Carmody's map of Dalkey township, 1863 (courtesy of Dalkey Castle Heritage Centre).

- the name 'Castle Street' applied to the entire length ('Dalkey Street' had disappeared by then); and
- Porter's Road (now St Patrick's Road and Carysfort Road).

The town commissioners leased Dalkey Castle in 1870 and refurbished it; it served as the town hall until Dalkey Urban District Council was replaced by Dún Laoghaire Corporation in 1930. The assembly room at the rear was built in 1892 and accommodated a variety of entertainments and public meetings. Dalkey Masonic Hall occupied the front part of Dalkey House in 1873, following the town commissioners' refusal of permission to use part of the Town Hall. Dalkey House was extended in the 1940s and was used for a few years as a hotel.[5]

1880 to 1900

In 1879 the Dublin Southern District Tramways Company began operating a horse-drawn tram from Marine Road in Kingstown to the junction of Castle Street and Convent Road, via George's Street, Glasthule and Ulverton Road, with a depot on the north side of Castle Street. Metal tracks were laid along the street as far as Convent Road, with a siding into the depot with its large tram sheds at the rear. When the line was electrified in 1896, overhead electric cables were installed; these can clearly be seen in the Lawrence Collection photo (Fig. 10.5). The earlier horse stables were replaced with an electricity substation. The inaugural trip of the electric tram from the city centre to Dalkey took place in February 1896, and the line opened to the public on 16 May. The terminus was at the eastern end of Castle Street, at the junction with Convent Road, while the tram ticket office was located where the Allcare pharmacy now stands.

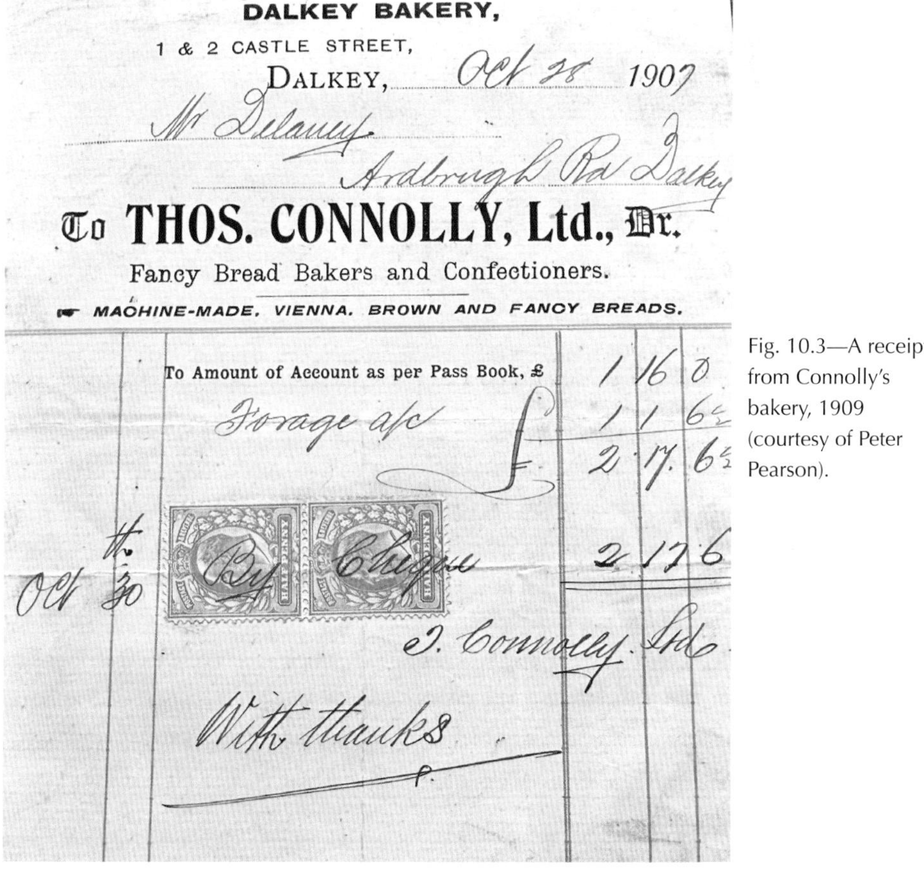

Fig. 10.3—A receipt from Connolly's bakery, 1909 (courtesy of Peter Pearson).

The Connolly family's bakery and grocery businesses at the bottom of Dalkey Avenue flourished in the 1880s, and included a corn and flour store on the opposite side of Castle Street. The horses were watered and fed in the adjoining field until the late 1940s, when Connolly's closed. At the eastern end of Castle Street the commercial core extended into parts of nearby streets, such as Railway Road, Coliemore

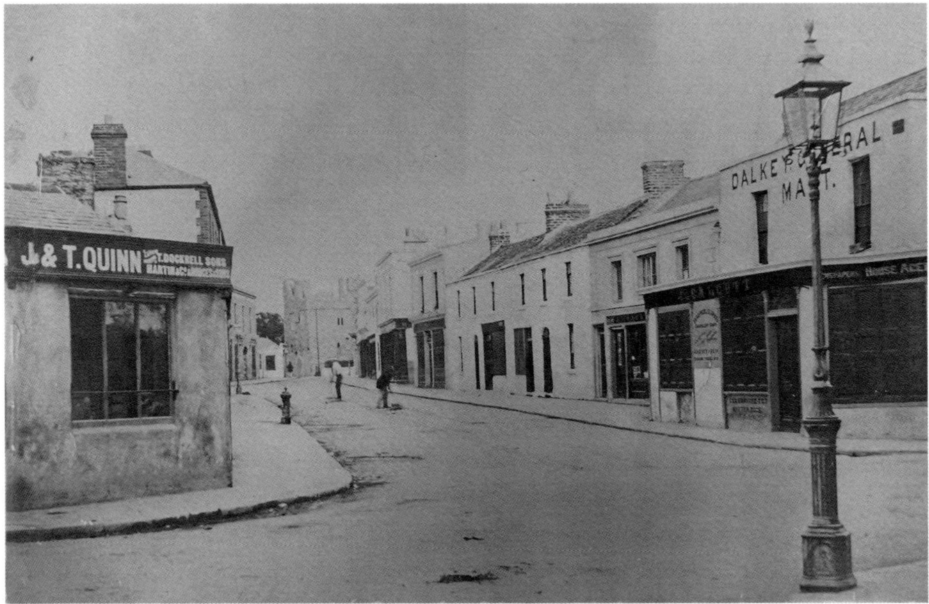

Fig. 10.4—Looking west along Castle Street, *c.* 1870 (courtesy of Local Studies, Dún Laoghaire–Rathdown Lexicon Library).

Road and Convent Road. For many years the post office was located near the railway station, with coal merchants such as W.A. McCormick based at the lower end of Railway Road.

There was considerable redevelopment at the eastern end of Castle Street, on both sides, in the closing decades of the nineteenth century and the first decade of the twentieth century. The photo in Fig. 10.4 is undated but is likely to date from the early 1870s, as no tram tracks are visible. Various members of the Calcutt family operated the Mart at the corner of Convent Road from 1870 until around 1900; at that time Fawcett Maxwell's pharmacy was where Deville's is today. There appear to be water-pumps on the footpath on the south side of the street. There is a plaque showing the date 1894 over the Dalkey News shop, indicating when the former two-storey building was replaced, while the current wine shop was given a more ornate façade.

1900 to the present day

By the turn of the twentieth century Castle Street could boast of a wide range of shops and services. *Thom's Directory* in 1901 listed seven specialist shops (pharmacy, etc.), six grocers/wine and spirit dealers, three meat and poultry shops, three drapers/dressmakers, three bootmakers, the Queen's Hotel, two restaurants, a bakery

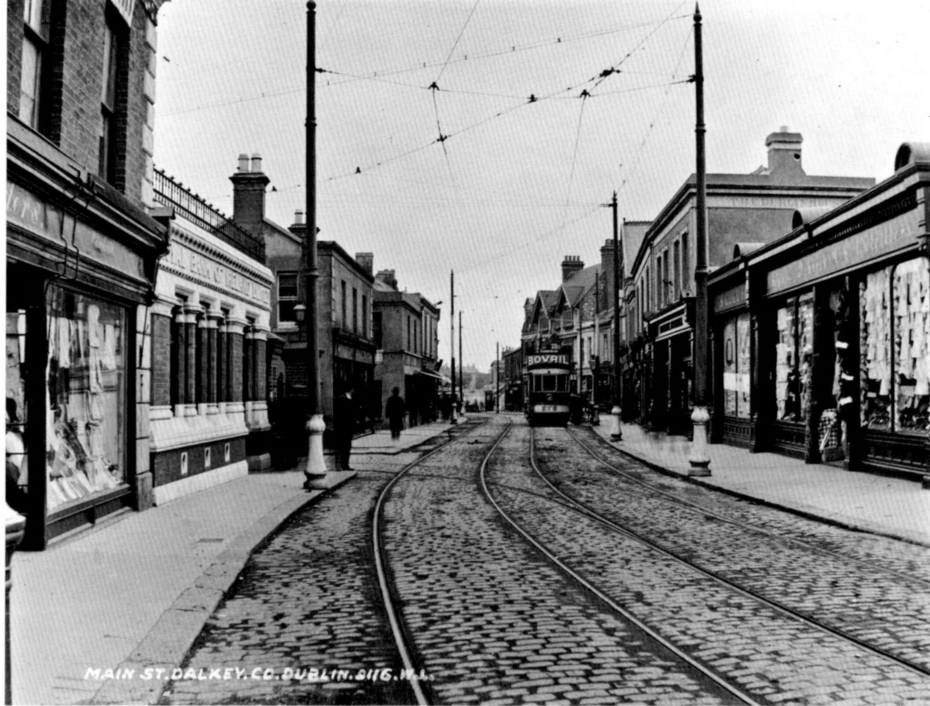

Fig. 10.5—Castle Street *c.* 1900 (courtesy of the National Library of Ireland).

and a public dispensary. This variety is indicative of the scale of social and economic development during the nineteenth century, which in turn reflected not only the increase in the population of the area but also its relative prosperity. In many of the larger houses it would have been standard practice to provide servants' quarters; their employers included the élite of Dublin city's professional and mercantile classes. In addition, the arrival of both the steam trains and the trams enabled middle-class commuters to live in Dalkey and work in the city. While the cumulative amount of development since 1800 was significant, it was incremental, with many land uses remaining constant over lengthy periods, Connolly's bakery and the Queen's being good examples.

While the ownership and usage of various commercial premises on Castle Street have changed over the past 100 years, the built form of the street has remained much the same. Around 1930 the Royal Bank of Ireland moved from its relatively small office at the entrance to the Tramyard to a much larger building at the junction of Castle Street and St Patrick's Avenue; the building was later occupied by AIB but is now vacant. The opening of Hyde Road in the 1940s led to the construction of the

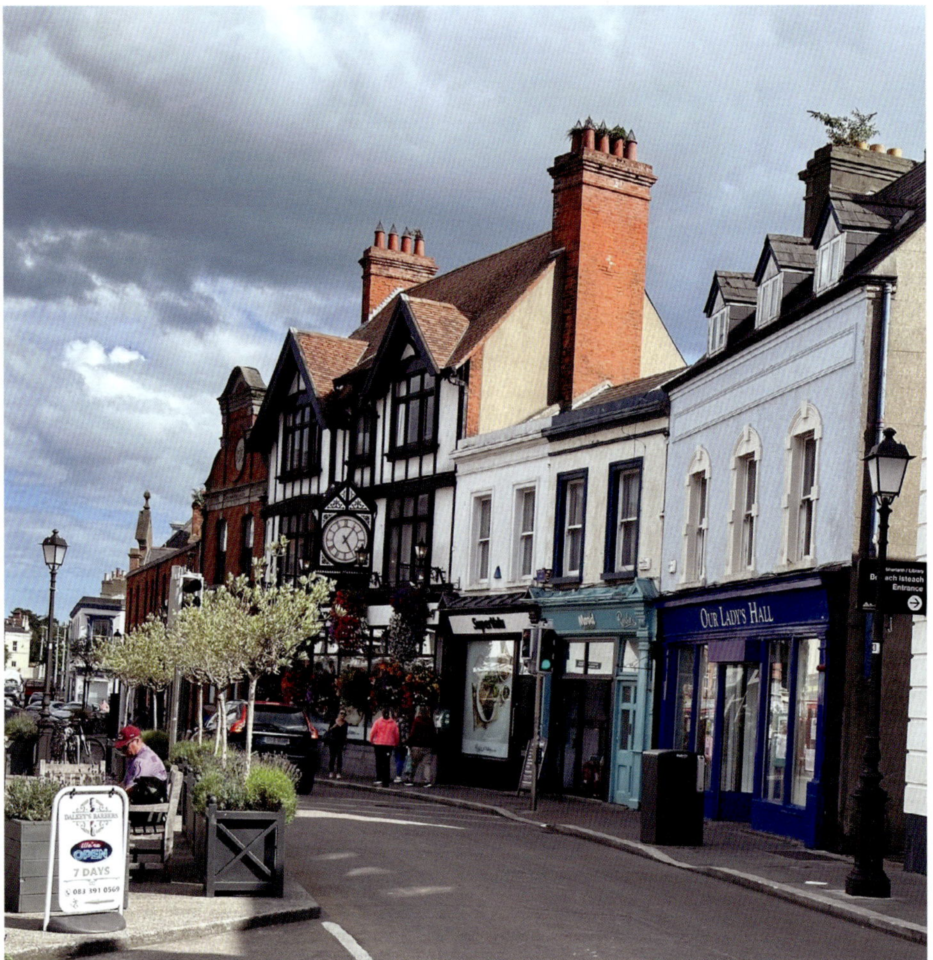

Fig. 10.6—Castle Street.

'Square-about' at the junction with Ulverton Road and Barnhill Road. When Findlater's shops around Dublin were sold in 1969, the Dalkey premises with its distinctive clock (Fig. 10.6) was purchased by H. Williams and later by SuperValu, who extended it at the rear. Otherwise the main changes to Castle Street have been residential development at Castle Mews, Termon and Kilbegnet Close, the new library and the Heritage Centre. Following the Covid pandemic which began in 2020, Dún Laoghaire–Rathdown County Council modified the street layout to narrow the carriageway and provide some outdoor seating areas.

11.

Pubs, taverns and hotels

Pubs and taverns in the eighteenth and nineteenth centuries

Dalkey village and its environs had a population of just a few hundred in the 1760s but it supported at least two public houses, the Ship and the Red Cross, both on the north side of the main street. As many of the poorer inhabitants at that time were illiterate, licensed premises often had decorative signs outside. The Red Cross was located to the east of Goat Castle, as shown on Reading's survey map of 1765 (Fig. 11.1).

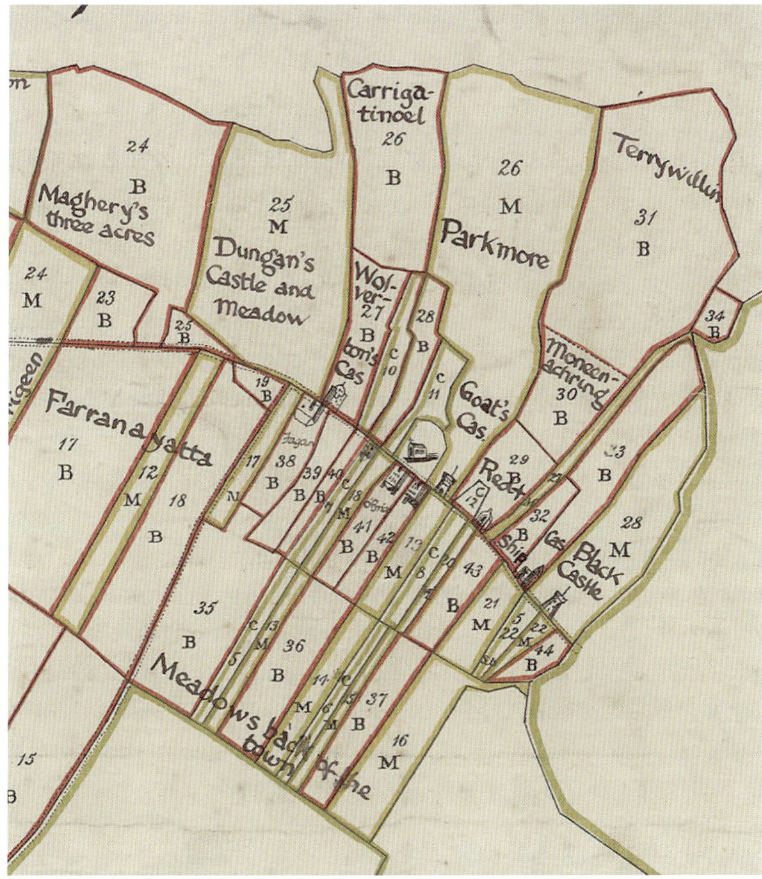

Fig. 11.1—Extract from Reading's survey map of 1765; the Red Cross can be seen at B29 and the Ship at B32, both on the main street of Dalkey (courtesy of the Royal Society of Antiquaries of Ireland).

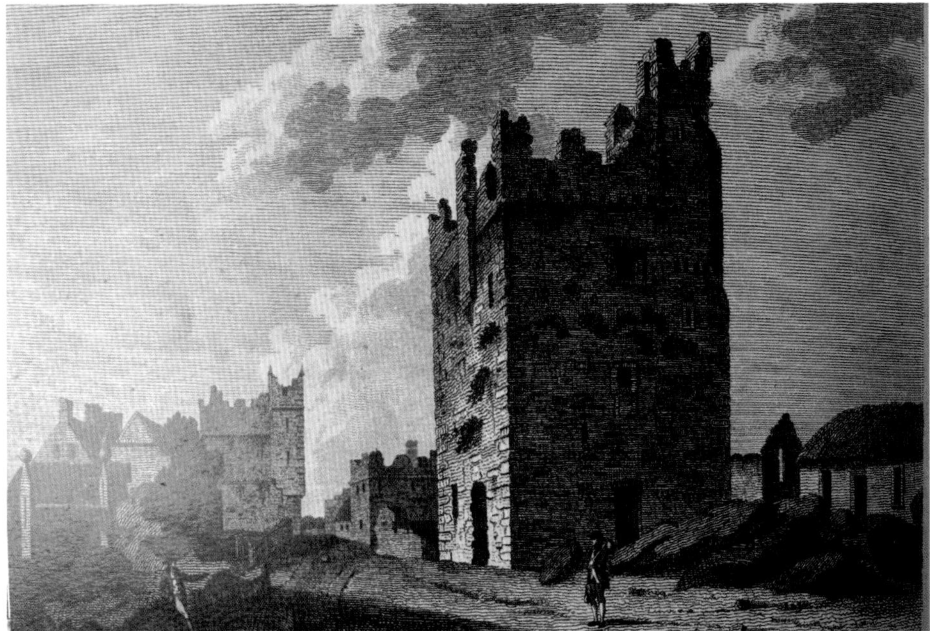

Fig. 11.2—Dalkey Castle by Francis Grose, 1791 (courtesy of the National Library of Ireland).

A plaque on the front elevation of the present Queen's premises claims that it was established in 1745; this is likely to refer to the original Red Cross, probably located in the small cabin shown in an engraving by Francis Grose dated 1791 (Fig. 11.2).

Sir John Hasler, an official in Dublin Castle who lived in a converted castle further east along the main street, leased the site adjoining Goat Castle in 1785. The lease referred to a cabin, almost certainly the one shown in Grose's engraving. Two years later Hasler obtained licences for a hostelry and for dispensing alcohol on the site, but at some stage after 1790 it appears that the cabin was demolished and replaced by a three-storey house, initially known as the Castle House and later as Rockview Lodge. Hasler died around 1800 and the property was leased out as a residence.

In the absence of a church or other public meeting place in Dalkey at that time, public houses provided a venue where locals could meet socially. As Reading's survey was primarily concerned with landholdings rather than buildings, it is quite possible that there were other pubs in the village. A Mr Shearman had a pub there in 1787, and a Mr Shannon had a tavern on the south side of Castle Street in the 1820s[1] (a tavern served food as well as alcohol). It had half an acre of garden as well as its own stables and coach-house, an important asset in the days before public transport; it also had a spring well to provide a supply of water (piped water did not arrive in Dalkey until the 1870s).

The number of public houses and taverns in Dalkey increased from the 1830s onwards, as new housing brought new residents and access by public transport facilitated a growth in visitors. One such was the Atmospheric Tavern, located at the end of Barnhill Road opposite the junction with Dalkey Avenue. A newspaper advertisement in 1843 drew attention to the fact that it was the nearest licensed premises to the terminus of the Atmospheric Railway, even before that railway opened for business in 1844. It went through a number of proprietors and changes of name, including the Rose Tavern and the Shamrock Tavern, with periods of vacancy, before closing in the 1870s. By that time the Atmospheric Railway had long closed and the new railway station was at the other end of the town. The site no longer exists, following the opening of Hyde Road in the mid-twentieth century and the subsequent creation of the 'Square-about'.

Writing in 1941–2, F.M. O'Flanagan, the 'Recorder of Dalkey',[2] listed a number of licensed premises that existed in Dalkey by the end of the nineteenth century,[3] including Pat Byrne's where SuperValu now stands, together with Whitehead's, Higginbotham's and Connolly's on Castle Street; the Castle Tavern at 115 Coliemore Road, together with the Queenstown Tavern at 107 Coliemore Road and Boland's tavern opposite Cliff Castle; and Annie Murphy's or Mangan's at the beginning of Sorrento Road. He also mentioned two pubs located at some distance from the centre of Dalkey: John Golden's pub near Bullock harbour and Larry Lamb's Beer House at the top of the Flags. Golden was based in one of Perrin's Cottages on Harbour Road about 1850 and would have catered to a diverse clientele made up of fishermen, pilots and coal-yard workers around the harbour and quarrymen from the nearby quarries off Harbour Road. The other premises was also known as the Village Inn on Ardbrugh Road near Dalkey quarry, where there was a collection of stonecutters' cottages overlooking a small green.[4]

Hotels in the nineteenth century

Prior to 1800, Dalkey was not on a through route to other towns and so didn't have coaching inns for travellers. With the opening of the Dublin to Kingstown railway in 1834, however, it started to attract visitors on account of its scenic setting, and taverns began to offer accommodation as well as meals. The first appears to have been the Dalkey Tavern, opened by George Sterling in May 1837.[5] He did not specify an exact address in his newspaper notices and so it is difficult to pinpoint its location. It must have been a reasonably large premises, probably on Castle Street, because he offered accommodation and dinners to groups as well as individuals, and he announced in July that coach-houses and stabling had just been completed. There was no mention of the enterprise after September 1837, however, and Sterling himself was declared insolvent in 1839, a fate he shared with several other pub and hotel proprietors in Dalkey in the mid-nineteenth century. The financial risks appeared to be higher in the years before the steam trains from Dublin finally reached the town in 1856, bringing with them crowds of day-visitors.

In July 1837 Thomas Cane, too, opened a hotel, again most likely on Castle Street and possibly on the site of the later Helton's Hotel (1840s) and the Albert Hotel (1850s):

> 'A splendid saloon and coffee room have been fitted up so as to afford elegant accommodations to the numerous parties crowding to visit the splendid and romantic scenery in the neighbourhood and at the same time so detached as not to interfere with the quiet and comforts of those residing in the hotel or weddings or other parties who may favour it with their patronage. There can be no place better adapted than Cane's Hotel for invalids and children, it being admirably situated in the purest air, and surrounded by fields and beautifully arranged gardens.'[6]

In the same public notice Cane acknowledged the help that he had received in fitting up his new premises from Martin Burke, owner of the Seapoint and Shelbourne hotels, and from Mr Hayes, owner of the Royal Hotel in Kingstown. The following year he thanked the directors of the railway company for their kindness in starting their omnibus from the [Kingstown] station to the hotel. Cane's hotel, which confusingly was also known as the Dalkey Hotel and Tavern, boasted a coffee-room which could seat 100 at dinner. Cane reputedly spent upwards of £400 on improvements to the premises, which may have over-extended his resources, because in December 1839 the lease was put up for sale with eighty years unexpired, and he too was listed as insolvent a month later.[7] Notwithstanding the help that Cane received in 1837 from Burke and Hayes, the hotels in Salthill and Kingstown were much superior in size and amenities to the new ventures in Dalkey, and would have provided stiff competition.

The Queen's Hotel began life in 1842 in Rockview Lodge, formerly the Castle House, beside Goat Castle. The house had been leased by John Hynes since 1821 and served briefly as an infant school later in that decade. Its use in the 1830s is not clear—it may have been the site of either Sterling's or Cane's hotel—and a hoard of Anglo-Saxon silver coins was found in 1838 when men were removing the castellated pillars of the gateway to the house in connection with the construction of a concert room.[8] A public dinner was held at Hynes' Tavern in June 1842, and in November it was announced that:

'The Queen's Hotel, which has been elegantly fitted up with every comfort and accommodation, under the management of George Beare, late part proprietor of the Gresham Hotel, was opened on Saturday evening last, on which occasion a large number of gentlemen were entertained at dinner; covers were laid for about 60 … A very large and handsome dining saloon has been built by Mr Beare.'[9]

The attention of the public was drawn to the hotel's proximity to the proposed terminus of the Atmospheric Railway and to the hot and cold baths at Coliemore; pleasure trips to Dalkey Island and Killiney Bay would be provided with 'superior boats and steady boatmen', while fishing parties would be supplied with every requisite. Beare had financial difficulties arising from his involvement with the Gresham Hotel, and he was replaced by George Hornick by 1846 and by George Glendining in 1860. Public meetings were held in the hotel in 1863 with a view to establishing a township in Dalkey, and the new town commissioners held their meetings there before converting Goat Castle for use as a town hall in 1872.

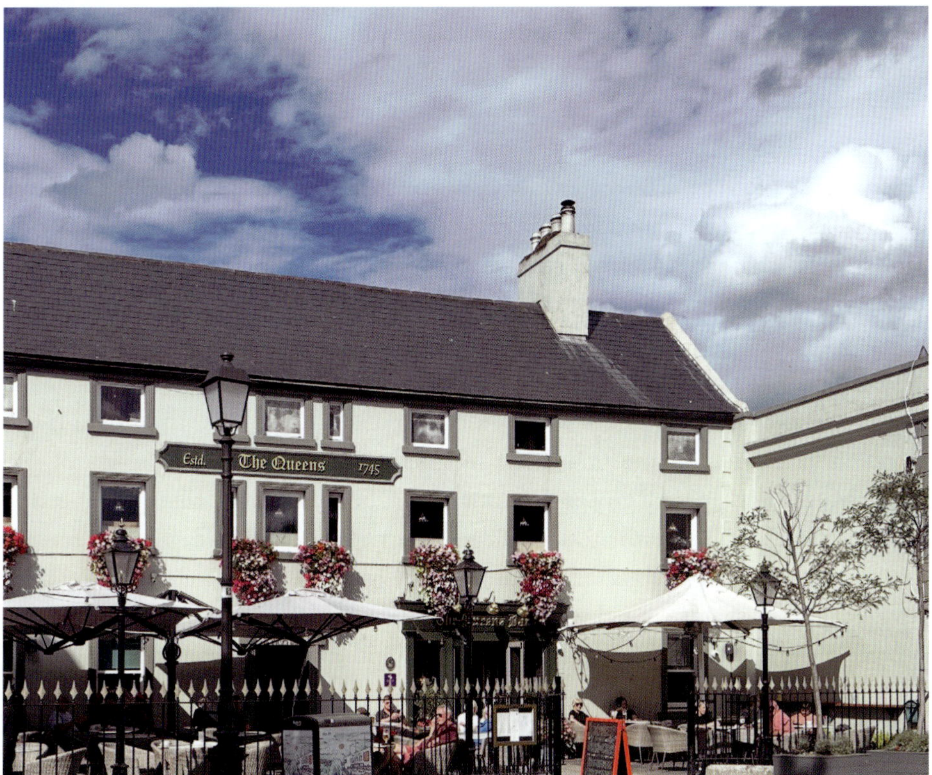

Fig. 11.3—The Queen's, Castle Street.

By 1843 John Helton had opened the Dalkey Hotel, Tavern and Livery Stables in the premises beside the Queen's Hotel on Castle Street; the similarity in the name of his business to Thomas Cane's at least suggests the possibility that they were on the same site. Helton was recorded as owning livery stables in Dalkey as early as 1839, and in May 1843 he published a newspaper notice saying that he was

'anxious to accommodate that part of the public who wish to examine the progress of the Atmospheric Railway. Dinners 1s.6d. to 2s. There is a dinner and ball saloon capable of entertaining 60 persons. Also coach house, stables and lock-up yard.'[10]

Helton died in 1847 and for a time the business was run by Miss Frances Peacock, who had previous hotel experience with Mr Gresham. It is not clear how long it survived, but by 1851 it was trading under the name of the Albert Hotel. It was managed by George Robinson from 1853 until 1862, when he became bankrupt. The lease of the premises was put up for sale, but there were no offers. The site was then acquired by Edward Harrison, who had a grocery shop further east on Castle Street; he was required to spend £300 on substantial building works, resulting in new retail premises. Some years later, part of the lands at the rear of the hotel were acquired by the tram company as a depot and stables, and subsequently for a power station when the Dalkey line was electrified in 1896.

In July 1848 Martin Burke, owner of the Shelbourne Hotel, advertised the lease of the Dalkey Railway Hotel and Tavern, 'situated at the intended [railway] station on Sorrento which leads to the Tunnel, within 5 minutes' walk of the hot baths'.[11] Burke lived at Khyber Pass, off Sorrento Road, where part of his lands were purchased in 1846 to construct the railway line between Dalkey and Killiney. However, the new station was not opened until 1854, following the closure of the Atmospheric Railway, so the hotel must have been something of a risky venture until then. It was operated by Thomas Flynn for a short time before being let to William Murphy in 1850. Murphy had been a grocer in Castle Street, became a town commissioner and ran the hotel until his death around 1881, when the lease was sold; it was described as a popular and well-established business, with eleven bedrooms for guests and staff. It would appear that the hotel was sold as a going concern, because legal notices appeared in the names of Anna Dowdall in 1892 and John Mulligan in 1894 stating that liquor licences were being sought for the Railway Hotel in Dalkey, but it had ceased to exist by 1900.

Concerts were staged in the Queen's Hotel in the 1870s, often to raise funds for charitable causes in the area, but this function was assumed by the Town Hall assembly room at the rear of Goat Castle, which opened in 1892. When the Queen's was advertised for sale in 1906 it had only four bedrooms, so its use as a hotel had also probably ceased in the late nineteenth century. It was acquired by Daniel Murphy, owner of the Clarence, Wynn's and Exchange hotels in Dublin. Initially he ran it as a licensed premises and was even prosecuted around 1912 for having customers on the premises after hours, but in the 1920s he used the Queen's as his family home. In fact, the public house licence was purely nominal, as he opened the pub just once a year to maintain the licence. After the business was sold on by his widow in the mid-1930s, the new owners operated it as a licensed premises again, with a restaurant attached in recent decades.

Hotels in the twentieth century

Dalkey had no hotel between around 1890 and 1920 but developed a selection of small hotels at different times during the twentieth century, all of them in existing houses, mainly with sea views and catering for weddings and other functions, and most replaced by apartment developments by the end of the century.[12]

Cliff Castle was built as a private residence by 1843. It was acquired by Tim and Bridie Murphy, who converted it into a hotel in 1920. It became a popular seaside hotel with twenty bedrooms (Fig. 11.4). As early as the 1930s it was advertising itself in UK newspapers as a base for touring in Ireland. In January 1961, 170 guests fled

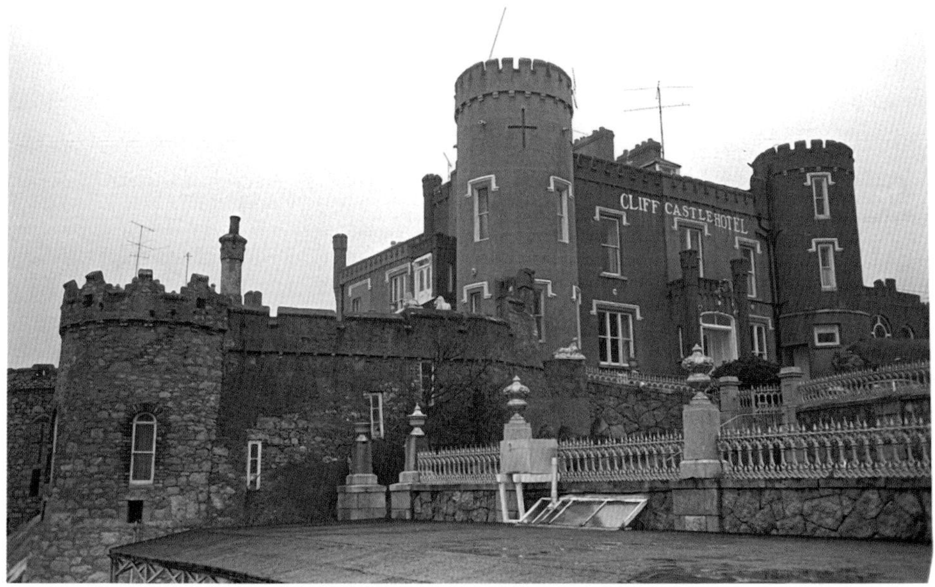

Fig. 11.4—Cliff Castle Hotel, Coliemore Road (courtesy of RTÉ Archives).

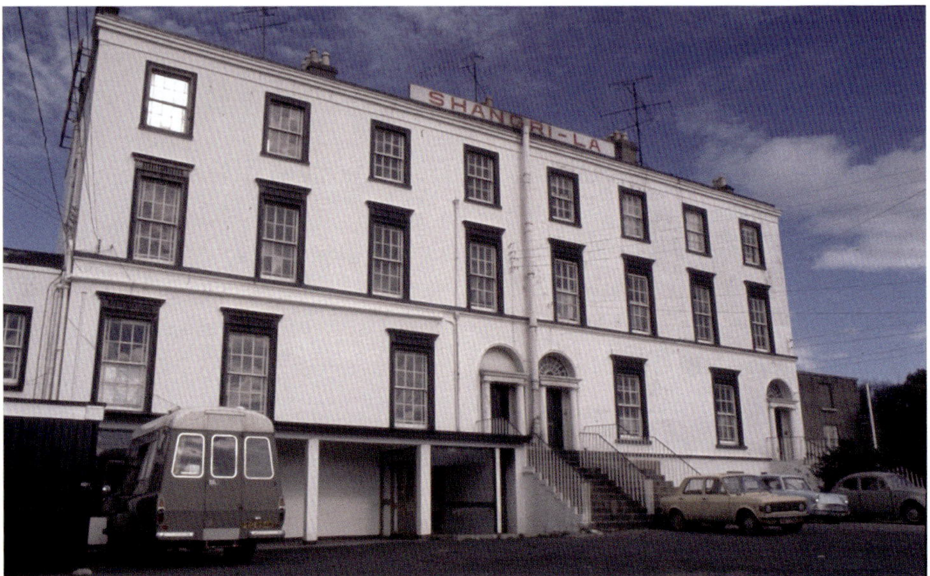

Fig. 11.5—The Shangri-La Hotel, Harbour Road (courtesy of RTÉ Archives).

from a wedding reception when fire broke out in some of the upstairs rooms of the hotel. Considerable damage was caused, including loss of the wedding presents; nevertheless, as the ballroom and kitchen were unaffected, the wedding banquet continued. The bride was Ina Murphy, daughter of the owners. The Murphy family sold up in the mid-1960s and ownership changed hands several times before 1978, when a night club called the Coral Reef was opened. The hotel was sold on again in 1980, but the history of conflict with local residents about noise and antisocial behaviour continued. The premises was purchased in 1989 by a couple who wanted it as a residence. It went through various owners and was rented for a time in the early 2000s by the Moroccan Embassy.

The Shangri-La Hotel (Fig. 11.5) opened in the mid-1940s and consisted of four Georgian-style terraced houses at Henrietta Place on Harbour Road. It was offered for sale as a going concern in 1950; the auction notice said that a very considerable sum had been spent on reconstruction and extension. The hotel had over forty bedrooms, a ballroom, bar and extensive gardens adjoining a private beach. It was also claimed that it was luxuriously furnished and equipped throughout.

The Shangri-La attracted film stars such as Elizabeth Taylor and Richard Burton and was noted for its fine dining. If you wanted to celebrate the New Year in 1948, you would have needed evening dress for the gala dinner dance, and admission cost fifteen shillings. Four days at Christmas 1966, to include a cabaret compèred by Joe

Lynch, a cocktail party, a film show and two days of golf, would have set you back £17.15.0. Like its neighbour the Cliff Castle Hotel, the Shangri-La advertised itself in the UK press as a base for touring Ireland. It was demolished in 1979 and replaced by the Bailey View apartments.

Khyber Pass, once the home of Martin Burke and also briefly lived in by Charles Stewart Parnell as a youth, was converted into a hotel by a builder called M.P. Kennedy in the mid-twentieth century. It was first known as the Khyber Pass Hotel in the 1950s and as the Killiney Heights Hotel in the 1970s. Its superb location overlooking both Killiney and Dublin bays ensured its popularity as a wedding venue. It was demolished around 1990 and replaced by apartments.

Colamore Cottage (later Lodge) was built around 1830, again as a private dwelling. In 1954 Matt and Detta Cullen opened the Colamore Hotel, boasting private bathing, boating, fishing and panoramic views over Dublin Bay and Dalkey Island. It was sold in 1962 and was later called the Coliemore Hotel. Like the other small hotels, it specialised in weddings and functions; an advertisement in 1974 emphasised that it catered for only one wedding reception each day, with the seaside setting providing an ideal backdrop for the wedding photos. The hotel was sold to Jim Delaney

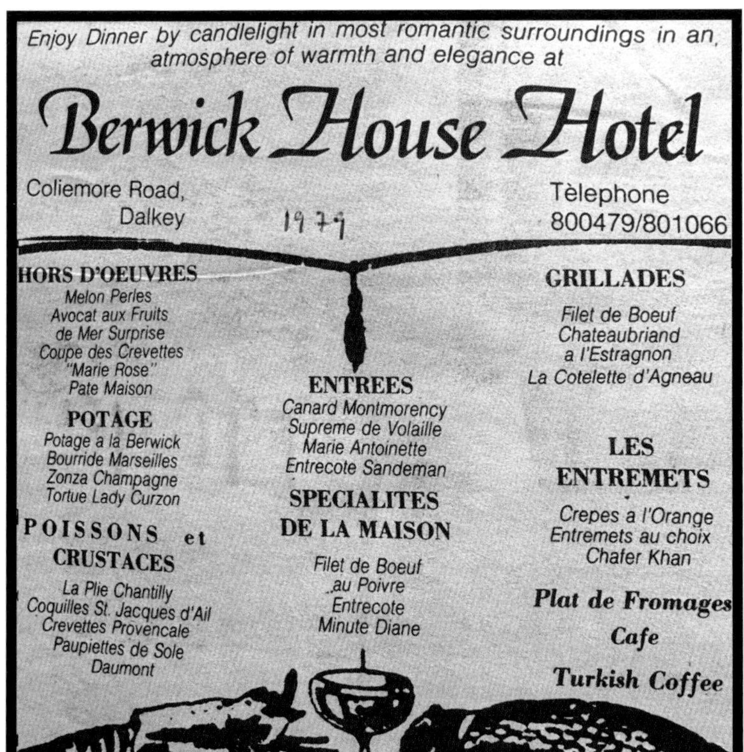

Fig. 11.6—Menu from the Berwick House Hotel, 1979 (courtesy of Peter Pearson).

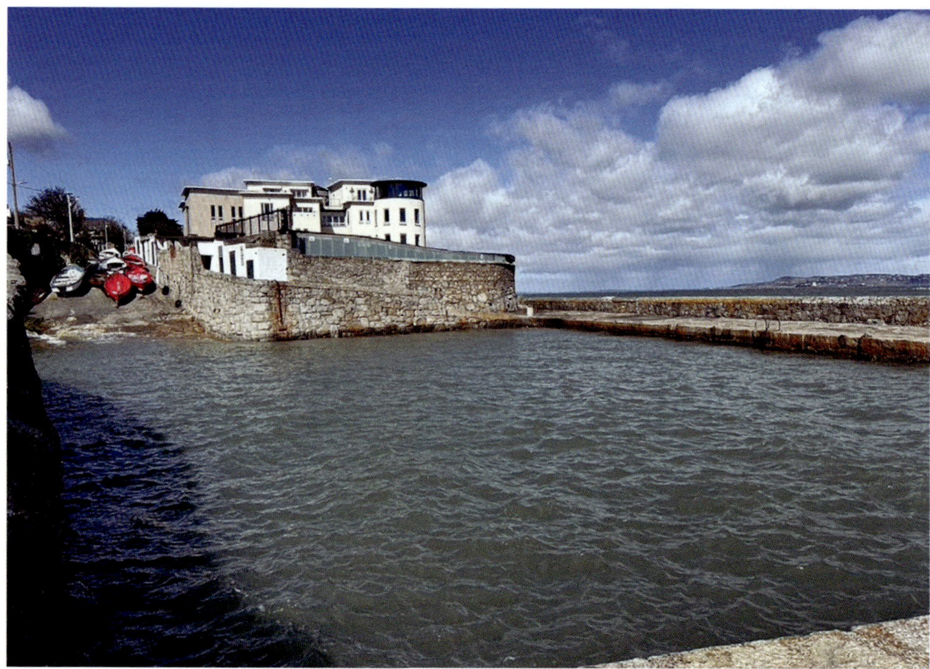

Fig. 11.7—Apartments on the site of the former Dalkey Island Hotel, Coliemore harbour.

in 1976 and enlarged, becoming known as the Dalkey Island Hotel. It closed in 1998 and was demolished in 2000, to be replaced by apartments.

There were a number of other small hotels in and around Dalkey which had only brief lives. Dalkey House was on the site between Hillview Cottage and the Masonic Hall, where in the late 1940s the ten-bedroom Dalkey House Hotel was built, occupying part of the land where Ormeau Drive is now. There was a small fire in the hotel in 1948 which caused only minor damage. However, it was sold for £1,325 in 1950 and ceased trading.

In 1948 the Queenstown Castle Hotel on Coliemore Road was offered for sale as a going concern, fully licensed and furnished, with beautifully situated castellated premises and attractive grounds, and private bathing. It was still trading in 1949 but, as far as I know, it ceased to be used as a hotel shortly afterwards and had been converted into a number of apartments by the 1980s. The Berwick House Hotel, also near Coliemore harbour, had a brief existence in the 1970s and 1980s before the building was demolished and replaced by apartments.

The lifespan of Dalkey's small hotels in the twentieth century ranged from a few years to about seventy years. There are several reasons for their gradual disappearance:

- Their generally small size militated against long-term survival; larger hotels such as Killiney Castle had scope to add function rooms and bedroom extensions, as well as providing parking, whereas it could be difficult to include *en suite* bedrooms, for instance, to what started life as nineteenth-century houses.
- Irish people began to travel abroad for sun holidays from the 1960s.
- There was a market demand for apartment developments from the 1970s onwards, and many of the small hotels were demolished over the following decades to make way for more lucrative use of what were often very scenic sites along the coast.

Dalkey has had no hotels for the past thirty years or more, but in 2024 the Queen's was granted planning permission for a thirty-bedroom extension at the rear.

12.

Public services and local government in Dalkey since 1800

Role of the grand jury prior to 1863

Prior to the establishment of the Dalkey Town Commissioners in 1863, a limited range of public services was provided in County Dublin by the grand jury, a body of the principal landowners in the county. Under an act of 1765, money raised under local rates (or 'cess') could be approved for expenditure on constructing or maintaining public roads at 'presentment' sessions; money could also be spent on the building and maintenance of courthouses and jails. As seen in Chapter 7, landowning developers in Dalkey, such as Hercules MacDonnell and Gerrard Tyrrell, were proactive in the 1840s and 1850s in seeking grand jury presentment funds for the improvement of roads such as Coliemore Road and Sorrento Road, and the construction of Ulverton Road; such funding sometimes included provision for footpaths and drains at the side of the roads, although the installation of street lighting was not covered.

Public health

Grand juries were also authorised to match funds for local dispensaries raised by voluntary subscriptions. Throughout the nineteenth century Dalkey was generally regarded as a healthy place to live, certainly compared with the poor housing conditions in parts of Dublin city. Its proximity to the sea, absence of polluting industries and relatively recently built housing all contributed towards its attractiveness as a residential suburb. Its healthy environment drew Mother Mary Ball to found her new Loreto novitiate close to the coastline in 1843 and was often cited in newspaper notices advertising houses to let for the summer season. Nonetheless, the area was not entirely immune from public health issues. In 1832, for instance, cholera affected many parts of Ireland, including Dalkey, as reported in the *Freeman's Journal*:

> 'The disease exists in the town of Dalkey, and the Kingstown Board of Health have caused some of the patients to be brought into the Kingstown hospital although Kingstown itself is free of the disease. Why was there not a Board of Health established in Dalkey itself? The people of Dalkey objected to a cholera hospital in the town. Almost all the cases brought from Dalkey have proved fatal.'[1]

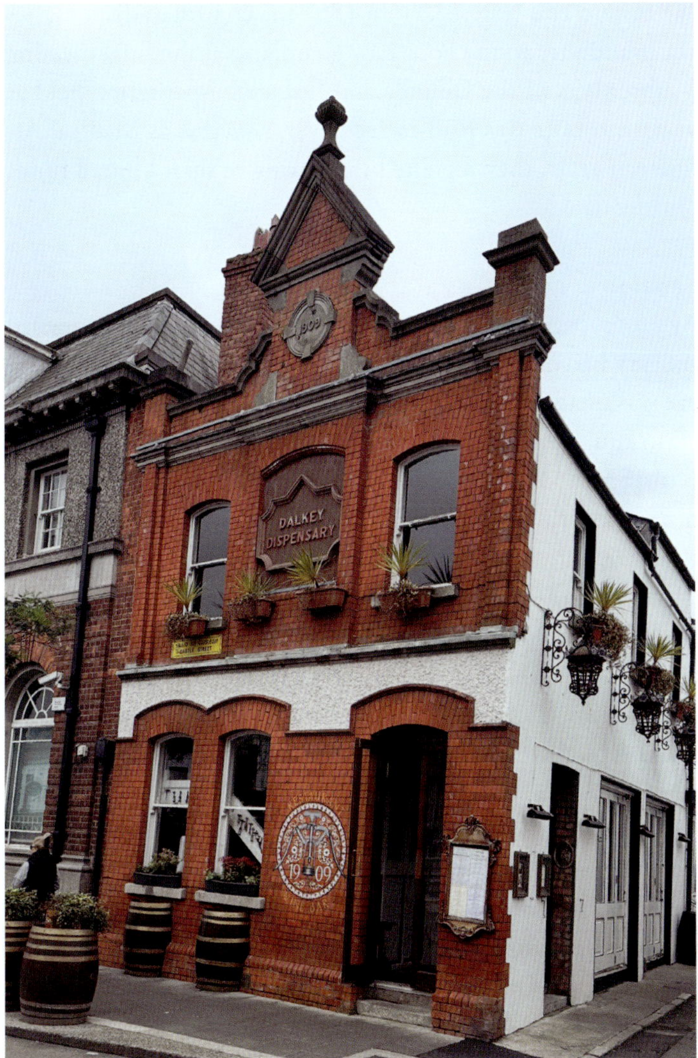

Fig. 12.1—Former Dalkey Dispensary, Castle Street.

The disease particularly affected the quarry-workers living in poor and unsanitary housing conditions; a meeting of the governors of the national school in September 1833 noted that the cholera epidemic in the previous year had deprived many of the children of their parents.[2] In that year there was a dispensary in Killiney village which also served Dalkey; dispensary doctors were public officials who provided medicine and advice free of charge to the poor. Dr Frederick Hasler, the local dispensary doctor, was a grandson of Sir John Hasler, who had lived at Dalkey Castle towards the end of the eighteenth century. A dispensary was opened in Castle Street in the 1840s, initially at the eastern end, later near the Catholic church and finally in a new building in 1909, again at the eastern end (Fig. 12.1). In 1851 the control of dispensaries was transferred from the grand jury to the Poor Law guardians; at the final meeting of the committee and subscribers of the Killiney and Dalkey Dispensaries, held at the Queen's Hotel that year, tribute was paid to Dr Hasler's success as Medical Attendant for the past nineteen years; they regretted that owing to their limited funds his salary was entirely inadequate.[3]

Post office and police station

Dublin city had a penny post system since 1773, with 'receiving houses' being opened in nearby suburbs. Dunleary had one since 1814;[4] letters could be sent by rail from 1834. A receiving house was established in Dalkey by 1837.[5] From the 1840s, local businesses could tender to run the post office as a franchise; Thomas Connolly was postmaster from 1846 to 1854 at No. 2 Castle Street, beside his thriving bakery at No. 1. Later in the century the post office was based in Railway Road before moving back to Castle Street by 1921. The 1907–8 Ordnance Survey maps show that most of the residential streets in the area had postboxes.

In his *Topographical Dictionary*, published in 1837, Samuel Lewis reported that there was a constabulary police station in the village. Its location is unknown, but it may have belonged to the County Constabulary, a uniformed police force established in 1822 which was replaced by the Dublin Metropolitan Police (DMP), set up in 1836. The DMP was initially based in Dublin city; it was not until 1840 that 'F' Division was created to cover the south-east county, including Kingstown and Dalkey. A local landowner, Samuel McComas, leased a plot of land on Sorrento Road to the DMP in 1845 for a police barracks, which lent its name briefly to Barrack Road (now Tubbermore Road), built in the 1850s; the public entrance faced that road. Anti-Treaty forces raided the Dalkey barracks in October 1922 and captured a small number of firearms. The DMP was absorbed into the Garda Síochána in April 1925 and the barracks remained a Garda station until its closure in 2013.

Dalkey township

In 1834 a number of wealthy inhabitants of Kingstown established a township to develop and improve the area,[6] with Glasthule being added in 1855. A public meeting chaired by James Milo Burke, a local developer, was held in the Queen's Hotel in April 1863 with the aim of placing Dalkey under the provisions of the 1854 Towns Improvement Act, which would have facilitated the provision of street lighting. In June 1863 a memorial with suggested township boundaries was sent to the lord lieutenant; he consented and directed that the public lighting provisions of the 1854 act

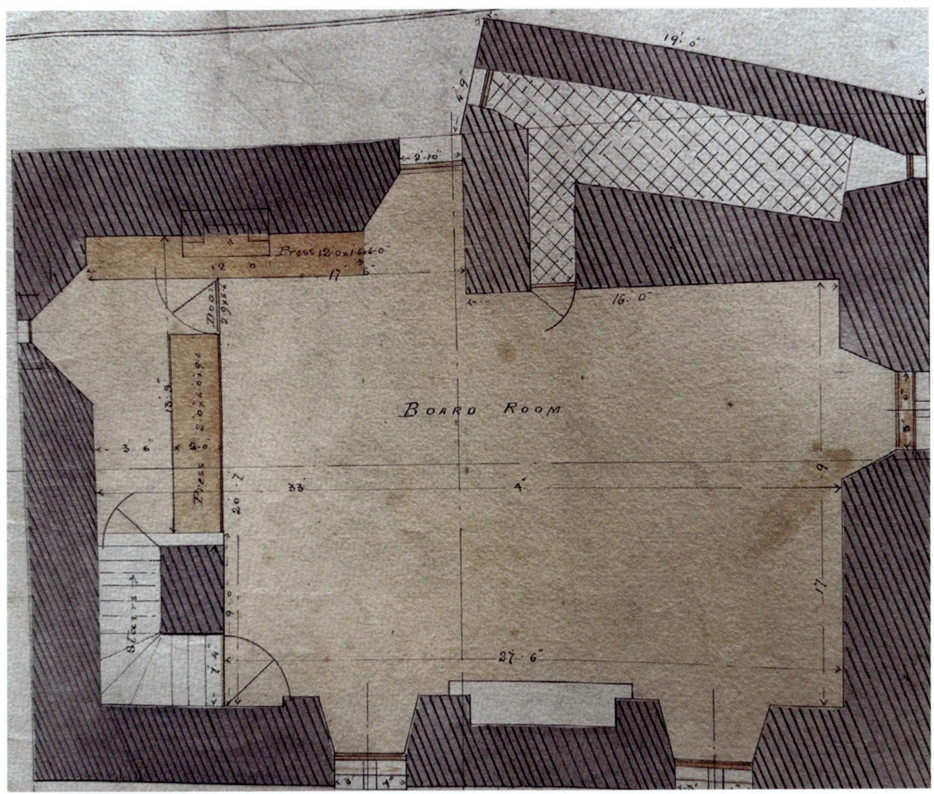

Fig. 12.2—Town commissioners' boardroom, Dalkey Castle (courtesy of Dalkey Castle Heritage Centre).

would apply to Dalkey township. A meeting of ratepayers held in the hotel in September 1863 elected twelve commissioners, including Burke and fellow developers Hercules MacDonnell, Gerrard Tyrell and Hugh O'Rorke, together with local merchants Edward Harrison and Thomas Connolly. Burke was elected as the first chairman, with meetings being held in the Queen's Hotel before Goat Castle was renovated as the Town Hall in 1872. By the end of 1863 public lighting had been installed in Castle Street, Ulverton Road and Dalkey Avenue.

The Dalkey Township Act 1867 gave the commissioners extended powers for lighting, paving, sewerage, draining, cleansing and supplying the town with water, the erection of two piers at Coliemore harbour, the transfer of the making and construction of roads and footpaths from the grand jury to the town commissioners and the erection of a town hall. They would be authorised to raise funds by making a township rate, set at two shillings in the pound which could only be increased with the consent of two thirds of the ratepayers. John Cunningham, a well-known railway contractor,[7] was engaged to build new piers at Coliemore in 1868.

Water-supply

In 1870 Dr Joliffe Tufnell, a distinguished surgeon who lived at Sorrento Terrace, wrote to the commissioners in relation to the Dalkey water-supply: 'Not one of the pumps in the township produce water fit for domestic use; and one at the Coolamore Road was fatally unfit for use'. Dr Cameron, Dublin City Analyst, had tested several waters from Dalkey; one was so bad that it corroded the crucible.[8] Dublin Corporation was in the process of piping drinking-water from the Vartry reservoir near Roundwood, Co. Wicklow, and Dr Tufnell urged all those either engaged in business or having property in the township to support the commissioners in bringing the Vartry water in at once. He also argued that if a fire took place in the township there was no possibility of preventing the premises from being reduced to a heap of ruins, perhaps with the loss of human life.

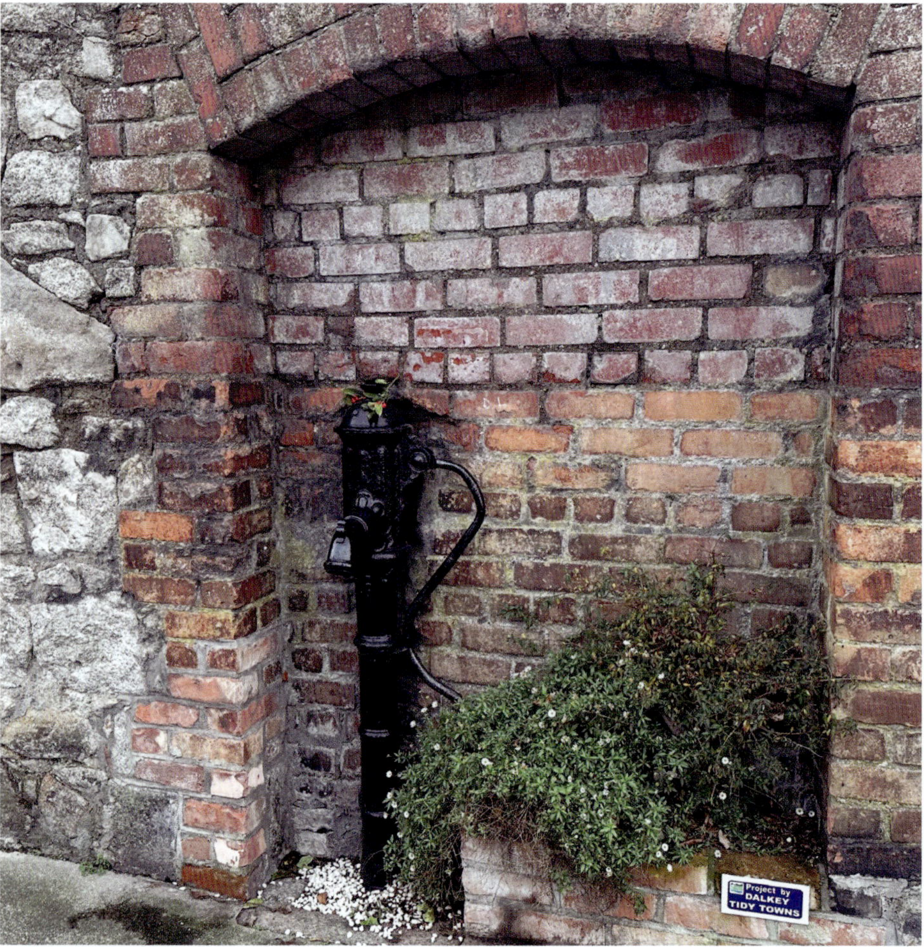

Fig. 12.3—Old water pump, Tubbermore Road.

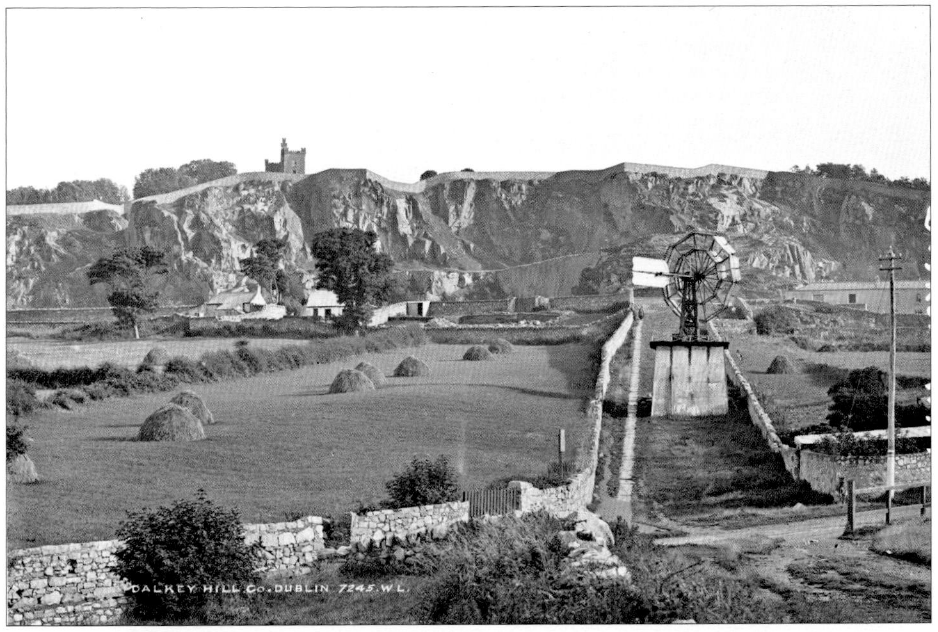

Fig. 12.4—The windmill near the Flags, Dalkey quarry (courtesy of the National Library of Ireland).

While the commissioners entered into an agreement with Dublin Corporation for the supply of Vartry water, parts of the township—notably on Torca Hill—were on a higher level than the pipe bringing the water from Stillorgan. A windmill to pump water from Castle Street to a height of 250ft was installed by John Cunningham and commenced operation in August 1886 (Fig. 12.4). Three years later, a new gas engine was installed at the pumping station to fill the reservoir on Torca Hill.

Provision of sewerage

During the late eighteenth and early nineteenth centuries, lack of proper sanitation in urban areas gave rise to contagious diseases such as cholera. In 1851 Dublin Corporation appointed Parke Neville as City Surveyor; his first priority was the provision of a sewerage network for the city, which took over three decades to complete. Prior to 1863 there was only a rudimentary drainage system in Dalkey; although the town commissioners prioritised keeping the rates as low as possible, they were mandated by new public health legislation, based on UK practice, to introduce a more comprehensive sewerage system, including sea outfalls at Bullock and Coliemore harbour and necessitating compulsory purchase of land for new sewers.[9] In 1876 the Local Government Board approved the carrying out of the main drainage of the township at a cost of £7,000. The commissioners were also empowered under the Public Health

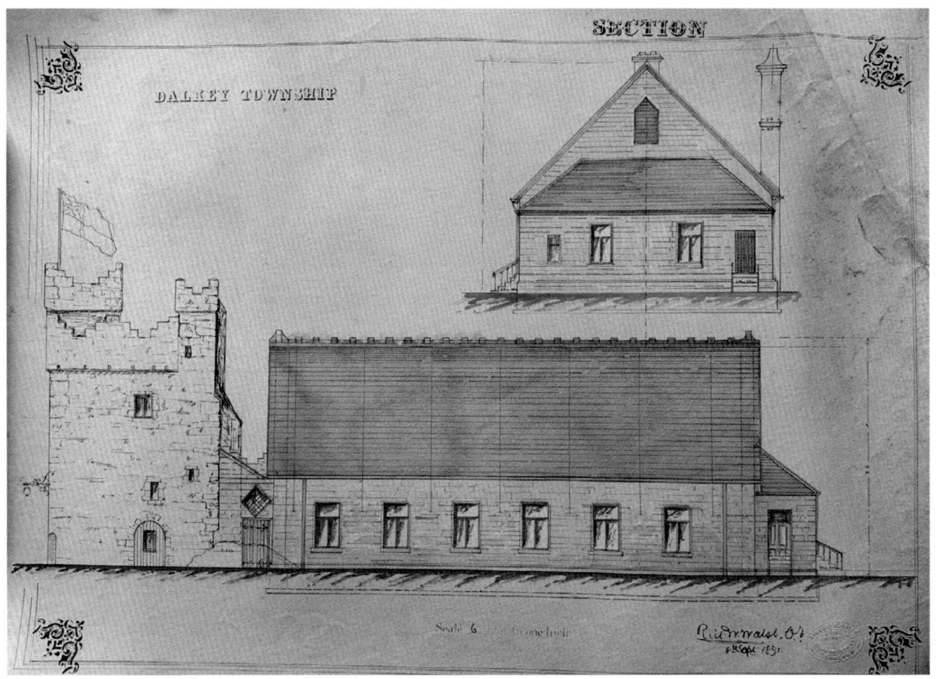

Fig. 12.5—Original engineer's drawings for the Town Hall assembly rooms, *c.* 1891 (courtesy of Dalkey Castle Heritage Centre).

(Ireland) Act 1878 to enforce building by-laws to ensure that new houses were connected to the sewers and to eliminate public nuisances.

In their final two decades as commissioners, they busied themselves with a wide variety of activities, including the provision of a men's bathing place at Vico Rock, the linking of Coliemore Road and Sorrento Terrace, and the purchase of a field near Sorrento Terrace as a public park (now Dillon's Park). In 1892 a new assembly room was opened beside Goat Castle (Fig. 12.5).

Dalkey Urban District Council 1899–1930

The town commissioners were replaced by an urban district council (UDC), elected by a wider franchise that included women, under the 1898 Local Government Act, which also transferred the powers of the grand jury to the newly established Dublin County Council. The Dalkey UDC continued to meet in the Town Hall and immediately invited tenders for the erection of fourteen working-class dwellings on St Patrick's Road. A further 113 houses were built in or near Dalkey between 1910 and 1922, including twenty-four in St Patrick's Square, sixteen on Corrig Road and fourteen on Carysfort Road.[10] A library was opened in Castle Street in 1901 (Fig. 12.6),

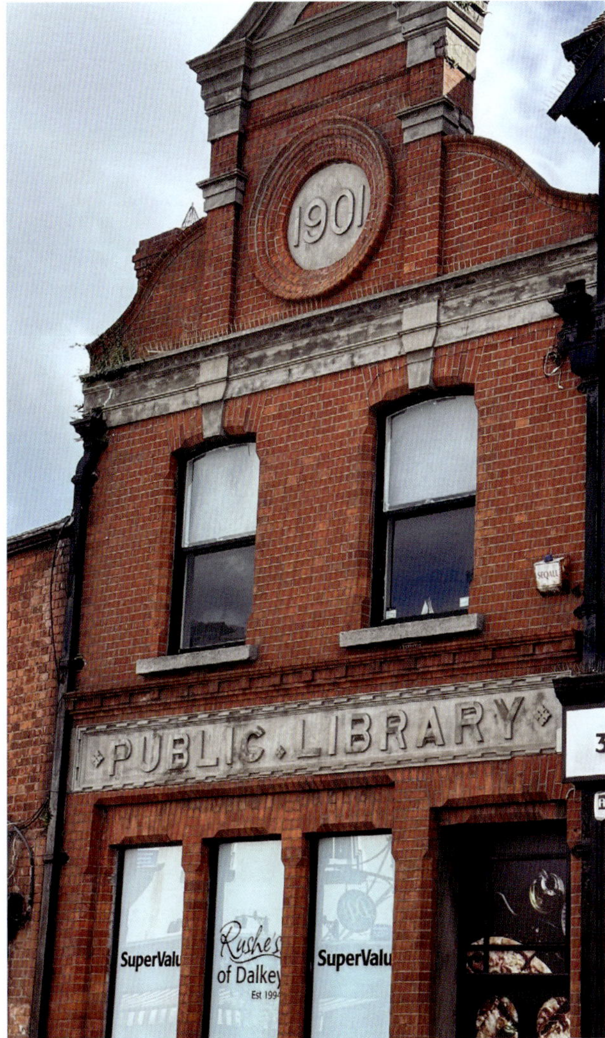

Fig. 12.6—Former public library, Castle Street.

partly funded by the Carnegie Trust, and in 1913 the UDC acquired Dalkey Island from the War Office in London. Ironically, the island fell within the administrative area of the County Council, as it had not formed part of the original township area in 1863.

Dún Laoghaire Corporation 1930–94

Further local government reform took place in 1930, when the townships of Dún Laoghaire (known as Kingstown until 1920), Blackrock, Dalkey and Killiney were merged to form the new Dún Laoghaire Borough Corporation, resulting in the closure of the Town Hall in Goat Castle. Perhaps the corporation's most significant con-

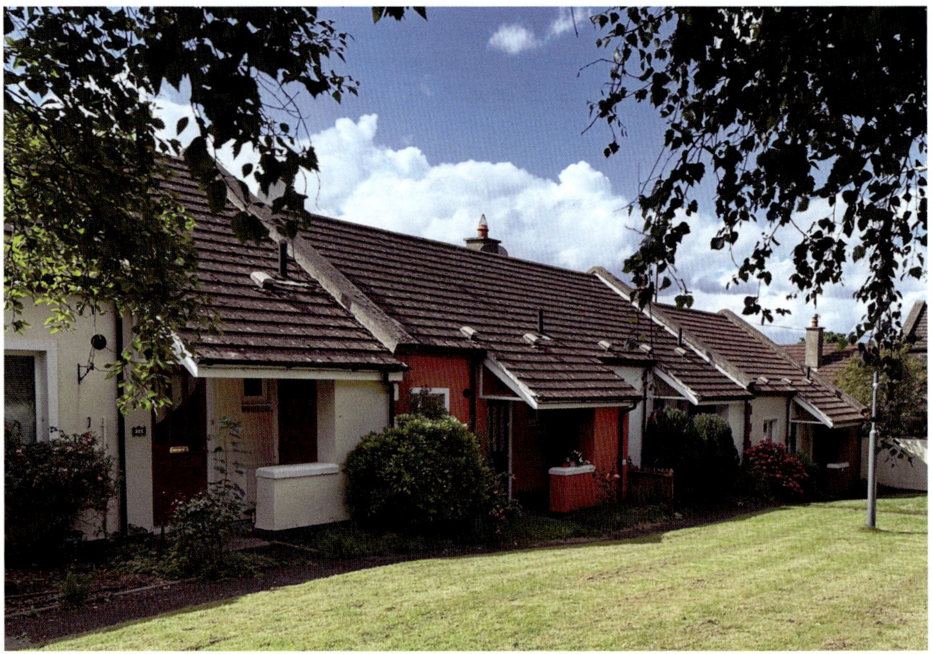

Fig. 12.7—Old persons' houses, Kilbegnet Close, off Castle Street.

tribution to the development of Dalkey was the construction of Hyde Road in the 1940s, linking Castlepark and Ulverton Roads; this led in the following decade to the purchase of playing fields for Dalkey United Football Club and Cuala GAA, and the construction of a major local authority housing scheme at St Begnet's Villas. The Catholic parish donated lands just west of the church, which enabled the corporation to develop the award-winning Kilbegnet Close old persons' housing scheme (1985–7) (Fig. 12.7). A new public library was built on Castle Street, west of the 1901 building, which is now incorporated into the SuperValu premises; the new library was extensively renovated in 2012 and includes a courtyard garden dedicated to Maeve Binchy, who had lived on Sorrento Road.

Dún Laoghaire–Rathdown County Council
The former Dublin County Council was dissolved in 1994 and three new county councils were created, including Dún Laoghaire–Rathdown, which incorporated the former Dún Laoghaire Corporation. In 1998 the new council developed the Dalkey Heritage Centre, attached to Goat Castle, which hosts a multitude of events, including writers' festivals, exhibitions and theatre performances. The existing walls of the castle tower room were opened up to reveal layers of history in the original stone-

work, including an unusual barrel-vaulted roof with fifteenth-century wickerwork shuttering. The Heritage Centre also includes a Writers' Gallery with portraits and interactive screens featuring the work of forty-five writers and creative artists, including Joyce, Beckett, Binchy and Bono.. In 2020 the council undertook public realm enhancements on Castle Street, creating more space for pedestrians by narrowing the roadway and reallocating on-street parking spaces for the use of people and local business.

13.

Bullock and Coliemore harbours

Given the relatively small size of the medieval settlement in Dalkey, it is surprising that the area could boast of two cross-channel harbours, Bullock and Dalkey Sound. Both were small, with little in the way of permanent piers until the nineteenth century. Bullock was originally owned by the Cistercian abbey of St Mary in Dublin; it was primarily a fishing harbour, although from time to time important members of the English administration landed there. Dalkey Sound (probably at Coliemore), under the control of the archbishop of Dublin, served as an outport for Dublin for several hundred years up to about 1600 because of the difficulties faced by larger ships crossing the sand bar at the Liffey estuary; it also provided access from the mainland to Dalkey Island.

Bullock harbour

The manor of Blowike (Bullock) was held by St Mary's Abbey prior to the Anglo-Norman invasion of 1169. In 1345 the right of the abbot to claim tolls from fish landed at the small harbour was recognised by the king's court in Dublin, namely the choice of one fish, and that the best, from each boat putting into the harbour at Bullock.[1] The monks would have needed a strong building within which they exercised their right to tolls, and also a place where they afforded hospitality to visiting dignitaries from England who landed at Bullock *en route* to Dublin. For example, in 1401 'Thomas of Lancaster, the King's son and Lord Lieutenant of Ireland, landed at Blowyk near Dalkey and thence he came to Dublin on the same day'.[2]

The Civil Survey of 1654–6 described Bullock as a sea port and a good haven.[3] Over a century later, the bookseller Peter Wilson wrote in 1768 that a new quay, faced with hewn stone, had lately been built for conveying stone to the lighthouse works;[4] granite from small quarries around Bullock was taken by barge and used in the construction of a new lighthouse at Poolbeg. That quay was in poor condition by the end of the century, however, and in 1803 the Corporation for Preserving and Improving the Port of Dublin (also known as the Ballast Board) wrote to the Earl of Carysfort, stating that they were desirous of becoming his tenants in order to work his quarries at Bullock and Sandycove. Leases for over 37 acres were granted in 1804–5.

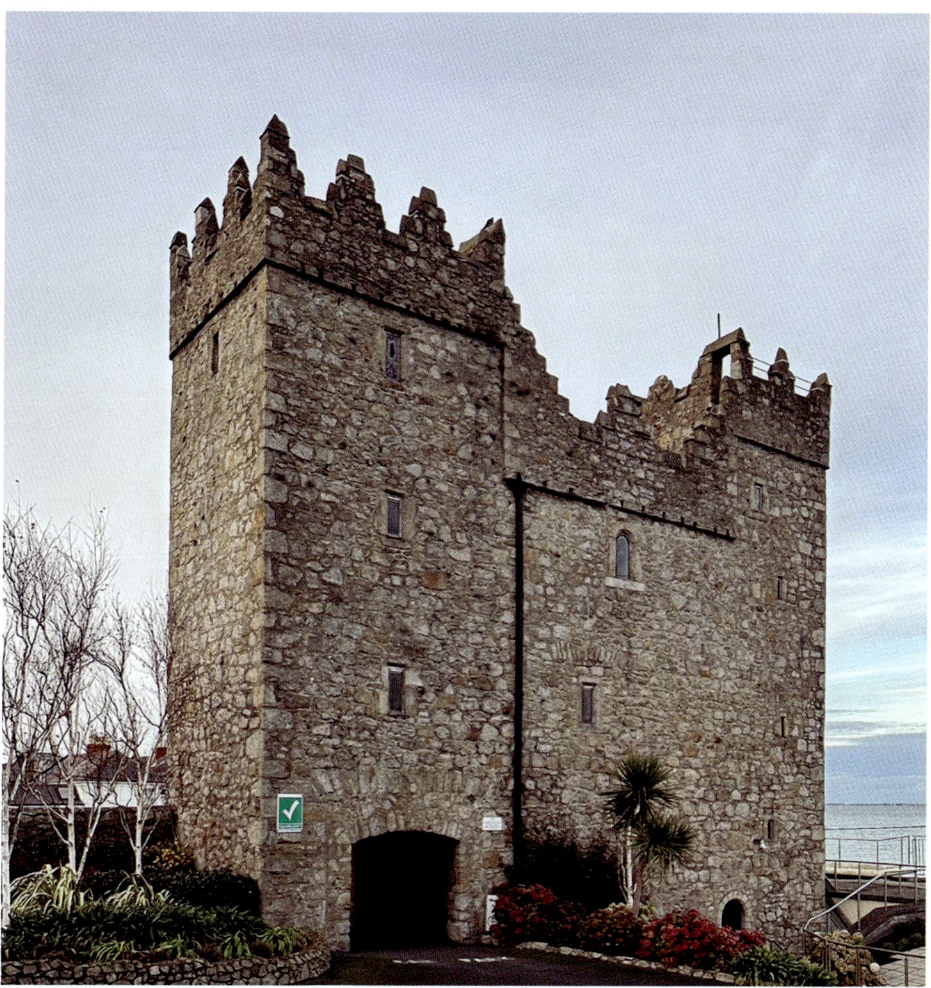

Fig. 13.1—Bullock Castle.

The Ballast Board built a terrace of ten pilots' cottages at the harbour in 1806, and in 1818 invited proposals for building a new quay wall, pier and other improvements at the harbour of Bullock.[5] The harbour was to be deepened, and a new road formed from what is now Breffni Road down to the harbour. The works were completed a year later and George Smith, the contractor, was awarded £2,000 for labour and materials. The cottages, road and harbour works were shown on a survey in 1835 (Fig. 13.2).

Lieutenant William Hutchison RN was appointed by the Ballast Board as Inspector of Quarries at Bullock and Sandycove in 1817, and resided in the large house beside the medieval castle overlooking the harbour. He also supervised the lifeboat

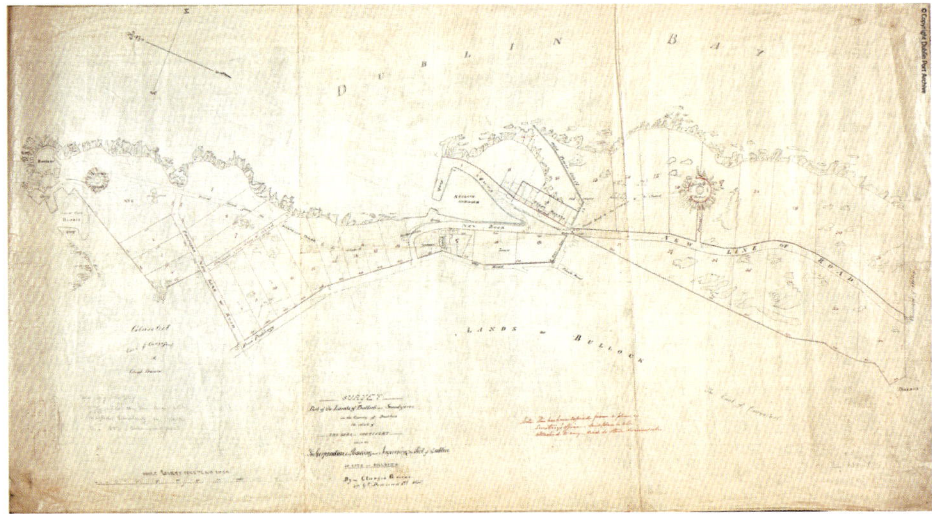

Fig. 13.2—Detail from Clarges Greene's 'Survey of part of the lands of Bullock and Sandycove in the county of Dublin: the estate of the Earl of Carysfort held by the Corporation for preserving and improving the port of Dublin' (1835) (courtesy of Dublin Port Archives).

which the Board had established at Sandycove in 1803; the Bullock pilots often volunteered to man the lifeboat.[6] Hutchison was involved in several heroic rescue attempts; he survived the wreck of the lifeboat at Sandycove in December 1821 when two of the pilots were drowned as they were going to the assistance of the *Ellen*.

In 1801 there were seven yawls at Bullock employed in catching whiting, pollock and herring.[7] Apart from its fishermen, the harbour was also noted for its pilots who guided ships into Dublin port, a tradition that continued into the nineteenth century. For centuries since the medieval era, a sand bar in the Liffey estuary had created a hazard for ships trying to enter the port, especially at low tide. A marine chart of Dublin Bay dating from the 1630s advised masters of such ships to anchor off Bullock harbour and to take a pilot on board.[8] The sand bar continued to pose difficulties until the Ballast Board built the South Wall and later the Bull Wall during the eighteenth and early nineteenth centuries. From the eighteenth century onwards the need for regulated pilotage at Dublin port was recognised, with the first act for the regulation of pilots being introduced in 1763, making pilotage obligatory for most ships entering the port. Unofficial pilots, such as local fishermen and boatmen, known as 'hobblers', also offered their services. Generations of families such as the Archbolds rowed out of Bullock to ships entering Dublin Bay.[9] The pilots' cottages were sold off by the port authority in 1866; all but one were demolished in the twentieth century and replaced by modern dwellings.

The Ballast Board sublet some of its lands around Harbour Road for housing development in the 1830s, and gradually the Bullock area was absorbed into Dalkey following the opening of Ulverton Road in the following decade. Houses were mainly heated by coal fires in the nineteenth century. An advertisement in *Saunders's News-Letter* in 1846 referred to the large concerns, long established as a coal-yard, having a shed for several cargoes of coal, offices etc., standing on upwards of half an acre at the harbour, which were to be let. The coal-yard was located approximately where the former Western Marine premises now stand. In the early years of the twentieth century the coal-yard was replaced by boat-building, including by the well-known Atkinson family.

In March 2018 the west pier at Bullock harbour incurred substantial damage as a result of Storm Emma, and the Dublin Port Company commissioned a high-tech exploration of its foundations and inner condition before commencing specialist repair work that maintained its historical fabric. The works on the eastern end of the pier were completed in 2019, but further work was needed on cornerstones at the entrance to the harbour which had subsided owing to the tidal wash.

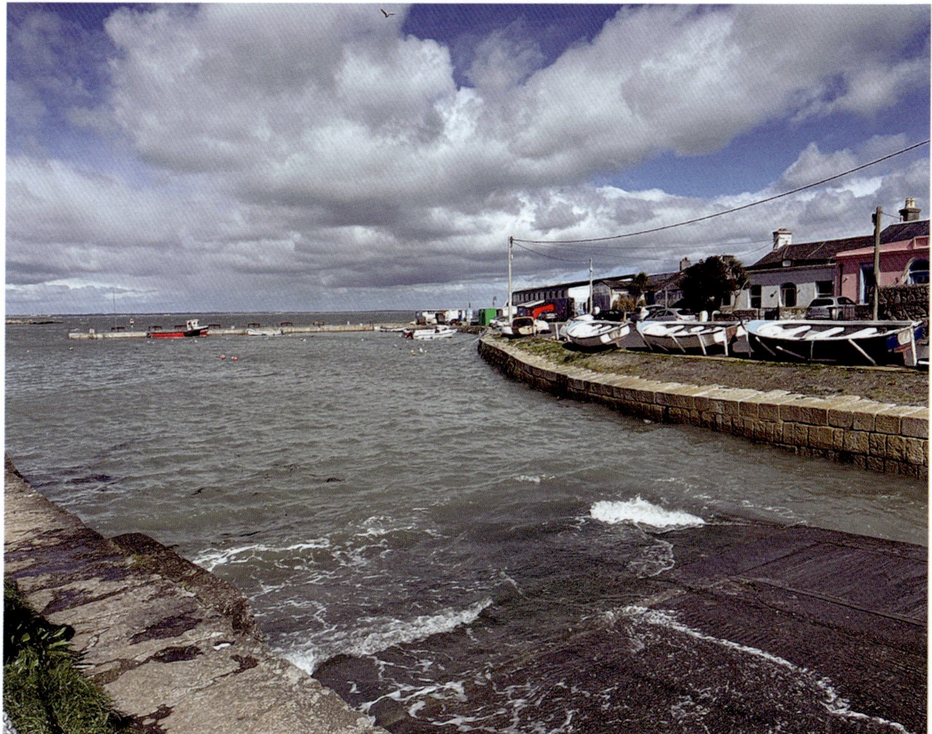

Fig. 13.3—Bullock harbour.

Today Bullock harbour is used by local fishermen and boatmen, with fish and crabs being sold from the pier. The Western Marine business closed in 2016 and the site was sold for redevelopment.

Coliemore harbour

Dalkey Sound, about 0.5km to the south-east of the town, provided a deep-water anchorage in the lee of Dalkey Island and served as an outport of Dublin for over three centuries because of the sand bar in the Liffey estuary. 'The port of Dalkey' was referred to in official documents as early as 1244 without specifying its exact site. In all probability this would have been at Coliemore, a small cove at the lowest point of the rocky shoreline and almost directly opposite the landing place on the island. The Irish version of the name, *An Caladh Mór* ('the big harbour'), testifies to its former status, and the present alignment of Coliemore Road mirrors the likely route from the port to Dalkey. Wilson referred in 1768 to 'the remains of a very strong causeway that runs across part of the common, evidently calculated to facilitate

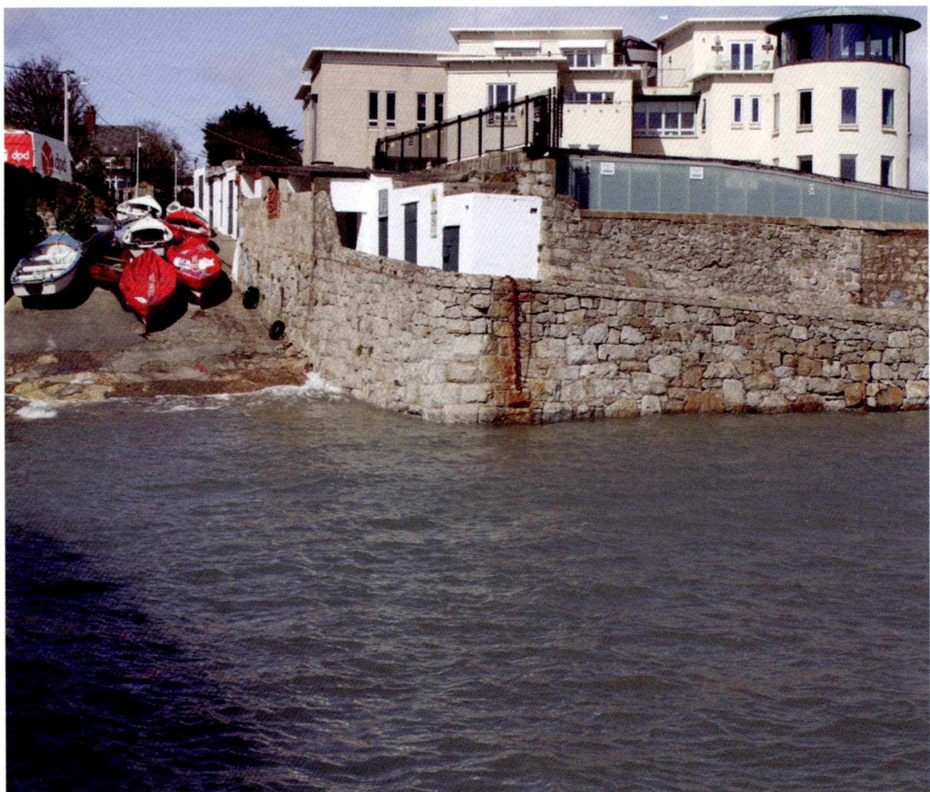

Fig. 13.4—Coliemore harbour.

the carriage of goods between the coast and the town'.[10]

As early as 1304-5, heavily laden ships could not discharge their cargo at the port of Dublin, and the practice of partly unloading barrels of wine at Dalkey developed; the wine was then transported to the city in smaller boats.[11] Merchandise unloaded at Dalkey was stored in fortified townhouses ('castles') in the village before being transported into the city, but this practice had ended by 1600, when ships could unload their cargoes at Ringsend. Coliemore reverted to being a small fishing harbour.

Following the Act of Union in 1800, the British government took a more active role in Irish affairs. Among the issues they dealt with in the early years of the nineteenth century was the need to provide what was termed an 'asylum harbour' in Dublin Bay, to provide shelter for ships that could not cross the sand bar at the entrance to the Liffey during storms. Various experts were commissioned to propose possible solutions, including Sir Thomas Hyde Page of the Royal Engineers. His report concluded that

> 'Dalkey Sound is capable of great improvement, and the anchorage may be better sheltered than it is now against the E. and points of the compass from the S. to the S.E., by uniting over the ledge of rocks, Dalkey, the Lamb and Maiden Islands by a rough breakwater wall, to be formed chiefly with the loose stones which are in sufficient quantity on the spot, and by carrying out from the S.W. point of Dalkey Island a breakwater pier, a sufficient distance into Killiney Bay, which will afford better shelter to the anchorage against the dangerous winds between the S. and S.E. points of the compass at the S.E. end of the island'.[12]

His own estimate of the cost of such works was put at £246,796, an astronomical sum for the time; unsurprisingly, his recommendation was not accepted. Another expert, Captain William Bligh of the Royal Navy and of 'Mutiny on the *Bounty*' fame, compiled the first modern chart of Dublin Bay and recommended that there should be an asylum harbour on the south side of the bay, possibly at the little fishing village of Dunleary. While he considered that Dalkey Sound was too exposed, he suggested instead making a breakwater for pilot and fishing vessels.[13] Nothing was done with Bligh's report either, and it took the tragedy of the loss of the troopships *Rochdale* and the *Prince of Wales* between Blackrock and Seapoint in 1807, with almost 400 dead, before the force of public opinion compelled the authorities to act, and work began in 1817 on an asylum harbour at Dunleary (later renamed Kingstown).

A Mrs McDonnell established hot baths and shower baths for ladies and gentlemen at Coliemore in 1843, which survived into the early twentieth century.

The nearby Clifton Baths, owned by Michael Kavanagh, lasted until the 1860s. In 1846 the County Dublin Grand Jury voted to contribute £85 for improving the natural harbour in Dalkey Sound but it was rejected by the Board of Works, while £17 was granted for gravelling and shaping the road from the town to the harbour.[14]

The Dalkey Town Commissioners wrote to the Dublin Port and Docks Board in 1866, arguing that Coliemore harbour, although a landing place for merchandise since the time of Edward III, was totally unfit and dangerous for landing and embarkation by fishermen, for the Ordnance (the garrison on Dalkey Island) and the Coast Guard, recently established in the locality. The fishermen and boatmen were obliged to haul up their boats onto the public road to obtain shelter. Two small piers would provide the necessary protection. A special act was passed in 1867 to enable the town commissioners to improve the harbour, and plans prepared by the Dublin port engineer, Bindon Blood Stoney, were approved by the board. Stoney prepared two plans, the cheaper one costing about £1,800, the amount the commissioners were willing to contribute. Two piers were constructed by John Cunningham, a well-known Dalkey contractor and builder (see profile in Chapter 15), who marked completion of the works by holding a function in his home on Ardeevin Road.

In 2023 Dún Laoghaire–Rathdown County Council completed repairs to Coliemore harbour. A section of the granite bedrock supporting the southern pier had collapsed in August 2020, resulting in the temporary closure of the pier while a series of rock anchors were inserted into the bedrock.

Today the harbour is used by ferry boats bringing visitors to Dalkey Island, by fishermen and by swimmers. It provides a superb viewing point towards Dalkey Island, with many sailing boats—and even the occasional Navy ship—navigating the strong currents in the deep waters of the Sound.

14.

Recreation and sports

Dalkey around 1800 was too small to support recreational facilities. It had no parish hall, no hotel and no sports grounds. The few wealthy residents, such as Sir John Hasler on Castle Street, entertained in their own homes. However, as the population increased in tandem with housing development during the nineteenth century, and as both residents and visitors had more disposable income, recreational and sports facilities became more common, particularly towards the end of the century and into the twentieth century.

Sea bathing

Sea bathing became fashionable during the eighteenth century, primarily because of its perceived health benefits. John Rocque's map of County Dublin in 1760 showed a bathhouse on Killiney strand (Fig. 14.1). While men mainly swam naked, women

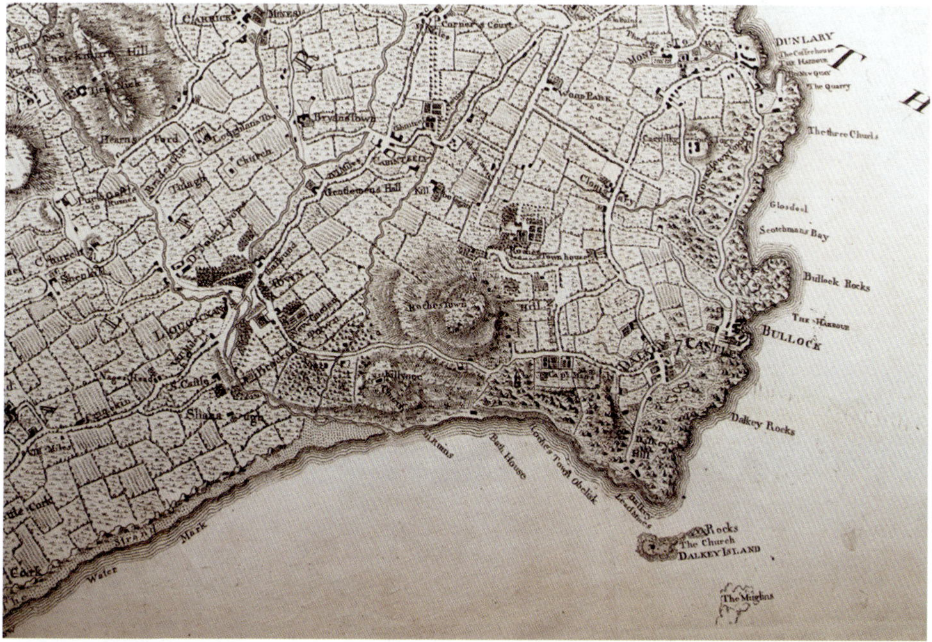

Fig. 14.1—Bathhouses at Killiney beach as shown on Rocque's map of County Dublin, 1760 (courtesy of the Royal Irish Academy).

wore full-length bathing-costumes to protect their modesty, and hence there were often separate bathing places for men and women. Furthermore, the latter tended to change their clothes in specially constructed huts or 'bathing machines' which could be drawn into position at the water's edge.

In the decades before and after 1800, houses—both large and small—in and near Dalkey could be rented by affluent families for the summer season; the newspaper advertisements often drew attention to the proximity of saltwater bathing, sometimes with bathing houses. The exact location of the latter cannot be determined, as there were few beaches on Dalkey's rocky coastline, although one notice claimed that bathing was available within five minutes' walk.[1] An 1832 advertisement for Rockview Lodge on Castle Street offered the exclusive use of a bathing house for the tenant.[2] Proximity to the sea, with the potential for secluded bathing for nuns, was a major factor in the decision of Mother Teresa Ball to locate a new Loreto convent near Carraig-na-Gréine in the early 1840s.

Commercial hot and cold baths were opened by a Mrs McDonnell near Coliemore harbour in 1843; she had previously helped her parents, Mr and Mrs Maddock, to operate such baths at Peafield, Blackrock. Also that same year, John Crosthwaite built the Royal Victorian Baths near the new harbour at Kingstown. As it happened, the lord lieutenant and his wife stayed at Carraig-na-Gréine that summer and were

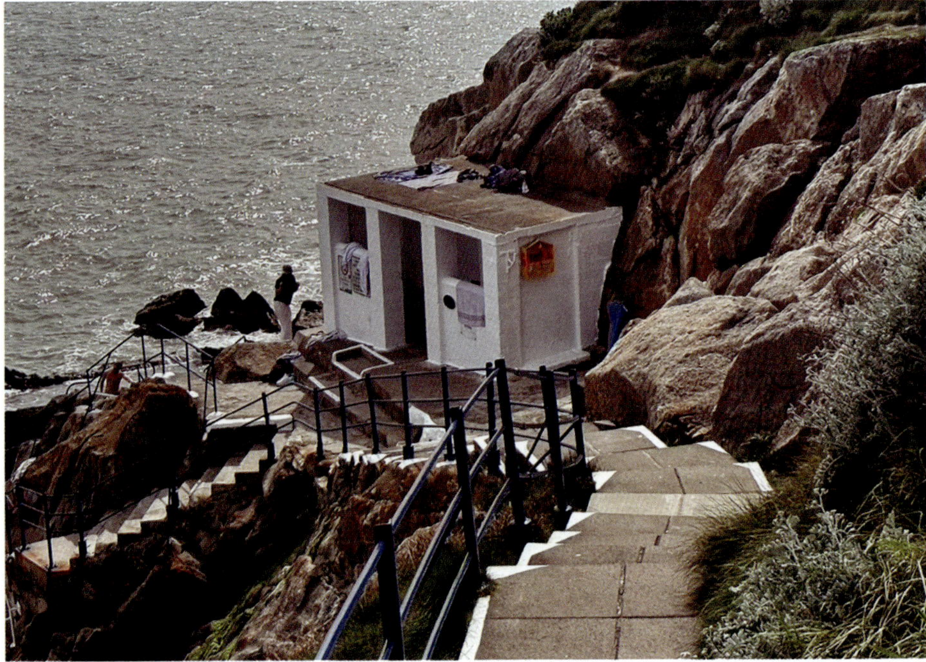

Fig. 14.2—Vico Rock bathing place.

patrons of the new Queenstown Baths, a point emphasised in public advertisements, as was the cleanliness of the water.[3] In 1876 the proprietor announced that he had opened new baths for men at one end of his property, which possessed 'the great advantage of being completely hidden from the public road'.[4] The baths proved to be a magnet for visitors to Dalkey and a bonus for owners of houses to let in the vicinity. Whereas the nearby Clifton Baths, opened by Michael Kavanagh in 1843, closed in the 1860s, the Queenstown Baths survived under different owners until the 1920s. A letter in the *Irish Times* in 1928 regretted the closure of the ladies' swimming baths there,[5] as the female writer was left with few other options, Vico Place (and the Forty Foot at Sandycove) being reserved for men only.

Following the establishment of the Dalkey Town Commissioners in 1863, a campaign began to develop a men's bathing place near the Vico Road, below the railway line. A public meeting was held in the Queen's Hotel in 1870 to urge the commissioners to complete works at the bathing place but apparently without success, because over two decades later the Vico Place Swimming Club was formed by local residents, including Alexander Conan of nearby Monte Alverno, to maintain the facility by means of voluntary subscriptions. The Swimming Club held swimming galas, the last of which took place in 1913.[6] Although the club lapsed around 1920, Vico Point continues to be a popular bathing place (Fig. 14.2). In addition to the commercial and public bathing places, several houses on the coastline from Harbour Road to Coliemore Road had their own private facilities, as shown on nineteenth-century Ordnance Survey maps.

Rowing and sailing regattas

Annual regattas, normally held during the summer, date back to at least the 1840s. At first they consisted of boat races in which local fishermen participated, either in Killiney Bay or Dalkey Sound. Spectators from Dublin, Kingstown and surrounding areas flocked to vantage points, such as on Sorrento Hill or near Coliemore harbour; extra trains were laid on to meet the demand, supported by local jarveys who met the trains at Dalkey. Military bands provided musical entertainment, and betting was heavy on local favourites. The day was rounded off with fireworks.[7]

Local landowners, such as the MacDonnell family at Sorrento Terrace and the Leslie family at Carraig-na-Gréine on Coliemore Road, not only took a leading role on the regatta organising committees but also opened their grounds to those willing to pay for admission, as their properties offered the best views over the racing courses and also accommodated refreshment marquees. During the 1850s, while rowing races still featured, larger yachts from the major yacht clubs in Kingstown and else-

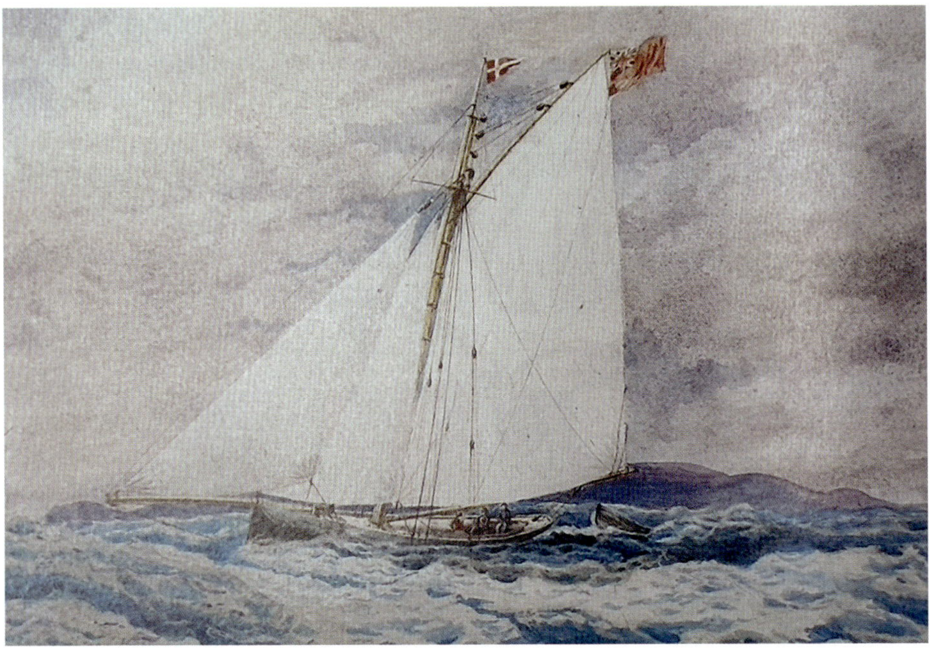

Fig. 14.3—Painting of the yacht *Ida* off Kingstown harbour by A.H. Orpen, 1860 (courtesy of the Royal St George Yacht Club, Dún Laoghaire).

where were invited to participate. The prize money for yacht races was usually a multiple of that offered for the rowing races.

Outdoor recreation

In the eighteenth and nineteenth centuries, a number of public leisure gardens, such as the Rotundo Gardens, were established in Dublin, often as a means of fund-raising for charities. Dalkey had a version of its own in the summer of 1850, according to this newspaper notice:

> 'Royal Victoria pleasure gardens, ball and concert rooms, Dalkey. Grand gala day, military musical parade, etc., to conclude with a magnificent display of fireworks. This delightful locality has lain dormant for several years for want of an enterprising person to establish a select and social series of respectable amusements. The subscriber … has taken the delightfully situated enclosed meadow, garden and cottage close to the Atmospheric Railway terminus, a beautiful sloping ground, on which he is now erecting a ballroom on a magnificent scale which will be fitted up in every respect as the Pillar Room, Rotundo … The first entertainment and opening of the gardens will take place on 2 July. Gardens will open at 5 pm, concert at 6 pm, and fireworks at 9.30 pm.'[8]

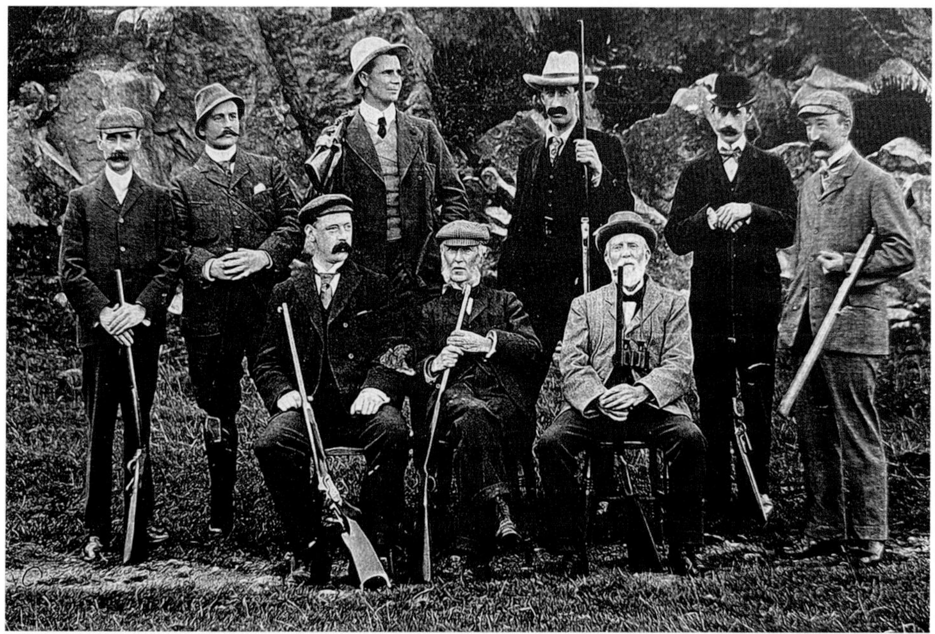

Fig. 14.4—Dalkey Rifle Club, 1899 (courtesy of Peter Pearson).

The following week it was announced that Mr Gallaher, the celebrated ventriloquist and illustrator of Irish life, would make his first appearance in Dalkey in the Victoria concert room, while Mr E.C. Hime, celebrated composer, vocalist and pianist, would sing several of his new and popular compositions. However, the pleasure gardens and concert room seem to have vanished as quickly as they had appeared.

A rifle practice club was recorded in the Griffith Valuation of 1848, and later in the century a rifle-range was set up at Dalkey Hill quarry, on the south side of Ardbrugh Road.

Quarrying effectively ceased at Dalkey Hill in the 1860s, following completion of the construction of Kingstown harbour. Some of the adjoining fields provided sites for a variety of outdoor sports for almost a century, pending the opening of the playing fields at Hyde Road in the 1950s. The former Dún Laoghaire Corporation acquired the quarry and the lands at Burmah Road and added them to Killiney Hill Park, which had been opened to the public in 1887.[9]

Torca Tennis Club had its grounds near 'Woodside' on Ardbrugh Road (to the east of the rifle-range). To quote Frank Mullen, 'If one stands on the Upper East Quarry of Dalkey Hill and looks down on what remains of Darcy's fields, one can see the ridges of two of the four tennis courts of the club, which prospered from *c.* 1890 to the early 1940s'.[10]

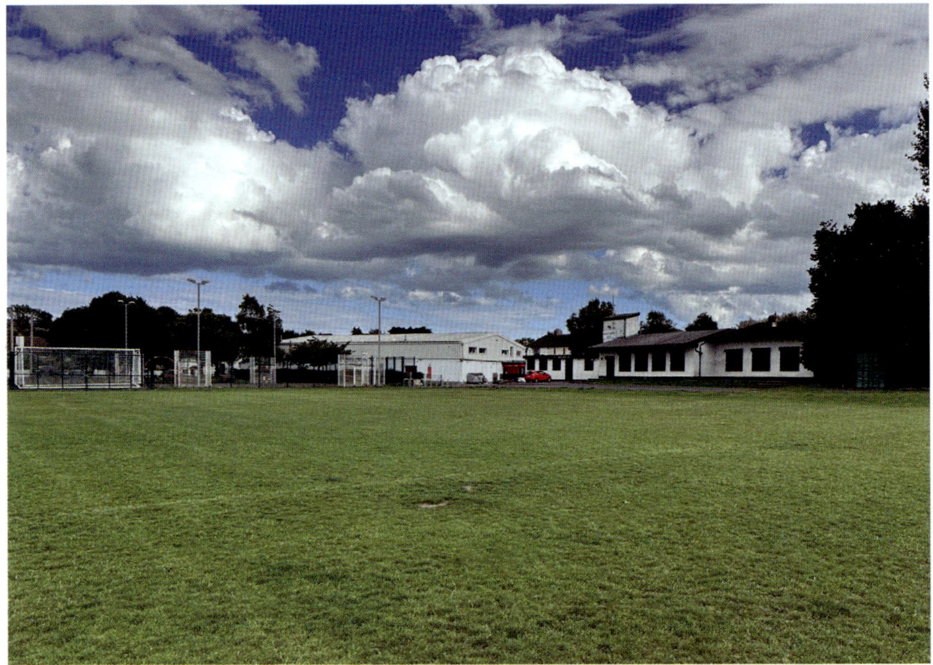

Fig. 14.5—Cuala GAA and Dalkey United sports grounds, Hyde Road.

Cuala GAA Club on Hyde Road has a complicated history involving breaks in continuity and mergers between clubs.[11] There was a tradition of both hurling and football in Dalkey in the late nineteenth century. Cuala Hurling Club was founded in 1918, Cuala being the historic name of the south Dublin/north Wicklow area in the Early Christian era. As with other sports mentioned above, their original practice ground was in the fields adjoining Dalkey quarry, although it was later transferred to a field near Hillside. St Benedict's GAA Club was active in 1917 but seems to have faded out later, and Cuala Boys GAA Club was founded in 1962. Following various mergers, Cuala Hurling and Football Club was launched in 1976, with the St Mary's Camogie Club based in Sallynoggin joining two years later.

Hurling matches were first played on the Hyde Park sports grounds in 1961, with an enlarged pitch being created by Dún Laoghaire Corporation the following year. In 1976 Cuala acquired the sports hall from the dormant Dalkey Boxing Club, and the Social Centre was opened in 1985. Cuala won two all-Ireland Club Senior Hurling Championships, in 2017 and 2018, and the Senior Football Championship in 2025.

Dalkey United Athletic Football Club was founded in 1953; it too started life on fields near Dalkey quarry before securing the use of a pitch at Hyde Road. The club has a proud tradition of competing at the highest levels of the amateur game and developing young players, including former member and Republic of Ireland international Paul McGrath.

One sport that did not start at Dalkey quarry was cricket. Dalkey Cricket Club was established in 1861, 'playing on one of Mr Burke's fields'.[12] This may well have been what is now known as Dillon's Park (see below) on Coliemore Road, which at that time was owned by James Milo Burke; Frank Mullen records playing cricket there almost a century later.[13]

Indoor facilities

A parochial hall attached to St Patrick's church on Harbour Road was built in 1868, thanks to a generous donation from Charles Leslie of Carraig-na-Gréine. Part of the hall was used to house the parochial school, which opened in 1870, with the remainder being available for events such as choral concerts.

The Dalkey Town Commissioners (see Chapter 12) adapted Goat Castle for use as a town hall in 1872, and about twenty years later they built an assembly room at the rear. The hall, which is still in use, accommodated public meetings, plays, concerts and flower shows; it also served as a temporary church in the 1990s, when the church of the Assumption was being renovated in advance of its 150th anniversary. The Heritage Centre was added by Dún Laoghaire–Rathdown County Council in 1998 to display the history of Dalkey and its literary heritage and to accommodate a small lecture room.

It appears that there was a small cinema on Convent Road in the 1920s, built by John Kavanagh, a building contractor. It was located on the site of the present car park associated with the Club bar.[14]

Public parks and amenities

Sorrento Hill was originally laid out by Hercules MacDonnell in the late 1840s as part of the 'pleasure ground' (private open space) for the benefit of the residents of Sorrento Terrace. With the passage of time, however, Lady MacDonnell, wife of Sir Richard MacDonnell of Sorrento House, had permitted public access to the hill, which commands superb views over both Dublin Bay and Killiney Bay, and by 1874 military bands were playing there on Saturdays. Twenty years later, she accepted a suggestion from Alexander Conan, owner of the nearby Monte Alverno, that she lease the hill to him and another trustee.[15] Bands played in the park at weekends (see Fig. 14.6). The grounds were not well maintained, however, and eventually it was taken into public ownership. A military lookout post was erected at the summit dur-

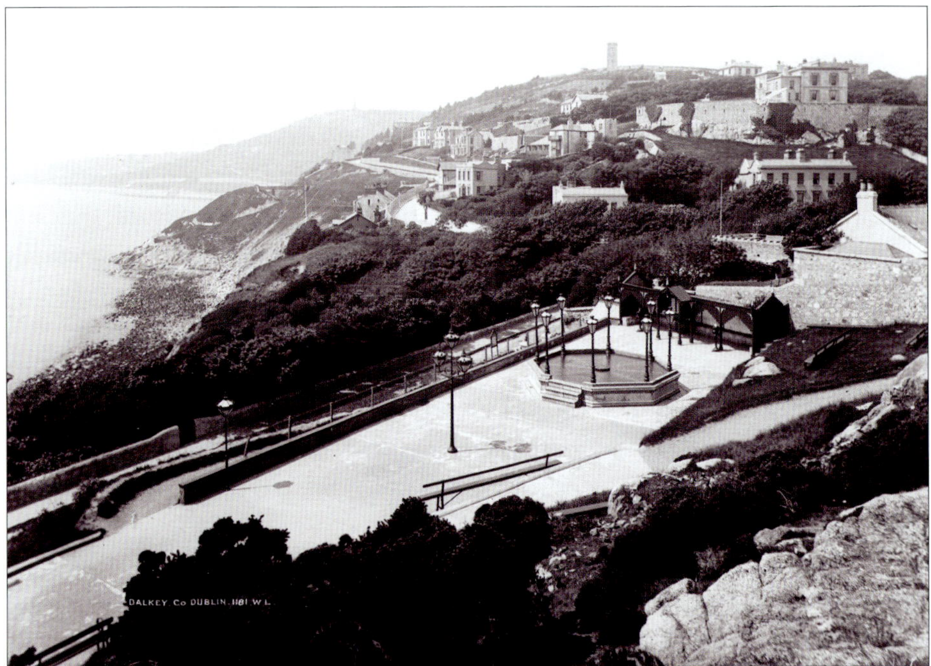

Fig. 14.6—Sorrento Park, *c.* 1900 (courtesy of the National Library of Ireland).

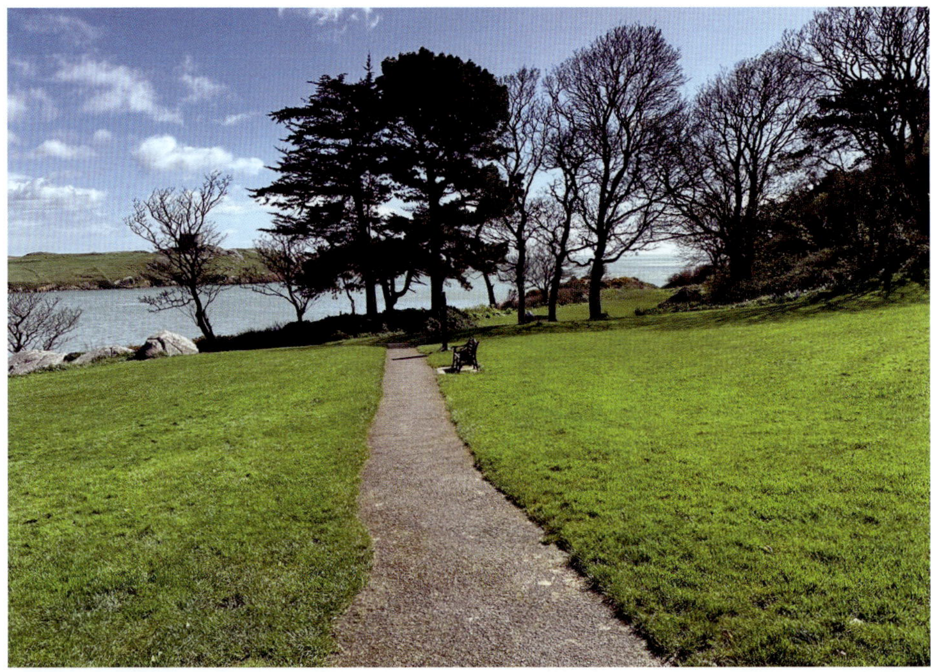

Fig. 14.7—Dillon's Park, Coliemore Road.

ing World War II (see Chapter 5 for both the lookout post and the nearby 'Éire' sign).

A mosaic in Sorrento Park, designed by Sarah Purser in 1937, commemorates the alleged links between John Dowland, the Elizabethan composer, and Dalkey. William Grattan Flood, an organist from Enniscorthy, Co. Wexford, claimed in an article in 1906 that Dowland had been born in Dalkey, but this seems to be little more than speculation.

In 1873 there was only a pedestrian right of way between Coliemore Road and Sorrento Terrace; vehicular access to the Terrace was from Sorrento Road. A bitter public controversy arose in 1885 about 'privatisation' of lands along the Dalkey coast-line;[16] old people remembered a time fifty years previously when it had been possible to walk across the Commons from the later site of the Loreto convent to White Rock on Killiney Bay. It was alleged that land speculators—including members of the town commissioners—had acquired valuable building sites with dubious title and thereby shut off public access.

Perhaps in response to the controversy, the town commissioners decided to open a public road between Coliemore Road and Sorrento Terrace, and to buy a field on the sea side overlooking Dalkey Island as a public park. The field belonged to James Milo Burke, a former town commissioner, who had acquired the land from Revd Francis Smith of Mount Alverno (as it was first called) as early as 1836. There is a well in the field which originally provided water for Mount Alverno, and which featured in a law case in 1861 when Patrick Blake (the then owner of the house) tried in vain to claim a right of way over Burke's land to the well.[17] The park was initially known as the People's Park, but later became Dillon's Park in memory of a Miss Dillon who ran a teashop there in the 1940s.[18] The park enjoys superb views over Dalkey Sound (Fig. 14.7).

Dalkey Urban District Council (which succeeded the town commissioners from 1899) tried in 1907 to lease Dalkey Island from the British War Department as a public park. The War Department, which had purchased the island in 1804 to build a Martello tower and gun battery (see Chapter 1), considered the money offered as insufficient, but eventually agreed to sell the island to the council in 1913. It was not used as a public park, but the right of public access was maintained.

15.
People who helped shape Dalkey in the nineteenth century

Dalkey was transformed from a sleepy village into a prosperous town during the course of the nineteenth century; this chapter looks at a number of people who helped shape its development.

William Edward Porter senior (1783–1859)
W.E. Porter, born in Kent, was an official in the Four Courts in Dublin who built Kent Terrace on Barnhill Road in 1836, one of the first terraces to be built in Dalkey (Fig. 15.1). He himself lived at No. 1, later renumbered as No. 4. He and his family acquired a substantial portfolio of land, much of it derived from the Bull estate, in and near the village. He acted as a middleman between the landowners and the tenants; his properties included the Queen's Hotel and the adjoining Goat Castle, together with many commercial premises on Castle Street. It seems certain that he was

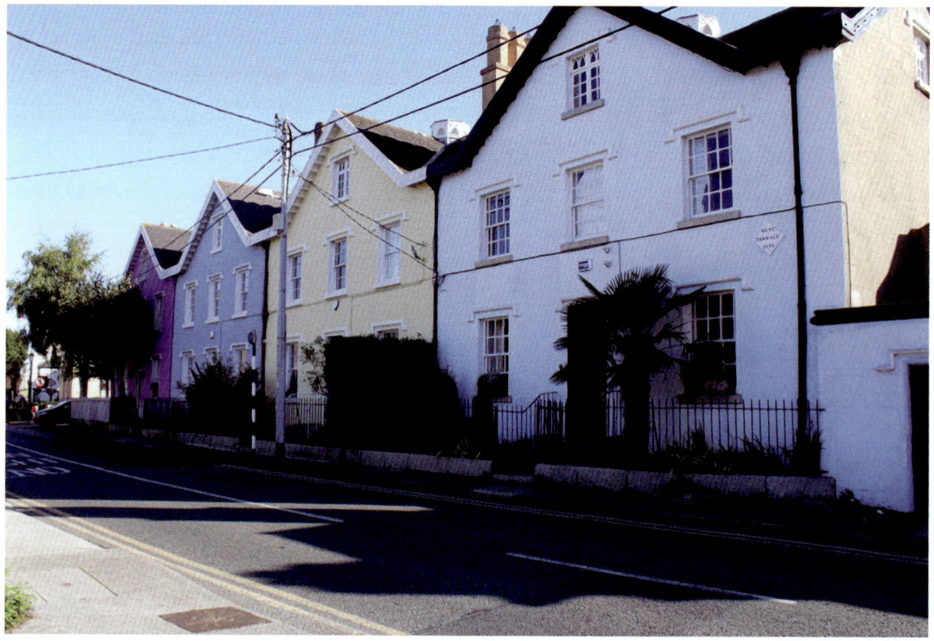

Fig. 15.1—Kent Terrace, built by William Edward Porter senior in 1836; he lived in the house on the right.

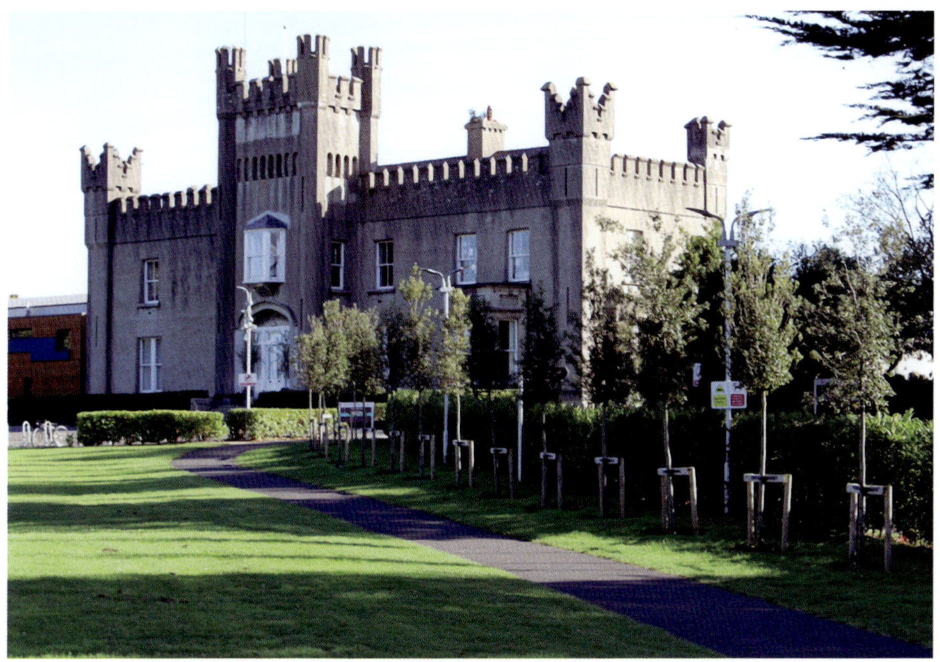

Fig. 15.2—Castle Park, originally the residence of Arthur Perrin in the 1830s.

involved in the construction of Ulverton Road around 1844, and he also developed Porter's Road (later St Patrick's Road) in the 1850s. He was a member of the committee of management responsible for building in 1843 the Episcopal church on Harbour Road, where he is commemorated with a plaque.

His eldest son, William Edward Porter junior,[1] expanded his father's property portfolio; his second son, Frederick, was an architect who worked mainly in England but who later lived at Kent Terrace.

Arthur Perrin (*c.* 1790–1866)

Arthur Perrin was a wealthy Dublin businessman who rented 45 acres at Bullock from the Carysfort estate in 1809. He later built a seven-bedroom castellated mansion on 26 acres, known initially as Castle Perrin and later as Castle Park (Fig. 15.2).

There were small granite quarries within his larger holding; stone was shipped to London for the wall bounding the Thames in front of the new Houses of Parliament.[2] He built Perrin's Cottages near Bullock harbour for his quarry-workers.

Perrin served as lord mayor of Dublin in 1834–5. He spent in excess of £8,000 (about €1 million in today's currency) in building Haddington House in Glenageary and developing 39 acres there for housing,[3] but he had overextended himself and

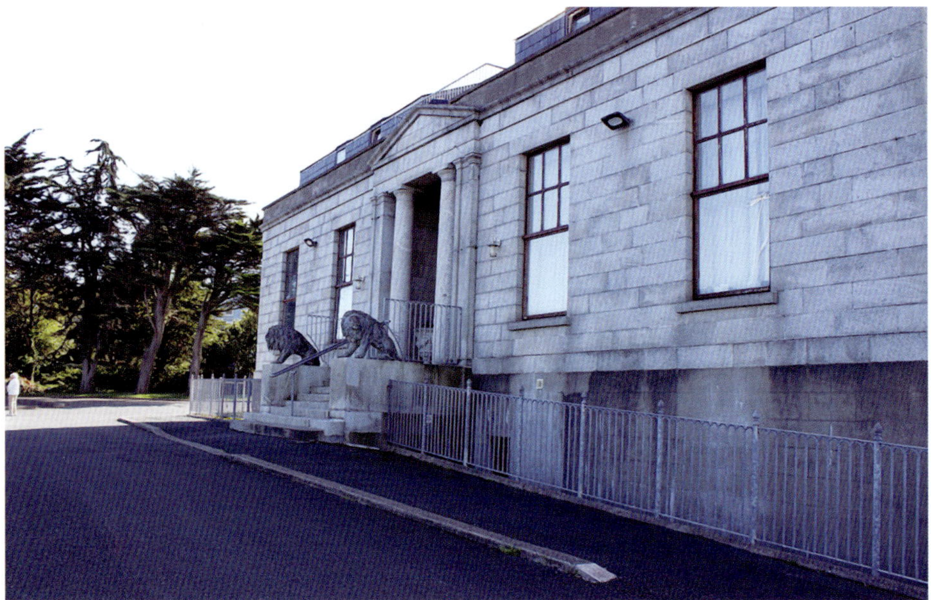

Fig. 15.3—Carraig-na-Gréine, built by Charles Leslie c. 1840.

was declared bankrupt in 1841, with debts of almost £4,000. He fled to New York and established a chemical factory in Brooklyn with one of his sons; he died in 1866.

In the nineteenth century Castle Park was let to members of the establishment, including senior judges. It was sold in 1904 to Wilfred Toone, who established a school there which continues to this day.

Charles Leslie (1804–79)

Charles Leslie was a partner in his family's pharmaceutical supplies business in Bride Street, Dublin, which he inherited after the death of his father in 1844. From around 1828 he began assembling a large coastal site by buying land from squatters on Dalkey Commons,[4] just east of the village, and built Carraig-na-Gréine c. 1840, one of the first of the large mansions that were to become a feature of the area during the nineteenth century (Fig. 15.3). The 1848 Griffith Valuation valued the house at £140 per annum, by far the most expensive in the Dalkey area.

It is interesting to note that Leslie, who probably did not speak Irish, used the Anglicised form (Corruicnagrena) of the Irish name *Carraig-na-Gréine* ('rock of the sun') as the name of his house, thus setting a precedent for many other houses on Coliemore Road, such as Inniscorrig, Rarc-an-Ilan, Cnoc Aluin etc.

While he rehoused some of the former squatters—probably miners working at Dalkey quarry—in small cottages on the nearby Leslie Avenue, he attempted to cut off public access to a well within the grounds. Mary Cullen, a local resident, successfully claimed a legal right of way.[5] To protect the privacy of his house, Leslie opted to build a tunnel under the grounds to the well, later nicknamed the Lady Well. He sold a portion of the lands adjoining the coast to Mother Teresa Ball for a Loreto convent around 1840 (see below). The convent site was located to the north of his own grounds, however, thus preserving his view towards Dublin Bay.

Leslie was a generous patron of St Patrick's church on Harbour Road. In 1870 a cut-stone schoolhouse and sexton's lodge, designed by the architect Edward Carson (father of the politician), were built at a cost of £1,000 at Leslie's expense. He also contributed to the cost of the rectory and gifted a pulpit and reading desk to the church.

He never married, and after his death in 1879 Carraig-na-Gréine passed to a nephew. It was later purchased by the Weir family, prominent jewellers in Dublin. In a curious twist of fate, it subsequently came into the possession of Loreto Abbey and was used as a school for much of the twentieth century. Carraig-na-Gréine now forms part of Sue Ryder House.

Revd Edward Leet (1800–78)

Revd Edward Leet (Fig. 15.4) was the first rector of St Patrick's church, Dalkey, and was closely involved in its construction. He served initially as a curate in Loughgall, Co. Armagh, in 1837–8. Meanwhile, in 1836 a committee had been formed to find a site for and build an Episcopal chapel of ease for the inhabitants of Dalkey, Bullock and Sandycove, which up to then had been in Monkstown parish. Revd Richard Tyner was appointed chaplain of the church, but after his resignation in 1839 Revd Leet was appointed in his place. The committee examined various potential sites but finally opted for one offered at a peppercorn rent by

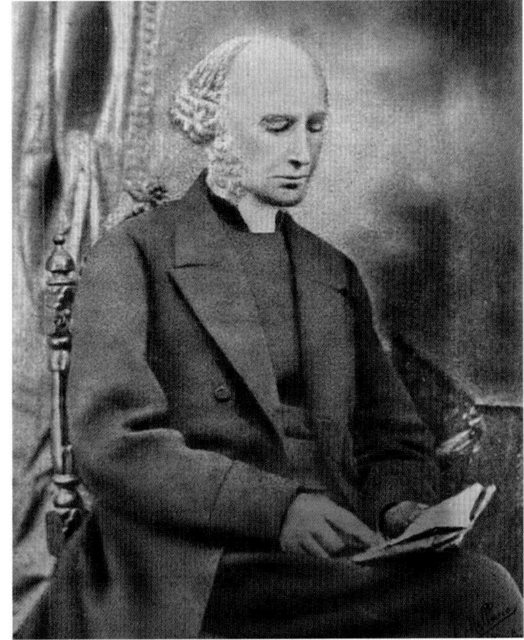

Fig. 15.4—Revd Edward Leet, first rector of St Patrick's church, Dalkey (courtesy of Brian Meyer).

the Ballast Board on Harbour Road which had the advantage of a plentiful supply of granite from an adjoining quarry. The church was opened by Archbishop Whately in 1843.

Revd Leet married Sarah Blake Knox in 1825; they had four sons and two daughters. One son, Major-General William Knox-Leet, was awarded the Victoria Cross, the UK's highest award for bravery, for his rescue in 1879 of one of his troops during the Anglo-Zulu war. Revd Leet and his family lived in rented accommodation in Sandycove until 1866, when a rectory was built beside the church. He had argued that during the twenty-five years of his incumbency he had expended in house rent a sum of £1,300, nearly double the cost at which a suitable residence might have been built. Leet was a doughty champion of his faith; in 1850 he published a pamphlet entitled *The Right and Duty of All Men to Read the Holy Scriptures: A Letter to the Roman Catholic Inhabitants of Dalkey, Co. Dublin*, and in 1855 he objected in vain when the Loreto nuns sought National School status. He organised a small parish school in a nearby house until a new school building, donated by Charles Leslie, was opened in 1870 (see Chapter 8).

According to Harry Latham, who wrote a history of St Patrick's church, Revd Leet was known for riding around the parish on his white horse. Part of Church Road near the rectory was called Leet's Lane.[6] He resigned in 1874 owing to infirmity of age and died in 1878; his wife had predeceased him in 1866.

Richard MacDonnell (1787–1867) and Hercules MacDonnell (1819–1900)

On the face of it, Revd Dr Richard MacDonnell, ordained minister in the Church of Ireland and provost of Trinity College Dublin, was an unlikely speculative developer, but he and his son Hercules left an indelible mark on the built environment of the Sorrento area of Dalkey as a result both of the houses they built themselves and of the houses built by others on their lands in the mid-nineteenth century.

Richard was born in Cork but studied in TCD, where he was elected a fellow at the young age of 19 and was awarded numerous degrees. He was a reforming academic, and served as professor of laws and later of Greek before being appointed bursar (1836–52) and provost (1852–67).[7] Despite a busy teaching career, he found time to start acquiring parcels of land in the Sorrento area in the late 1820s at bargain prices; three properties, which he bought from a mariner, a farmer and a spinster, cost £6, £6 10s and £13 respectively.[8] He built Sorrento Cottage on a cliffside site overlooking Killiney Bay around 1837; the name, with its echoes of the Bay of Naples, subsequently prompted a series of Italian names for streets and houses in the locality.

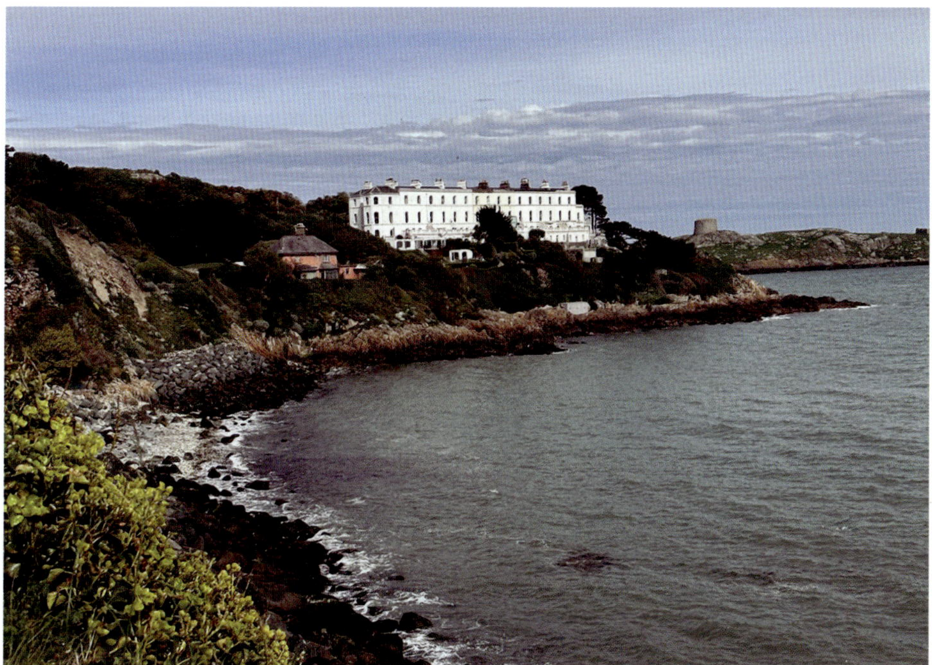

Fig. 15.5—Sorrento Terrace, with Sorrento Cottage in the foreground.

Just before the Famine, both he and Hercules began a more ambitious development, a terrace of high-quality houses over the cliffs to the east of Sorrento Cottage (Fig. 15.5). The first—and largest—of these, Sorrento House, overlooking Dalkey Island, was Richard's home until he was elected provost in 1852.

Hercules was a polymath, but in different ways from his father. A qualified barrister, he served as secretary to the Commissioners of Charitable Donations and Bequests from 1854 till 1885,[9] and was elected as a Dalkey Town Commissioner in 1863. He eloped to marry Emily Moylan in Gretna Green in 1842 and played a leading role in the musical life of Dublin.

Both he and his father had to overcome many obstacles in developing some of the best-known houses in Dalkey, as Hercules recalled in 1885:

'When the mines were discontinued in 1793, the cottages passed into the hands of fishermen and their families. Their direct descendants held these continuously, enclosing plots with rough stone walls, within which they planted potatoes etc., until the year 1829. Their rights, under this uninterrupted succession for 36 years, were then purchased by my father. Large quarries had been opened in Killiney hill [*sic*] for the construction of Kingstown Pier, and nearly every other spot of Dalkey Commons had been enclosed by the workmen who flocked there for employment. But, as the pier approached completion, the amount of work diminished, and practically closed about that time. The consequence was that the poor inhabitants had to seek a living elsewhere, as their patches of cultivation were quite too small to maintain them. The majority were too glad to sell their holdings, and I remember many who were thus enabled to establish themselves in better positions.

At that time there was only a rugged trackway for a short distance beyond Dalkey village, and to reach my father's place [Sorrento Cottage] it was necessary to walk over rough stones and rocks, through alternate mud and furze … The road continued narrow and untenable until in 1848 I obtained a shilling presentment, and thus at my own heavy cost, unaided by the public, I widened and formed the whole Sorrento Road from Dalkey Main Street to Sorrento Terrace, which had then not been built. The granite curbing on the pathway was cut and laid by me.'[10]

The sale of Richard MacDonnell's Dalkey properties in the Landed Estates Court in July 1873 revealed the extent of the portfolio which the family had built up since the late 1820s. In all, the 35 acres on sale were worth an estimated £512 in annual rental and included the ground-rent not only of Sorrento Terrace itself but also of houses such as Strawberry Hill, Nerano, Sunnyside, Sorrento Villa, Wave View, Marine Villa and Fern Hill. The sites of the latter four had been leased in 1861 by Dr MacDonnell to Henry Gonne, town clerk of Dalkey, for 999 years. The portfolio also included land on Torca Hill (including Torca Cottage) and the site of the coastguard station on Beacon Hill.

In 1882 Lady MacDonnell, widow of Sir Richard Graves MacDonnell (eldest son of Dr MacDonnell and a former governor of Hong Kong), entered into an agreement with the town commissioners to open up a vehicular link between Coliemore Road and Sorrento Terrace, which had hitherto been a pedestrian right of way. The family also donated Sorrento Hill as a public park; previously it had been the private open space associated with Sorrento Terrace.

Martin Burke (*c.* 1788–1863) and his son James Milo Burke (1814–1908)
Martin Burke was born in County Tipperary but moved to Dublin, where he opened a hotel at Seapoint. In 1824 he bought three adjoining houses on St Stephen's Green and developed the Shelbourne Hotel (Fig. 15.6), which soon became one of the city's most prestigious establishments.

In the following decades, he and his son James began buying land from squatters and poor landowners in the area between Coliemore Road and Sorrento Road in Dalkey and building spacious houses on scenic sites, which were then rented or pur-

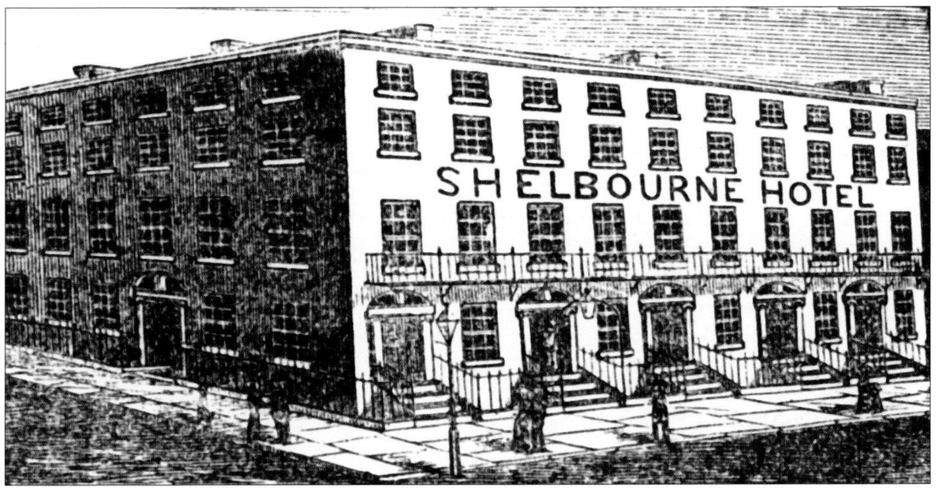

Fig. 15.6—Advertisement for the Shelbourne Hotel, Dublin, *Irish Ecclesiastical Gazette*,1 December 1856 (courtesy of the British Library Board and the British Newspaper Archive).

chased by Dublin's wealthy mercantile and professional classes. One of the first such houses was Queenstown Castle (Fig. 15.7), built on the rocky foreshore near Coliemore harbour; it was described in the *Dublin Penny Journal* on 15 February 1834:

> 'There is a dwelling house of a most extraordinary kind now being completed on a portion of Dalkey Common. It is seen in our drawing, two stories in height, standing alone, with the front door opening within a few feet of a craggy mountain precipice, and its rere wildly hanging over a dreadful rocky steep washed by a boisterous sea.'

The Commons were relatively undeveloped prior to the surge of new residential growth arising from the activity of such entrepreneurs as Charles Leslie and the Burkes. For all his undoubted flair as a businessman, however, Martin Burke was a rough diamond. Both he and his workmen adopted aggressive tactics towards adjoining landowners in carving out development sites, resulting in several acrimonious court cases. In one such case Burke was sued by Mary Cavanagh for assault, and the jury awarded her £250 (equivalent to about €30,000 today) in damages.[11]

James Burke claimed that in 1844 his father laid out Nerano Road at a cost of £1,000,[12] which is credible given the number of housing sites which the pair developed in the mid-nineteenth century. Unlike Charles Leslie, they adopted names associated with British royalty and the empire for many of their dwellings, such as Queenstown, Victoria, Albert and Khyber Pass. The latter was the home of Martin Burke himself from the late 1840s; it was situated on high ground to the south of

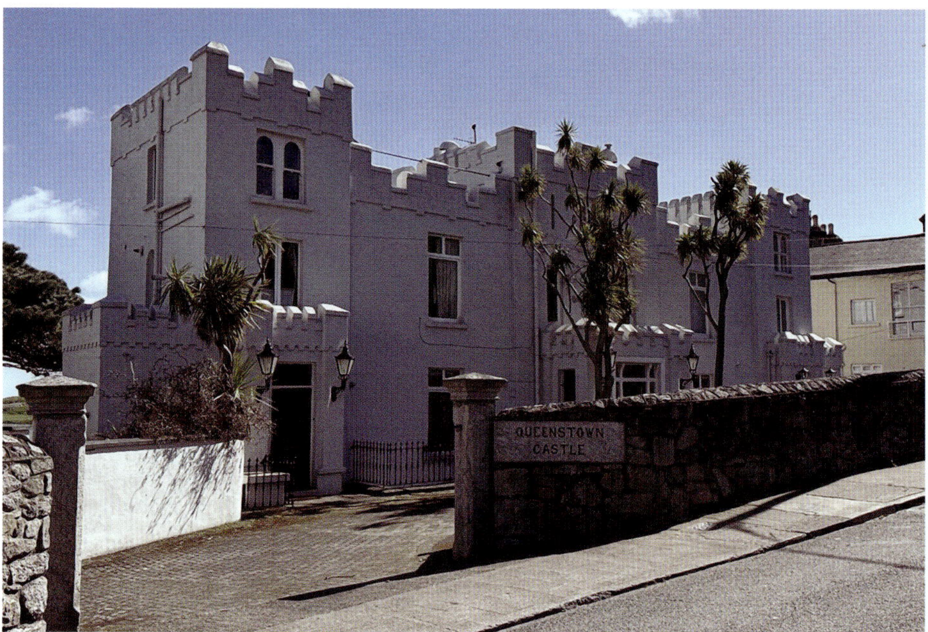

Fig. 15.7—Queenstown Castle, Coliemore Road, as it appears today.

Sorrento Road, with superb views over Killiney Bay. Some of the grounds were compulsorily acquired in the late 1840s for the railway line to Bray. Burke senior died in 1863; Khyber Pass was rented out before being sold in 1880 and became a hotel in the mid-twentieth century, before being demolished to make way for apartments in the 1980s.

Martin Burke was the sole Catholic juror when Charles Gavan Duffy, the Young Irelander, was charged in 1846 with writing a seditious article in *The Nation*; it is claimed that Burke was responsible for Duffy's acquittal, which led the British lord chancellor to criticise him in the House of Lords.[13]

James Milo Burke, a barrister and businessman, was very much an establishment figure: he fired small cannons from the grounds of Victoria House to salute the arrival of Queen Victoria in Kingstown in 1849. He was a justice of the peace and a deputy lieutenant of County Dublin, and a director of the National Bank. Given his significant property interests in the area, it is not surprising that he took a leading role in the establishment of the Dalkey Town Commissioners in 1863 and was elected as their first chairman. In 1882 he facilitated the extension of Coliemore Road southwards to join with Sorrento Terrace, and in 1885 he sold a field on Coliemore Road to the commissioners for a public park; it is now known as Dillon's Park, overlooking Dalkey Island. This was a significant gesture at the time because of public controversy over lack of public access to the shore as a result of housing development. Burke died at Springfield House (named after his father's birthplace) in 1908, leaving over £9,000 in his will.

Mother Mary Teresa Ball (1794–1861)

Frances Ball, the daughter of a wealthy Dublin silk merchant, was educated at a convent of the Institute of the Blessed Virgin Mary (later known as the Loreto Order) in York, where she was professed as a nun in 1816 and given the name Mary Teresa (Fig. 15.8). She accepted an invitation from Dr Daniel Murray, the future archbishop of Dublin, to establish a branch of the order in Ireland. The first Loreto convent and girls' school was opened at Rathfarnham in 1823.[14]

For various reasons, however, there were no fewer than five deaths among the sisters in Rathfarnham in 1839–40, and Mother Mary Teresa decided to found a new convent near the sea at Dalkey, where she believed the air was healthier and which offered the possibility of sea bathing. She bought a 3-acre site on the coast, part of the grounds of Carraig-na-Gréine, from Charles Leslie (see above) for £1,500.[15] While construction was in progress in 1841–3, she rented Bullock Castle and the adjoining large house as a temporary convent and school; it was from there that she watched the departure from Dún Laoghaire harbour of a group of Loreto nuns bound for Calcutta, where they

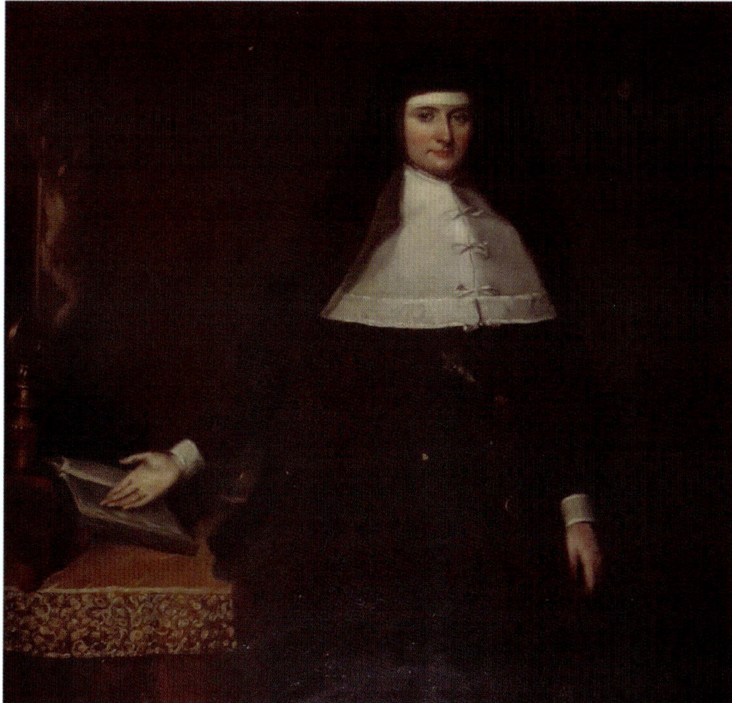

Fig. 15.8—Mother Mary Teresa Ball (courtesy of the Irish Province IBVM (Loreto) Archives).

rapidly established further new convents in India.

Loreto Abbey in Dalkey was initially founded as a novitiate and a boarding-school for girls, but a day-school and a girls' national school followed; both primary and secondary schools continue to provide education today (see also Chapter 8). A chapel was also built in the abbey and was consecrated in 1845. The road leading from Dalkey to the convent was originally known as Nunnery Road and subsequently as Convent Road. Many Loreto convent schools in Ireland were opened during Mother Teresa's lifetime, but Dalkey was one of her favourites; when she became seriously ill in 1861, she asked to be brought there, where she died.

Thomas Connolly (*c.* 1788–1868)

Thomas Connolly was a prominent businessman in Dalkey in the mid-nineteenth century who made several contributions to its development. First, he took a leading role in the establishment of the 'poor school' on Barnhill Road in the 1830s, serving as treasurer of the national school. Second, he leased part of his land at Bayview House, on the south side of Castle Street, for a new Catholic chapel in 1840; his son, Canon James Connolly, parish priest of Harrington Street, later donated the freehold of the site.

Third, he founded a highly successful bakery business at the corner of Castle Street and Dalkey Avenue (where there is now an apartment block); in 1846, during

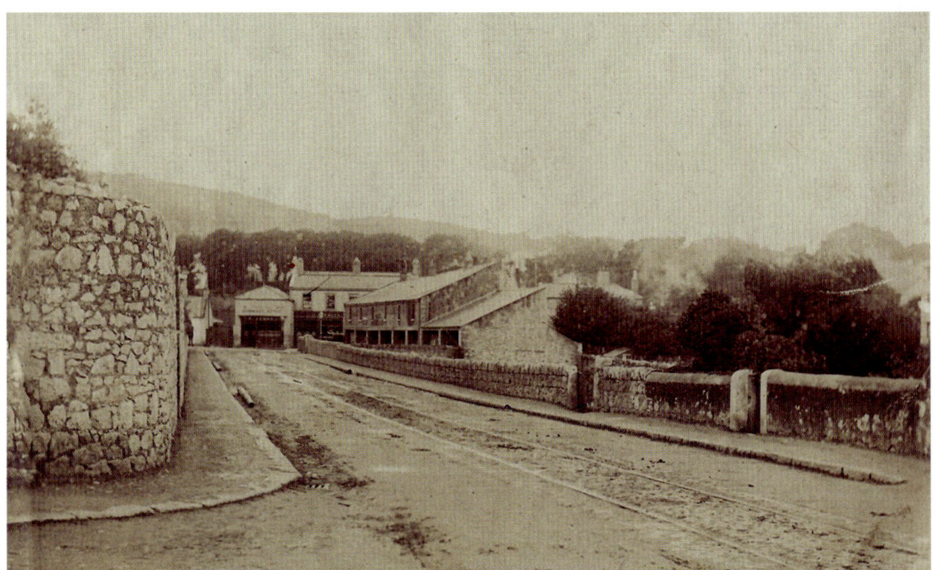

Fig. 15.9—The stables of Connolly's bakery, Ulverton Road, in the late nineteenth century (Harry Blake Knox collection, courtesy of the late Caroline Pritchard).

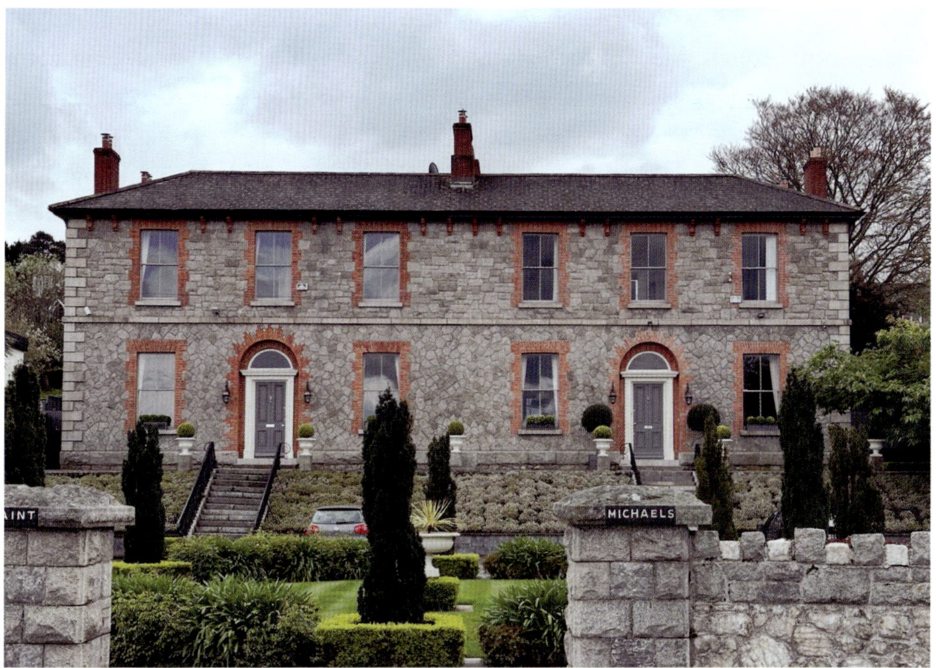

Fig. 15.10—St Michael's, Ardeevin Road, built by John Cunningham *c.* 1863.

the Famine, he claimed to be paying out more than £1,000 per year in wages.[16] The business continued until the 1940s, serving Dalkey and the wider district. Connolly was elected as one of the first Dalkey Town Commissioners in 1863.

John Cunningham (1815–89)

John Cunningham was a local builder who not only developed houses in Dalkey (Fig. 15.10) but was also a quarry owner and a significant building contractor, particularly in relation to railway projects. He built several large houses near Dalkey station, which had opened for regular services in 1856. Newspaper advertisements for new houses in the area often emphasised proximity to the station:

> 'For sale, two newly-built houses, red brick fronts, close to Dalkey railway station and commanding an extensive view of Dublin Bay. Five bedrooms and servants' apartments. Apply to John Cunningham.'[17]

He laid out the new road which bears his name and lived in John Ville on Ardeevin Road. His houses included Harvieston on Cunningham Road, built for the wealthy Eason family, and Ulverton on the road of the same name.

His numerous building contracts included Harcourt Street and Foxrock railway stations, the National Yacht Club in Dún Laoghaire harbour, and several railway bridges and viaducts. He also carried out major works at Coliemore harbour commissioned by the Dalkey Town Commissioners in 1868. According to a contemporary account,

> 'The fishing-boat piers in course of construction at Dalkey will be about 150 feet each in length. The new harbour will prove valuable not only to fishermen, but also to the residents and summer visitors at this highly-favoured township. The plans were supplied by B.P. Stoney, engineer to the Port and Docks Board. The contract was carried out by Mr John Cunningham at a cost of £1,858.'[18]

Following the laying of the foundation stone at the harbour by James Milo Burke, chairman of the town commissioners, a function was held in John Ville to mark the occasion.

Cunningham owned a granite quarry in Dalkey (the exact location was not specified), which enabled him to supply high-quality stone for his building projects. In 1865 he replied as follows to a letter of complaint in the *Irish Times*:

> 'My [Dalkey] quarries are always superintended by competent foremen, and the quality of the workmanship is well-known, and can be sustained by the principal builders in Dublin and elsewhere who have favoured me with their orders these many years. Last week I sent a large cargo of cut stone to London for the Thames Embankment.'[19]

Nevertheless, he was not immune to the travails of the building industry. Killen & Cunningham, railway contractors, went bankrupt in 1861, and at a hearing at the Court of Bankruptcy and Insolvency the following year counsel for the Killen estate said that they would pay full value.[20] The case seemed to involve Killen rather than his building partner, however, and Cunningham continued trading. He died at John Ville in 1889; his son took over and extended it, so that the house as it exists at present is not the same as when Cunningham built it in 1860.

16.

Notable Dalkey residents

The previous chapter looked at people who helped shape Dalkey in the formative nineteenth century. This chapter looks at people who were born in Dalkey, or who lived there for some of their lives, and who made their mark in a wide variety of fields, such as literature, theatre, medicine, architecture and high fashion. Two (William Hutchison and Richard Toutcher) played a role in the development of Kingstown (now Dún Laoghaire) harbour, one (Alexander Conan) was a pioneering photographer, and one (Fr Willie Doyle SJ) was a decorated war hero.

Maeve Binchy (1939–2012)
Maeve Binchy's family moved from Glenageary to No. 1 Eastmount, Sorrento Road, when she was 12. She became a teacher before joining the *Irish Times*, later becoming their Women's Editor and then their London correspondent. There she met her future husband, Gordon Snell, who encouraged her to start writing short stories in addition to journalism. Her first novel, *Light a Penny Candle*, was published in 1982

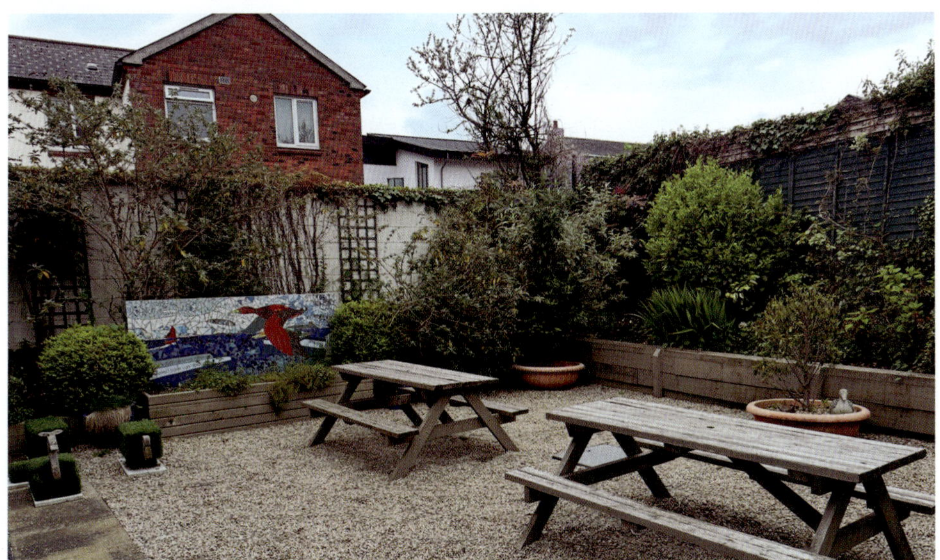

Fig. 16.1—Maeve Binchy memorial garden, Dalkey Library.

and remained on the best-seller lists for fifty-three weeks. Around 1977, on a visit home, she bought Pollyvilla, at the western end of Sorrento Road, and she and Gordon moved there in the early 1980s. They extended the first floor to make a studio where they could both continue to work side by side.

They were very supportive of the Heritage Centre at Dalkey Castle, where she now features in the Writers' Gallery, and attended the opening in June 1998. In 2017 the manager, Margaret Dunne, inaugurated an annual literary festival, 'Echoes: Maeve Binchy and Irish Writers', at Dalkey Castle. After Maeve's death in 2012, a landscaped garden at the rear of Dalkey Library was dedicated to her memory (Fig. 16.1).

Alexander Conan (1854–1941)

In 1889 Alexander Conan inherited Monte Alverno, Sorrento Road, from his father Joseph, a successful merchant tailor in Dublin. The original house had been built about sixty years previously by Fr Francis Smyth, a Franciscan priest who established a school for poor children on the site. Conan, who took over his father's business with his brother Walter, spent fifteen years and a considerable fortune combining a pair of semi-detached houses into an enlarged castellated mansion. His design of the tower was based on that of Kylemore Abbey, Co. Galway, also constructed in Dalkey granite.

Conan was a member of the Dalkey Town Commissioners and served for a time as chairman. He played an important role in persuading Lady MacDonnell to hand

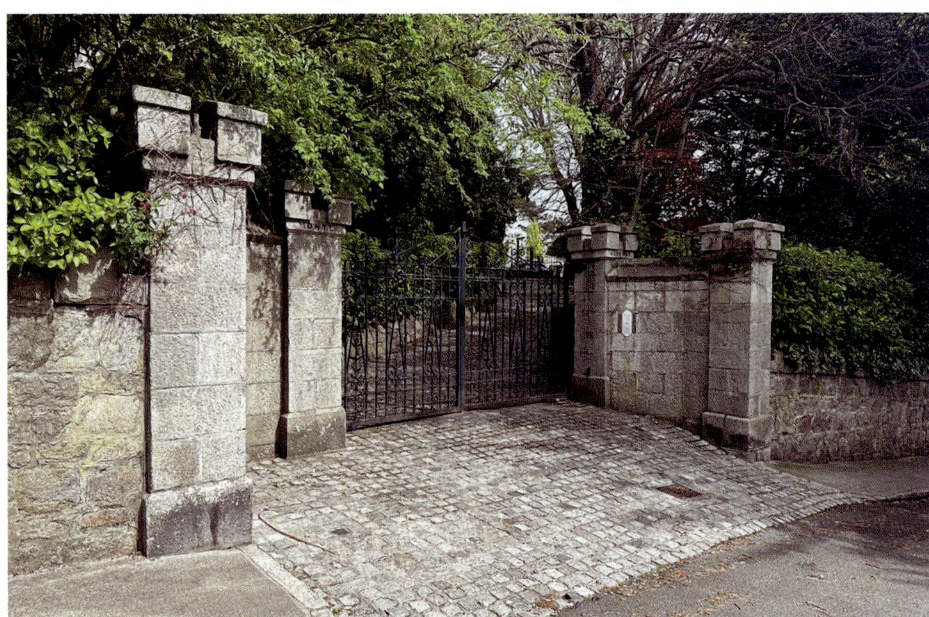

Fig. 16.2—The entrance to Monte Alverno, Sorrento Road.

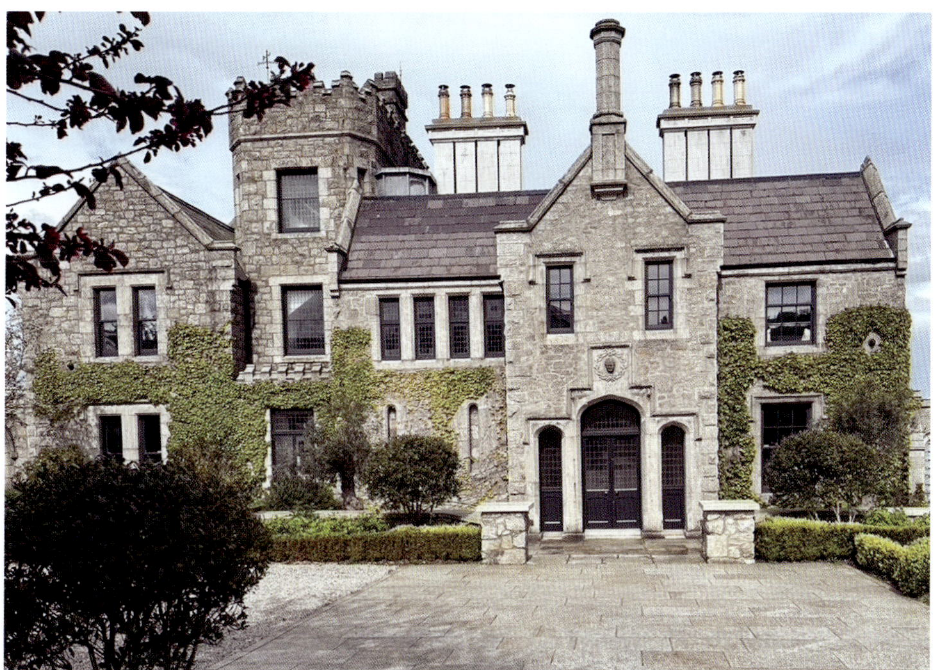

Fig. 16.3—Inniscorrig, home of Sir Dominic Corrigan, on Coliemore Road.

over Sorrento Hill as a public park in 1894, and in developing Vico Rock as a men's bathing place. In the early twentieth century he became a pioneer in the art of photography, and his collection of stereoscopic photos is now held by the National Library of Ireland. The collection is primarily a family one, depicting an upper-middle-class Dublin family on excursions both in Ireland and abroad. Some of the collection relates to World War I, while four photos relate to 1916 and the Easter Rising.

Sir Dominic Corrigan (1802–80)

Dominic Corrigan was educated at the lay college at Maynooth and was apprenticed to the local doctor. He graduated from Edinburgh University in August 1825, and on returning to Dublin began his private practice at Ormond Quay and later at Merrion Square West. His suburban home was Inniscorrig on Coliemore Road (Fig. 16.3).

He became a fellow of the Royal College of Physicians of Ireland in 1856, and in 1859 was elected president, the first Roman Catholic to hold the position. In 1866 he was awarded a baronetcy for his services to medicine. His specialism was the aortic valve, and he diagnosed the heart condition known as Corrigan's Pulse; the cardiac ward in Beaumont Hospital is named in his honour. He was elected a Liberal MP for Dublin at a by-election in 1870.

Cyril Cusack (1910–93)

Cyril Cusack was born to Irish parents in South Africa and raised in County Tipperary. He joined the Abbey Theatre in 1932 and remained with the company for thirteen years. He moved to London, performing with the Royal Shakespeare Company and the Royal National Theatre before founding his own touring company. He married the actress Mary Kiely in 1945 and lived at Clonquin on Sorrento Road; they had five children, three of whom also became performers (Sinéad, Sorcha and Niamh). Mary died in 1977, and in 1979 Cusack married Mary Cunningham; they had one daughter, Catherine, also an actress.

In a career of ninety films he worked with major directors, including Zefferelli, Truffaut and Zinnemann, and appeared in over seventy-five TV productions, including RTÉ's *Strumpet City* and the popular *Glenroe* series.

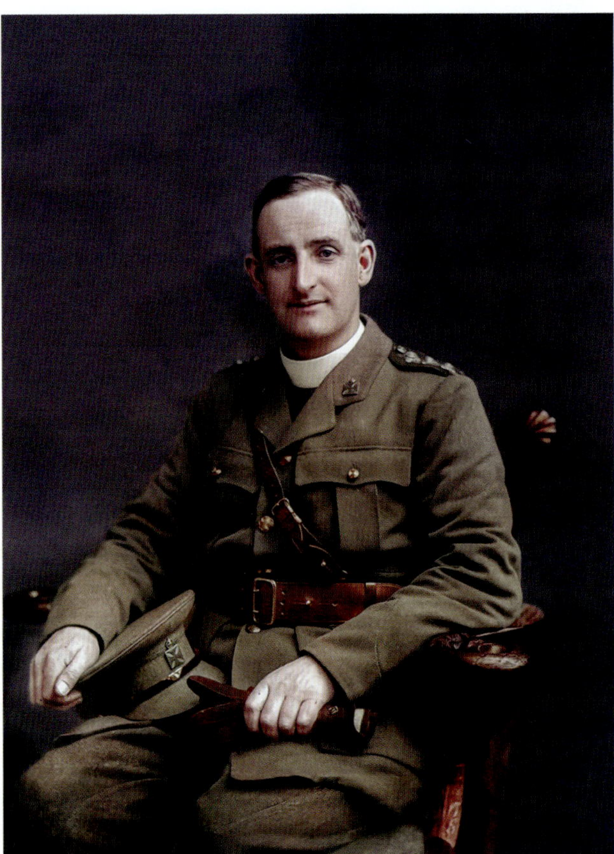

Fig. 16.4—Fr Willie Doyle SJ (courtesy of the Fr Willie Doyle Association).

Fr Willie Doyle SJ (1873–1917)

Willie Doyle was born at Melrose, Dalkey Avenue, the youngest of seven children. His family was deeply religious, and long lines of the local poor visited the house at Christmas to receive financial assistance and gifts. He was ordained as a Jesuit priest in 1907, and from 1909 until 1915 he served on the Jesuit mission team, travelling around Ireland and Britain preaching parish missions and conducting retreats.

In November 1915 he was appointed chaplain to the 8th Battalion Royal Irish Fusiliers (Fig. 16.4). Despite having the rank of Captain, he lived and suffered alongside his men, experiencing all of the dangers and trials of life in the trenches. Fr Doyle was awarded the Military Cross in January 1917 for his work with casualties during the Battle of the Somme. On 16 August 1917, at the Battle of Passchendaele, a group of soldiers led by Lieutenants Marlow and Green got into trouble beyond the front line, and Fr Doyle ran to assist them. It seems that Fr Doyle and the two officers were about to take shelter when they were hit by a German shell and killed. The cause for Fr Doyle's beatification and canonisation is currently being promoted by Bishop Tom Deenihan of Meath.

Daithí Hanly (1917–2003)

Daithí Hanly qualified as an architect in 1940 and worked in both the private sector and the Office of Public Works (OPW) before joining Dublin Corporation in 1944. He won the public competition for the design of the Garden of Remembrance at Parnell Square in 1946, although the project was not completed until 1966. In 1947 he moved to Dún Laoghaire Borough Corporation, where he designed a large local authority housing scheme at Sallynoggin. He rejoined Dublin Corporation and was appointed city architect in 1959, responsible for both housing and civic projects. On his retirement in 1965 he went into private practice, his most ambitious commission being the basilica of Our Lady Queen of Ireland at Knock, Co. Mayo, in 1976.

The original Abbey Theatre on Marlborough Street (Fig. 16.5) was severely damaged by fire in 1951 and was demolished in 1961. Hanly, who was a committed preservationist, took it upon himself to arrange for the salvage of over 700 numbered granite blocks from the façade and transported them to his garden at San Elmo on the Vico Road. He hoped that they might be reused in a new national theatre museum but, despite his best efforts, nothing happened before his death in 2003. His widow Joan kept in touch with the OPW, and it was announced in January 2024 that the feasibility of incorporating the granite stones into a new Abbey Theatre building is being considered.

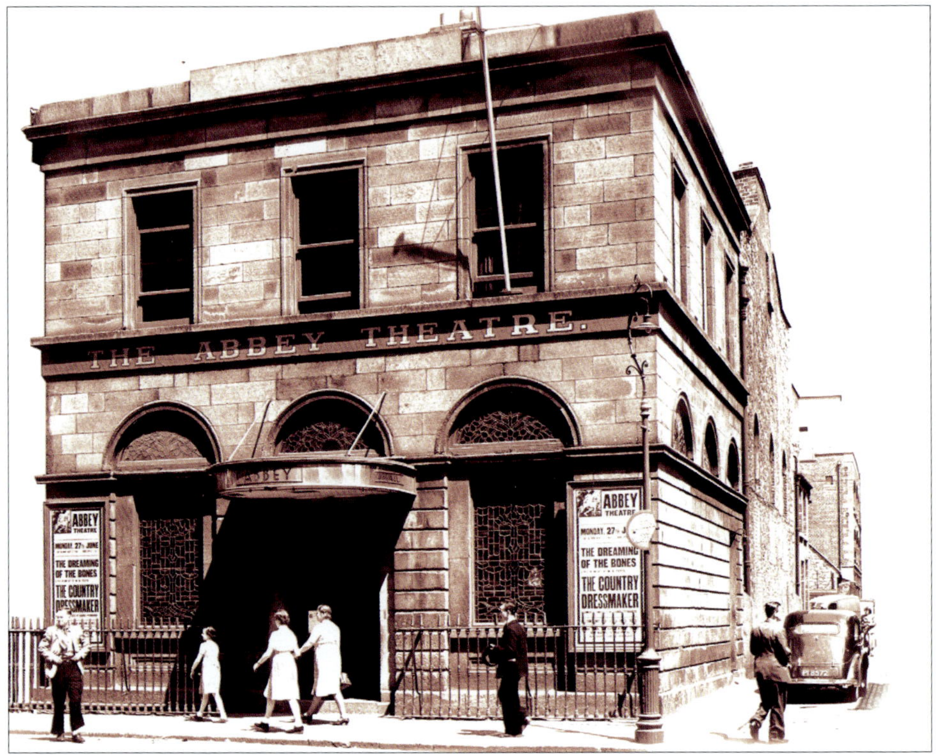

Fig. 16.5—Former Abbey Theatre, Marlborough Street, Dublin, *c.* 1949 (courtesy of the Abbey Theatre Archive).

Sir John Hasler (*c.* 1730–*c.* 1800)

In the late eighteenth century Sir John Hasler became one of the first prominent Dublin city residents to live in Dalkey; he was to be followed by many others about fifty years later. He served as chamberlain at Dublin Castle under several lord lieutenants from about 1770 for several decades, primarily as organiser of large ceremonial events such as balls for the Ascendancy. He lived at Castle Street in Dalkey from about 1785 until his death, initially in the 'House Castle' (Fig. 16.6) and later in Rockview Lodge beside the Goat Castle; the latter was converted for use as the Queen's Hotel in 1843 (see Chapter 11).

Hasler's grandson, Dr Frederick Hasler, served as a public health doctor in Killiney and Dalkey from the 1830s to the 1850s.

William Hutchison (1793–1881)

William Hutchison (Fig. 16.7) was born in Dublin and joined the Royal Navy as a midshipman in 1806, at the age of 13. He served in the Mediterranean and West

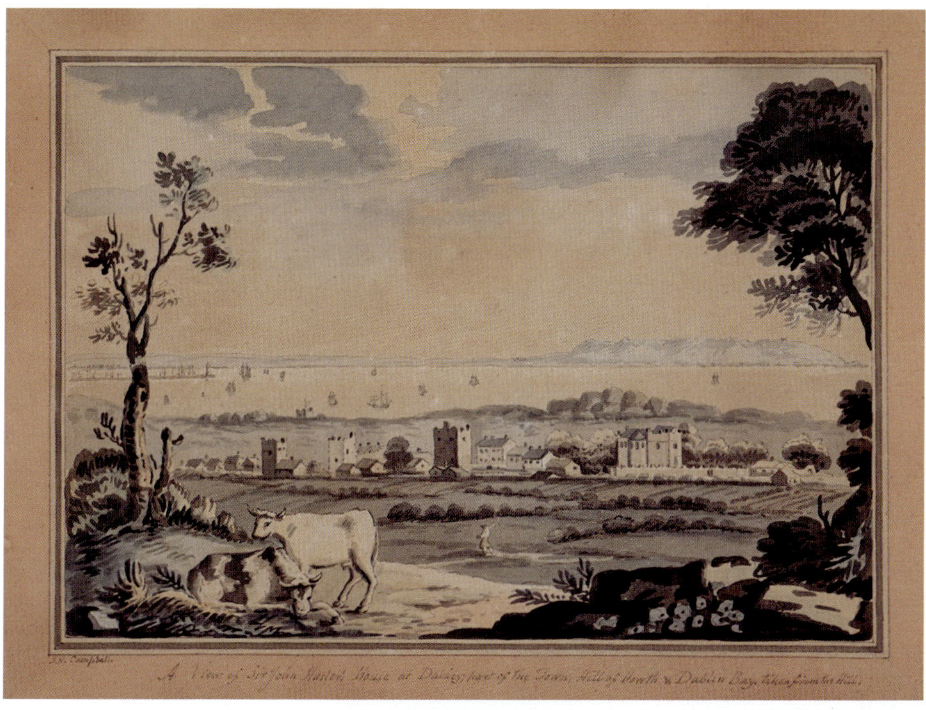

Fig. 16.6—John Henry Campbell's *A view of Sir John Hasler's House in Dalkey: Part of the Town, Hill of Howth and Dublin Bay, taken from the Hill,* late eighteenth century (courtesy of the Gorry Gallery, Dublin 2).

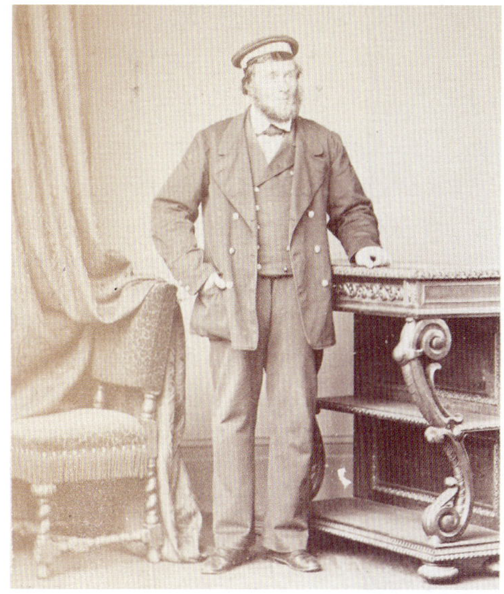

Fig. 16.7—A probable photograph of Captain William Hutchison (courtesy of the National Library of Ireland).

Indies. He was promoted to Lieutenant in 1815 but was discharged the following year, at the end of the Napoleonic wars. On his return to Ireland, he was appointed as Inspector of the Ballast Board's quarries at Bullock in 1817. His duties also included supervision of the lifeboat at Sandycove, where he participated in several heroic rescues, including that of the *Iron Duke* in August 1829 off Sandycove. The lifeboat saved all eleven men, women and children from the wreck, for which Hutchison was awarded the gold medal of the predecessor of the RNLI.

In 1822, Hutchison was appointed the first harbour-master of the new harbour being built at Kingstown. He was superintendent of the pilot boats of Kingstown and had his own boat and crew. In 1837 he reported to the Ballast Board that a number of Church of Ireland residents in the neighbourhood of Bullock proposed to build a church in the vicinity and asked the board for a suitable plot of land. The board agreed to grant a sublease of a 1-acre site on Harbour Road at a peppercorn rent for sixty-two years. Construction began in 1838 and St Patrick's church was opened in 1843.

Hugh Leonard (1926–2009)

Hugh Leonard (Fig. 16.8) was born John Byrne in November 1926, the son of Annie Byrne and an unknown father. Only a few days old, he was informally adopted by Margaret and Nicholas Keyes, who lived at Rosanna Cottage on Kalafat Lane, off Sorrento Road. Nicholas was employed as a gardener by the Jacob family at Enderly, Cunningham Road. By the time that Leonard (his pen-name) was in his late teens, the Keyes family had moved to a corporation house in the newly built St Begnet's Villas.

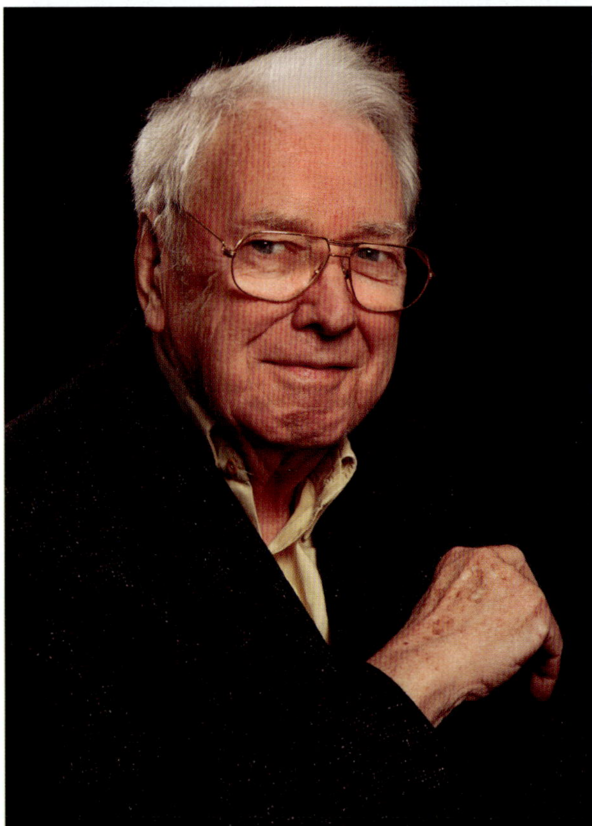

Fig. 16.8—Hugh Leonard (courtesy of Dalkey Castle Heritage Centre).

During the 1950s Leonard worked at the Land Commission, while writing plays and radio scripts in his spare time. He spent the 1960s in England, first working as a script editor for Granada Television and then freelancing in London. During this decade he continued to write for the stage. He returned to Ireland in 1970 and spent the rest of his life living in the Pilot View apartments overlooking Bullock harbour.

His memoirs *Home Before Night* (1979) and *Out After Dark* (1989) describe life in Dalkey as he was growing up, while one of his most popular plays, *Da* (1979), portrays his complex relationship with his foster-parents. His newspaper columns in the 1990s revealed the changes to Dalkey brought about by a more prosperous era, such as the opening of several well-known restaurants in the town.

Denis Florence MacCarthy (1817–82)

Denis MacCarthy was a popular poet, translator and biographer in the mid-nineteenth century. His link with Dalkey is that he lived at Summerville, Dalkey Avenue, for a brief period in the early 1860s. He was one of the first elected town commissioners in 1863, but he left Ireland for health reasons the following year.

Born in Dublin, he initially studied for the priesthood at Maynooth College but discovered that he had no vocation. He went on to qualify as a barrister but never practised, preferring instead to write both poetry and prose for a variety of publications, including Charles Gavan Duffy's *The Nation*. At the height of his fame Mac-Carthy was popularly regarded as one of Ireland's foremost poets, and was often referred to as the poet laureate of Ireland.

Frank O'Flanagan (1905–82)

Frank O'Flanagan, the self-styled 'Recorder of Dalkey', wrote an article in the 1942 *Dublin Historical Record* entitled 'Glimpses of old Dalkey' which is essential reading for anyone interested in the history of the area. He lived in Jamrud on Sorrento Road, built as a gardener's cottage by Major Bryan Cooper, who owned Khyber Pass in the 1920s. That house had been named by Martin Burke (see Chapter 15) after the famous mountain pass in India, where Cooper was born; Jamrud was a fort near the Pass.

O'Flanagan worked for the Hibernian Bank for forty years until 1962, but his real passion was the promotion of Dalkey and the preservation of its heritage and amenities. He was one of the founding members of the Dalkey Development Association in 1943 and of the Dalkey Literary Historical and Debating Society in 1949. The society invited President Eamon de Valera to an event in Dalkey Castle in 1966 to mark the 50th anniversary of the 1916 Rising (Fig. 16.9).

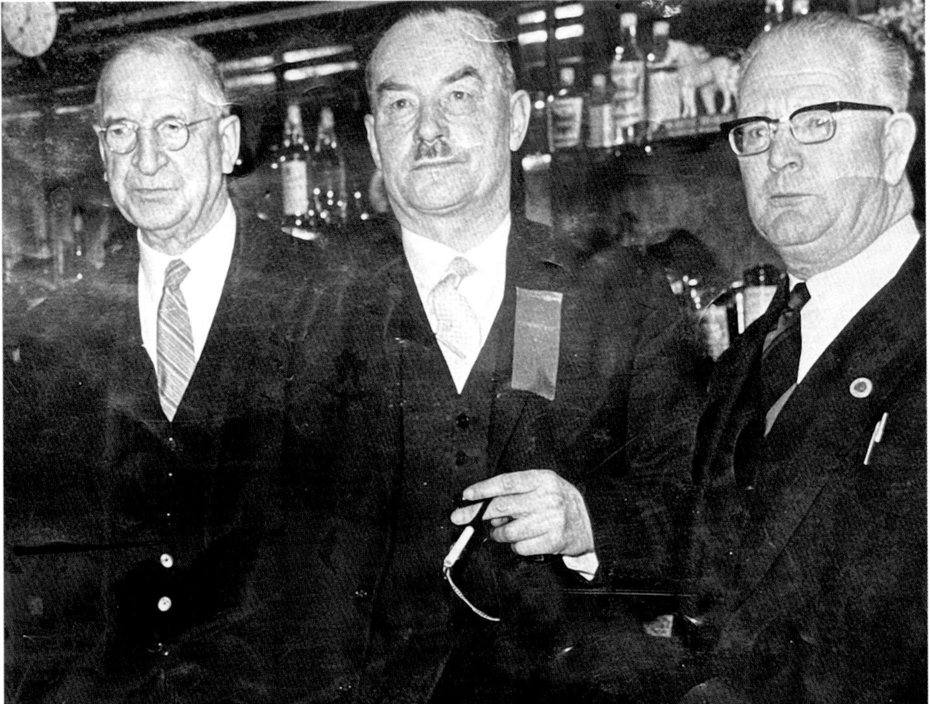

Fig. 16.9—Frank O'Flanagan (centre) with President Eamon de Valera (courtesy of Local Studies, Dún Laoghaire–Rathdown Lexicon Library).

O'Flanagan campaigned to ensure the maintenance of the Vico swimming place and took part in the revival of the King of Dalkey festival in the mid-1960s.

He died in 1982, and in 2018 his archive of research material was entrusted to the Dún Laoghaire–Rathdown Lexicon Library, where it can be consulted in the Local Studies Section.

Lennox Robinson (1886–1958)

Lennox Robinson was born near Douglas, Co. Cork. On a visit to the Cork Opera House in August 1907, he was greatly influenced by the Abbey Theatre company, then on tour with *Cathleen Ni Houlihan* by W.B. Yeats and *The Rising of the Moon* by Lady Gregory. Some months later Robinson wrote his first play for the Abbey, where he made his career. Yeats offered the inexperienced Robinson the post of theatre manager in 1909. In 1915 he took a position as organising librarian for the Carnegie Trust, then establishing a network of public libraries throughout Ireland. In the meantime he continued to write plays and won much success with *The White-headed Boy* (1916). He returned to the Abbey in 1919 as manager and producer/di-

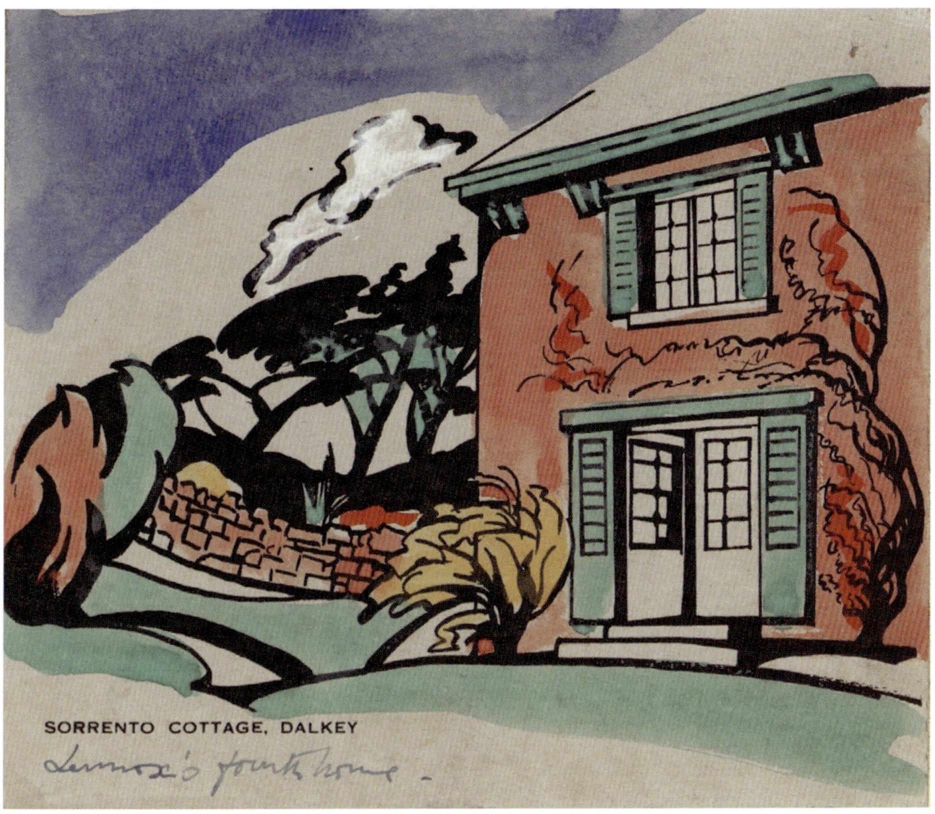

Fig. 16.10—Postcard of Sorrento Cottage, given by Lennox Robinson to Lily Yeats in 1938 (courtesy of the National Gallery of Ireland).

rector and remained there until his death in 1958. Robinson is usually credited with reviving the Abbey after 1919, encouraging new talents such as Seán O'Casey. He lived at Sorrento Cottage (Fig. 16.10) near the Vico Road in the 1920s/1930s and entertained major literary figures such as Yeats.

Carmel Snow (1887–1961)

Carmel Snow (née White) was raised at St Justin's, Victoria Road, Dalkey. Her father, Peter White, was a merchant tailor, but after his death from pneumonia in 1893 she and her mother Annie moved to America. Annie became a noted dressmaker for rich New York socialites, and Carmel began to travel to the Paris collections with her, thus igniting her own love for fashion.

In the early 1920s Carmel began working with the fashion magazine *Vogue* and was appointed fashion editor in 1926, the same year in which she married George Snow. She subsequently moved to *Harper's Bazaar*, describing her goal as creating a

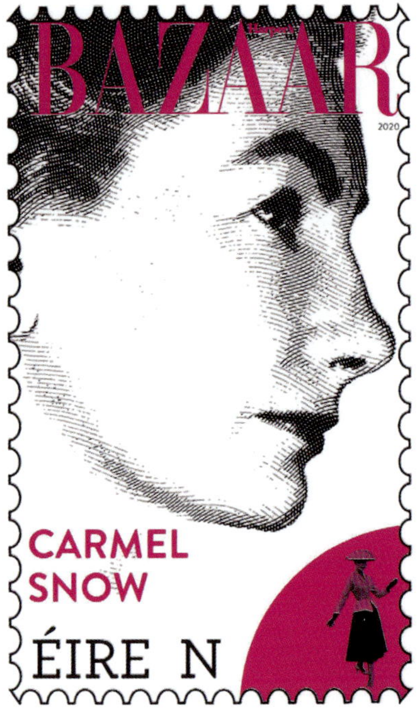

Fig. 16.11—'Pioneering Irish Women: Carmel Snow' stamp, issued 5 March 2020 (courtesy of An Post ©).

magazine for 'well-dressed women with well-dressed minds'. As editor-in-chief of the American edition from 1934 to 1958, she was considered the most powerful fashion arbiter in America (Fig. 16.11).

Richard Toutcher (1758–1841)

Born in Norway, Toutcher was a seaman and shipbroker who settled in Dublin around 1789. He was acutely conscious of the lack of a safe haven in Dublin Bay for ships caught in storms while waiting to enter the port, and is believed to have been the author of an anonymous pamphlet published in 1811 arguing the case for the construction of an 'asylum harbour' at Dunleary. He discovered that by renting land at Dalkey Hill he could acquire mining rights to the underlying granite on commonage land, and in 1814 he leased 10 acres off Barnhill Road, giving him 20 acres of commonage land. He offered the stone free of charge for the proposed harbour at Dunleary. An act of parliament to build the harbour was passed in 1816, and Toutcher was appointed second assistant engineer on the harbour construction. It is estimated that the free stone he donated was worth about £300,000.

In 1819 Toutcher granted part of his lands to the Harbour Commissioners for the purpose of making a tram road or railway to carry stone from Dalkey Hill to the harbour. He continued to work for the harbour until the early 1830s. For some of that time he lived at Shamrock Lodge, off Barnhill Avenue. Although he was awarded a pension of £100 from the Civil List in 1835, he died bankrupt in 1841 and was buried in Monkstown.

Further reading

Maeve Binchy

Maeve Binchy, 'My Dalkey', in Frank Mullen (comp.), *Dalkey: An Anthology*, vol. 2 (Dublin: F. Mullen, 2009), pp 127–8.

https://maevebinchy.com/biography/

Alexander Conan

Conan Kennedy, *Grandfather's House: Monte Alverno, Dalkey, Co. Dublin* (Killala: Morrigan Book Co, 2008).

Photographic collection: https://catalogue.nli.ie/Collection/vtls000298221.

Sir Dominic Corrigan

https://heritage.rcpi.ie/Whats-On/Blog/the-corrigan-window

Cyril Cusack

Dictionary of Irish Biography entry by Bridget Hourican (https://www.dib.ie/biography/cusack-cyril-james-a2340).

Fr Willie Doyle SJ

https://williedoyle.org/about-fr-willie/

Frank O'Flanagan

Frank O'Flanagan, 'Glimpses of old Dalkey', *Dublin Historical Record*, vol. 4, no. 2 (1941–2), pp 41–57.

https://libraries.dlrcoco.ie/library-services/local-history/fm-oflanagan-recorder-dalkey

Daithí Hanly

Obituary, *Irish Times*, 12 July 2003.

Sir John Hasler

Joseph Robins, *Champagne and Silver Buckles: The Viceregal Court at Dublin Castle 1700–1922* (Dublin: Lilliput Press, 2001).

Captain William Hutchison
H.A. Gilligan, 'Captain William Hutchison and the early Dublin Bay lifeboats', *Dublin Historical Record*, vol. 33, no. 2 (1980), pp 42–55.

Hugh Leonard
Hugh Leonard, *Home Before Night* (London: André Deutsch, 1979).
'Hugh Leonard's Dalkey', *New York Times*, 20 December 1981 (www.nytimes.com).

Denis Florence MacCarthy
Dictionary of Irish Biography entry by James Quinn (https://www.dib.ie/biography/maccarthy-denis-florence-a5126).

Lennox Robinson
Dictionary of Irish Biography entry by Christopher Murray (https://www.dib.ie/biography/robinson-lennox-a7727).

Carmel Snow
https://www.womensmuseumofireland.ie/exhibits/carmel-snow

Richard Toutcher
'Bicentenary of Dún Laoghaire Harbour', an exhibition curated by Colin and Anna Scudds of the Dún Laoghaire Borough Historical Society in association with dlr Local Studies, Dún Laoghaire–Rathdown Lexicon Library, 18 May–10 December 2017 (https://libraries. dlrcoco.ie/sites/default/files/Bicentenary of Dún Laoghaire Harbour.pdf).

Guide to sources for the local history of Dalkey

A. Maps

The Representative Church Body Library holds a copy of what is probably the oldest map of Dalkey: 'the plot of Dalkey in the parish of Dalkey', surveyed by John Tormer in 1656. The map is reproduced in Fig. 6.3, and also on page 47 of Raymond Refaussé and Mary Clark, *A Catalogue of the Maps of the Estates of the Archbishops of Dublin, 1654–1850, with an Historical Essay by Raymond Gillespie* (Dublin: Four Courts Press, 2000).

The Down Survey is a mapped survey of townlands in Ireland carried out in 1656–8 under the direction of William Petty at a scale of 40 perches to one inch (the modern equivalent of 1:50,000). The maps of the barony of Rathdown include Dalkey and Bullock; there is a printed copy in the dlr Lexicon Local Studies Section, and online copies can be viewed at https://downsurvey.tchpc.tcd.ie/.

The National Library of Ireland has a series of manuscript maps relating to Dalkey, including a photostat copy of a map of the lands of Dalkey, Co. Dublin, with names of tenants, by T. Reading, 1765. See https://catalogue.nli.ie/Search. Reading's map is reproduced in colour in Fig. 2.4, and also in *Archaeology Ireland*'s Heritage Guide No. 33: *Medieval Dalkey in the 1760s* (Bray: Wordwell, 2006).

Historic Ordnance Survey 6in. and 25in. maps of the area can be viewed at https://osi.maps.arcgis.com/apps/webappviewer/index.html?id=bc56a1cf08844 a2aa2609aa92e89497e.

UCD Digital Library has a large collection of historic maps of County Dublin, including the 1888 Ordnance Survey 1:1,056 (5ft to one statute mile) maps of Dalkey township: https://digital.ucd.ie/view/ucdlib:40994.

Dublin Port Archives: for old maps of Dublin Bay and of Bullock harbour, see https://www.dublinportarchive.com/.

Taylor's map of the environs of Dublin, published in October 1816, by John Taylor, Dublin.

B. Books and articles

Archaeology
Annual *Excavations Bulletins* are published by Wordwell, and the excavation
   reports can also be searched and viewed online at https://excavations.ie/.
Cooney, G., 'Dublin's islands', *Archaeology Ireland*, vol. 4, no. 4 (1990), pp 7–9.
Corlett, C., *Antiquities of Old Rathdown: The Archaeology of South County Dublin
   and North County Wicklow* (Bray: Wordwell, 1999).
Corlett, C. (ed.), *Unearthing the Archaeology of Dún Laoghaire–Rathdown* (Dún
   Laoghaire: Dún Laoghaire–Rathdown County Council, 2013).
Doyle, I.W., 'The early medieval activity on Dalkey Island, Co. Dublin: a re-
   assessment', *Journal of Irish Archaeology*, vol. 9 (1998), pp 89–102.
Leon, B.C., 'Mesolithic and Neolithic activity on Dalkey Island—a reassessment',
   Journal of Irish Archaeology, vol. 14 (2005), pp 1–21.

Medieval and early modern Dalkey
Ball, F.E., *A History of the County of Dublin: The People, Parishes and Antiquities
   from the Earliest Times to the Close of the Eighteenth Century. Part First: Being a
   History of that Portion of the County Comprised within the Parishes of
   Monkstown, Kill-of-the-Grange, Dalkey, Killiney, Tully, Stillorgan, and Kilmacud*
   (Dublin: Alex. Thom, 1902).
Beranger, G. (ed. P. Harbison), *A Collection of Drawings of the Principal Antique
   Buildings of Ireland, Designed on the Spot and Collected by Gabriel Beranger*
   (Dublin: Royal Irish Academy, 1991).
Bradley, J., 'Some reflections on the problem of Scandinavian settlement in the
   hinterland of Dublin during the ninth century', in J. Bradley, A.J. Fletcher and
   A. Simms (eds), *Dublin in the Medieval World: Studies in Honour of Howard B.
   Clarke* (Dublin: Four Courts Press, 2009), pp 39–62.
D'Alton, J., *The History of the County of Dublin* (Dublin: Hodges & Smith, 1838).
Dolley, R.H.M., 'The "lost" hoard of tenth-century Anglo-Saxon silver coins from
   Dalkey', *Journal of the Royal Society of Antiquaries of Ireland*, vol. 91, no. 1
   (1961), pp 1–18.
Gilbert, J.T. (ed.), *Chartularies of St Mary's Abbey, Dublin, with the Register of its
   House at Dunbrody, and Annals of Ireland* (London: Longmans & Co., 1884).
Guinness, H.S. (ed.), *The Register of the Union of Monkstown (Co. Dublin), 1669–
   1786* (Dublin: Parish Register Society, 1908).
Horner, A., '"Ireland's true survay", 1630s', *History Ireland*, vol. 26, no. 5 (2018),

pp 24–7.

Kelly, M.R.L., *Dalkey, Co. Dublin* (Ilfracombe: Arthur H. Stockwell, 1952).

McNeill, C. (ed.), *Calendar of Archbishop Alen's Register, c. 1172–1534, Prepared and Edited from the Original in the Registry of the United Dioceses of Dublin and Glendalough and Kildare* (Dublin: Royal Society of Antiquaries of Ireland, 1950).

Mason, A., 'Cross-inscribed slab in Archbold's Castle, Dalkey, Co. Dublin', *Journal of the Royal Society of Antiquaries of Ireland*, vol. 113 (1983), pp 143–4.

Mills, J. (ed.), *Account Roll of the Priory of the Holy Trinity, Dublin, 1337–1346* (Dublin: Royal Society of Antiquaries of Ireland, 1891).

Mills, J., 'The Norman settlement of Leinster: the cantreds near Dublin', *Journal of the Royal Society of Antiquaries of Ireland* (5th ser.), vol. 4, no. 2 (1894), pp 160–76.

Murphy, M. and Potterton, M., *The Dublin Region in the Middle Ages: Settlement, Land-use and Economy* (Dublin: Four Courts Press, 2010).

Ó Conbhuí, Revd C., 'The lands of St Mary's Abbey, Dublin', *Proceedings of the Royal Irish Academy*, vol. 62C (1961–3), pp 21–72.

Ó hÉailidhe, P., 'The Rathdown slabs', *Journal of the Royal Society of Antiquaries of Ireland*, vol. 87, no. 1 (1957), pp 75–88.

O'Reilly, J.P., 'Notes on the orientations and certain architectural details of the old churches of Dalkey town and Dalkey Island', *Proceedings of the Royal Irish Academy*, vol. 24C (1902–4), pp 195–226.

Otway-Ruthven, J., 'The organization of Anglo-Irish agriculture in the Middle Ages', *Journal of the Royal Society of Antiquaries of Ireland*, vol. 81, no. 1 (1951), pp 1–13.

Rocque, J., *A Survey of the City, Harbour, Bay and Environs of Dublin* (London, 1757).

Rocque, J., *An Actual Survey of the County of Dublin* (4 sheets) (Dublin, 1760; reprinted London, 1802).

Ronan, M.V., 'Royal visitation of Dublin 1615', *Archivium Hibernicum*, vol. 8 (1941), pp 1–55.

Ronan, M.V., 'Archbishop Bulkeley's Visitation of Dublin, 1630', *Archivium Hibernicum*, vol. 8 (1941), pp 56–98.

Rutty, J., *Natural History of the County of Dublin* (2 vols) (Dublin: W. Sleater, 1772).

Smith, C., 'An unpublished medieval deed from Dalkey, Co. Dublin', *Journal of the Royal Society of Antiquaries of Ireland*, vol. 125 (1995), pp 46–50.

Smith, C.V., *Dalkey: Society and Economy in a Small Medieval Irish Town* (Dublin: Irish Academic Press, 1996).

Wakeman, W.F., 'Primitive churches in Co. Dublin', *Journal of the Royal Society of Antiquaries of Ireland*, vol. 1, no. 8 (1891), pp 697–702.

Wakeman, W.F., 'Ante-Norman churches in the county of Dublin', *Journal of the Royal Society of Antiquaries of Ireland*, vol. 2, no. 2 (1892), pp 101–6.

Wakeman, W.F., 'Descriptive sketch of places visited: Dalkey, etc.', *Journal of the Royal Society of Antiquaries of Ireland*, vol. 6, no. 4 (1896), pp 403–41.

Wilson, P., 'A topographical description of Dalkey, and the environs. In a letter to John Lodge, esq., deputy keeper of the Rolls. Dalkey Lodge, March 28, 1768', *The Gentleman's Magazine* (May 1770) [reproduced in J.J. Gaskin and M. Simmonds, *Irish Varieties* (see below), pp 61–72].

Dalkey from 1800 to the present

Archer, J., *Statistical Survey of the County of Dublin* (Dublin: Graisberry & Campbell, 1801).

Bolton, J., Carey, T., Goodbody, R. and Clabby, G., *The Martello Towers of Dublin* (Dublin: Dún Laoghaire–Rathdown County Council and Fingal County Council, 2012).

Broderick, D., *Local Government in Nineteenth-century County Dublin: The Grand Jury* (Dublin: Four Courts Press, 2007).

Cannon, N., 'Mariners in the blood: pilot families of Bullock Harbour, Dalkey, Co. Dublin', *The Irish Genealogist*, vol. 14, no. 1 (2014), pp 34–45.

Clare, L., *Enclosing the Commons: Dalkey, the Sugar Loaves and Bray, 1820–70* (Dublin: Four Courts Press, 2004).

Conlon, T., *Victorian Dún Laoghaire* (Dublin: History Press Ireland, 2016).

Corcoran, M., *Through Streets Broad and Narrow: A History of Dublin Trams* (Dublin: Ian Allan, 2008).

de Courcy Ireland, J., *History of Dún Laoghaire Harbour* (Blackrock: Caisleán an Bhúrcaigh, 2001).

Donnelly, N., *History of Dublin Parishes*, vol. 1 (Dublin: Catholic Truth Society, *c.* 1907).

Forristal, D., *The First Loreto Sister: Mother Teresa Ball 1794–1861* (Dublin: Dominican Publications, 1994).

Galavan, S., *Dublin's Bourgeois Homes: Building the Victorian Suburbs, 1850–1901* (Abingdon: Routledge, 2017).

Gaskin, J.J., *Varieties of Irish History: From Ancient and Modern Sources and*

Original Documents (Dublin: W.B. Kelly, 1869).

Gaskin, J.J. and Simmonds, M., *Irish Varieties: A Victorian View of the Histories of Dalkey, Kingstown, Killiney and Bray* (Dalkey: Exchange Bookshop Ltd, 1987).

Gilligan, H.A., 'Captain William Hutchison and the early Dublin Bay lifeboats', *Dublin Historical Record*, vol. 33, no. 2 (1980), pp 42–55.

Goodbody, R., *The Metals: From Dalkey to Dún Laoghaire* (Dún Laoghaire: Dún Laoghaire–Rathdown County Council, 2010).

Horner, A., 'John Rennie's documents relating to the planning of Dunleary Harbour 1815–16', *Dublin Historical Record*, vol. 59 (2006), pp 182–200.

Kennedy, C., *Grandfather's House: Monte Alverno, Dalkey, Co. Dublin* (Killala: Morrigan Book Co., 2008).

Kennedy, C., *Conan Kennedy's Dalkey, County Dublin* (Killala: Morrigan Book Co., 2016).

Latham, H., *St Patrick's Church of Ireland Church and Parish, Dalkey, Co. Dublin* (Dalkey: H. Latham, 1993).

Lyons, G., *Steaming to Kingstown and Sucking Up to Dalkey: The Story of the Dublin and Kingstown Railway* (Dublin: Londubh Books, 2015).

Malone, E. (ed.), *Dalkey: St Begnet's Church Graveyard* (Dún Laoghaire: Dún Laoghaire Borough Historical Society, *c.* 1991).

Mallet, C.F., *Report of the Railroad Constructed from Kingstown to Dalkey, in Ireland, Upon the Atmospheric System: and Upon the Application of this System to Railroads in General* (London: John Weale's quarterly papers on engineering, 1844).

Nuttall, D, *A People's History of Dún Laoghaire–Rathdown* (Dublin: Eastwood Books, 2024).

O'Duffy, E., *Champagne, Cocktails and Crêpes Suzette: Wining, Dining and Dancing in Dún Laoghaire through the Ages* (Carrigtwohill: Lettertec Publishing, 2022).

O'Flanagan, F.M., 'Glimpses of old Dalkey', *Dublin Historical Record*, vol. 4, no. 2 (1941–2), pp 41–57.

Ó Maitiú, S., *Dublin's Suburban Towns, 1834–1930* (Dublin: Four Courts Press, 2003).

O'Riordan, D., 'Dalkey's first National School', *Dún Laoghaire Journal*, no. 31 (2022), pp 53–9.

O'Riordan, D., 'The school on Dalkey Commons', *Dún Laoghaire Journal*, no. 32 (2023), pp 45–51.

O'Sullivan, M. and Downey, L., 'Martello and signal towers', *Archaeology Ireland*, vol. 26, no. 7 (2012), pp 46–9.

Stafford Johnson, J., 'The Dublin Penny Post: 1773–1840', *Dublin Historical Record*, vol. 4, no. 3 (1942), pp 81–95.

Thom's Irish Almanac and Official Directory (Dublin: Alex. Thom, 1844–).

Dalkey—general

Archives of Dalkey Town Commissioners and Dalkey Urban District Council: These are held in the County Hall, Dún Laoghaire. See https://www.dlrcoco.ie/sites/dlrcoco/files/atoms/files/la2_-_archives_of_dalkey_township_and_la3_-_archives_of_killiney-ballybrack_township_0.pdf.

Dún Laoghaire–Rathdown Library: Directory of local studies, articles and book chapters in Dún Laoghaire–Rathdown, compiled by Nigel Curtin, former Local Studies Librarian at dlr Lexicon. See https://libraries.dlrcoco.ie/library-services/local-history/local-studies.

Edwards, B.L., *Dalkey: A Short Account of the Town Through its Changing History* (Dublin: James Duffy and Co. Ltd, *c.* 1933).

Joyce, W. St J., *The Neighbourhood of Dublin: Its Topography, Antiquities and Historical Associations* (Dublin: M.H. Gill, 1912).

MacAongusa, B., *Hidden Streams: A New History of Dún Laoghaire–Rathdown* (Blackrock: Currach Press, 2007).

Mullen, F. (comp.), *Dalkey: An Anthology*, vol. 1 (Dublin: Frank Mullen, 2008).

Mullen, F. (comp.), *Dalkey: An Anthology*, vol. 2 (Dublin: Frank Mullen, 2009).

O'Sullivan, J. and Cannon, S. (eds), *The Book of Dún Laoghaire* (Blackrock: Blackrock Teachers' Centre, 1987).

Pearson, P., *Between the Mountains and the Sea: Dún Laoghaire–Rathdown County* (Dublin: O'Brien Press, 1998).

Pearson, P., *The Granite Coast: Dún Laoghaire, Sandycove, Dalkey* (Dublin: O'Brien Press, 2022).

C. Newspapers

Contemporary newspapers, such as *Saunders's News-Letter*, *The Freeman's Journal* and *The Irish Times*, can be viewed on microfilm at the National Library of Ireland (https://www.nli.ie/collections/our-collections/newspapers) or online at the British Newspaper Archive (https://www.britishnewspaperarchive.co.uk/) (subscription required).

Endnotes

Chapter 1

1 See Chapters 13 (harbours) and 7 (castles).

2 G.D. Liversage *et al.*, 'Excavations at Dalkey Island, Co. Dublin, 1956–1959', *Proceedings of the Royal Irish Academy*, vol. 66C (1967–8), pp 53–233.

3 J.D. Bateson, 'Roman material from Ireland: a re-consideration', *Proceedings of the Royal Irish Academy*, vol. 73C (1973), pp 21–97, at pp 67 and 97.

4 National Monuments Service, site no. DU023-029004-.

5 Gabriel Cooney, 'Dublin's islands', *Archaeology Ireland*, vol. 4, no. 4 (1990), pp 7–9, at p. 8.

6 Christiaan Corlett, *Antiquities of Old Rathdown: The Archaeology of South County Dublin and North County Wicklow* (Bray: Wordwell, 1999), p. 37.

7 *Calendar of the Documents of Ireland 1171–1251* (London: Longman and Co., 1875–86), pp 266–7.

8 *Irish Penny Journal*, 21 November 1841.

9 Appendix to the *30th Report of the Deputy Keeper of Public Records in Ireland* (Dublin: Public Record Office of Ireland, 1898), pp 51–2.

10 *Irish Times*, 31 January 1930.

11 *Dublin Evening Post*, 22 August 1797.

12 *Freeman's Journal*, 16 August 1850.

13 Jason Bolton, *Martello Towers Research Project* (Dublin: Fingal County Council, Dún Laoghaire–Rathdown County Council and the Heritage Council, 2008), pp 21–31.

14 Pól Ó Duibhir, 'Martello tower no. 7 and the defence of Killiney Bay', *Dublin Historical Record*, vol. 7, no. 2 (2017), pp 162–75, at p. 162.

15 Samuel Lewis, *Topographical dictionary of Ireland* (London: S. Lewis, 1837), vol. 1, pp 447–8.

16 Bolton, p. 41.

17 *Dublin Builder*, 1 February 1867.

18 *Freeman's Journal*, 16 May 1863.

19 Available to download on www.dlrcoco.ie.

Chapter 2

1 Francis Elrington Ball, *A History of the County of Dublin: the People, Parishes and Antiquities from the Earliest Times to the Close of the Eighteenth Century. Part First: Being a History of that Portion of the County Comprised within the Parishes of Monkstown, Kill-of-the-Grange, Dalkey, Killiney, Tully, Stillorgan, and Kilmacud* (Dublin: A. Thom, 1902), p. 71; *Dublin Penny Journal*, vol. 2, no. 91 (29 March 1834), pp 308–9.

2 R.H.M. Dolley, 'The "lost" hoard of tenth-century Anglo-Saxon silver coins from Dalkey', *Journal of the Royal Society of Antiquaries of Ireland*, vol. 91, no. 1 (1961), pp 1–18, at pp 16–17.

3 W.F. Wakeman, 'Ante-Norman churches in the county of Dublin', *Journal of the Royal Society of Antiquaries of Ireland*, vol. 2, no. 2 (1892), pp 101–6, at pp 103–4.

4 Christiaan Corlett (ed.), *Unearthing the Archaeology of Dún Laoghaire–Rathdown* (Dún Laoghaire: Dún Laoghaire–Rathdown County Council, 2013), 109, fig. 127.

5 C. McNeill (ed.), *Calendar of Archbishop Alen's Register, c. 1172–1534, Prepared and Edited from the Original in the Registry of the United Dioceses of Dublin and Glendalough and Kildare* (Dublin: Royal Society of Antiquaries of Ireland, 1950), pp 194–6, no. 326.

6 Charles Smith, 'An unpublished medieval deed from Dalkey, Co. Dublin', *Journal of the Royal Society of Antiquaries of Ireland*, vol. 125 (1995), pp 46–50, at p. 48.

7 Charles Smith, *Dalkey: Society and Economy in a Small Medieval Irish Town* (Dublin: Irish Academic Press, 1996), pp 25–6.

8 *Calendar of the Documents of Ireland, 1302–7* (London: Longman and Co., 1886), p. 135.

9 McNeill, *Archbishop Alen's Register*, p. 233, no. 90 (240); p. 238, no. 90 (242).

10 National Monuments Service Sites and Monuments Record no. DU023-023016.

11 David B. Quinn, 'The bills and statutes of the Irish parliaments of Henry VII and Henry VIII', *Analecta Hibernica*, no. 10 (1941), pp 71–169, at p. 88.

12 M.V. Ronan, 'Archbishop Bulkeley's Visitation of Dublin, 1630', *Archivium Hibernicum*, vol. 8 (1941), pp 56–98, at p. 86.

13 Richard M. Flatman, 'Some inhabitants of Newcastle and Uppercross baronies, Co. Dublin, *c.* 1650', *Irish Genealogist*, vol. 7, no. 4 (1989), pp 496–504; Séamus Pender (ed.), *A Census of Ireland, c. 1659* (Dublin: Irish Manuscripts Commission, 1939), p. 379.

14 *Dublin University Magazine*, vol. 27 (1846), p. 544; J. Gaskin and M. Simmonds, *Irish Varieties: A Victorian View of the Histories of Dalkey, Kingstown, Killiney and Bray* (Dalkey: Exchange Bookshop Ltd, 1987), p. 49.

15 Peter Wilson, quoted in Gaskin and Simmonds, *Irish Varieties*, p. 62.

16 John Barrett, 'Quarries, mines and railways of Dalkey', *Journal of the Mining Trust of Ireland*, vol. 6 (2006), pp 17–21.

17 *Saunders's News-Letter*, 27 June 1774.

Chapter 3

1 Newport White (ed.), *Extents of Irish Monastic Possessions, 1540–1541* (Dublin: Irish Manuscripts Commission, 1943), p. 11.

2 John D'Alton, *The History of the County of Dublin* (Dublin: Hodges & Smith, 1838), p. 881.

3 Francis Elrington Ball, *A History of the County of Dublin: The People, Parishes and Antiquities from the Earliest Times to the Close of the Eighteenth Century. Part First: Being a History of that Portion of the County comprised within the Parishes of Monkstown, Kill-of-the-Grange, Dalkey, Killiney, Tully, Stillorgan, and Kilmacud* (Dublin: A. Thom, 1902), p. 37.

4 Robert C. Simington, *The Civil Survey AD 1654–1656, Vol. 7, County of Dublin* (Dublin: Irish Manuscripts Commission, 1945), p. 268.

5 Séamus Pender (ed.), *A Census of Ireland, c. 1659* (Dublin: Irish Manuscripts Commission, 1939), pp 379–81.

6 Henry Seymour Guinness (ed.), *The Register of the Union of Monkstown (Co. Dublin), 1669–1786* (Dublin: Parish Register Society, 1908), pp 85–9.

7 Peter Wilson, 'A topographical description of Dalkey and the environs. In a letter to John Lodge, esq., deputy keeper of the Rolls. Dalkey Lodge, March 28, 1768', *The Gentleman's Magazine* (May 1770) [reproduced in J. Gaskin and M. Simmonds, *Irish Varieties: A Victorian View of the Histories of Dalkey, Kingstown, Killiney and Bray* (Dalkey: Exchange Bookshop Ltd, 1987), p. 69].

8 Ball, *History of the County of Dublin*, p. 39.

9 See Nuala Cannon, 'Mariners in the blood: pilot families of Bullock Harbour, Dalkey, Co. Dublin', *The Irish Genealogist*, vol. 14, no. 1 (2014), pp 34–45.

10 F.M. O'Flanagan, 'Glimpses of old Dalkey', *Dublin Historical Record*, vol. 4, no. 2 (1941–2), pp 41–57, at p. 42.

Chapter 4

1 See http://www.downsurvey.tcd.ie/.

2 M.R.L. Kelly, *Dalkey, Co. Dublin* (Ilfracombe: Arthur H. Stockwell, 1952), p. 20.

3 Charles V. Smith, *Dalkey: Society and Economy in a Small Medieval Irish Town* (Dublin: Irish Academic Press, 1996), p. 27.

4 Kelly, *Dalkey*, p. 21.

5 *Ibid.*, p. 14.

6 J.J. Gaskin and M. Simmonds, *Irish Varieties: A Victorian View of the Histories of Dalkey, Kingstown, Killiney and Bray* (Dalkey: Exchange Bookshop Ltd, 1987), p. 49.

7 Kelly, *Dalkey*, pp 18–19.

8 *Ibid.*, p. 14.

9 Quoted in Gaskin and Simmonds, *Irish Varieties*, p. 65.

10 *Saunders's News-Letter*, 5 May 1773.

11 Smith, *Dalkey: Society and Economy*, p. 27.

12 Kelly, *Dalkey*, p. 23.

13 Francis Elrington Ball, *A History of the County of Dublin: The People, Parishes and Antiquities from the Earliest Times to the Close of the Eighteenth Century. Part First: Being a History of that Portion of the County comprised within the Parishes of Monkstown, Kill-of-the-Grange, Dalkey, Killiney, Tully, Stillorgan, and Kilmacud* (Dublin: A. Thom, 1902), p. 72; Kelly, *Dalkey*, p. 17.

14 John Kavanagh, 'A rediscovered castle in Dalkey', in Christiaan Corlett (ed.), *Unearthing the Archaeology of Dún Laoghaire–Rathdown* (Dún Laoghaire: Dún Laoghaire–Rathdown County Council, 2013), pp 124–8.

15 Quoted in Gaskin and Simmonds, *Irish Varieties*, p. 62.

16 Kavanagh, 'A rediscovered castle', p. 128.

17 See Chapter 15 for a profile of Thomas Connolly.

Chapter 5

1 *Freeman's Journal*, 16 October 1845; *Dublin Evening Mail*, 24 June 1842.

2 Courtesy of Mr Brian Porter, Dalkey.

3 *Freeman's Journal*, 26 March 1847.

4 If anything, the national population loss may have been even greater, as some historians consider that the 1841 Census figure of 8.175 million was an underestimate; see Joseph Lee, 'On the accuracy of the pre-Famine Irish Censuses', in J.M. Goldstrom and L.A. Clarkson (eds), *Irish Population, Economy and Society: Essays in Honour of the late K.H. Connell* (Oxford, 1981), p. 54.

Chapter 6

1 See J. Otway-Ruthven, 'The organization of Anglo-Irish agriculture in the Middle Ages', *Journal of the Royal Society of Antiquaries of Ireland*, vol. 81, no. 1 (1951), pp 1–13, at p. 6.

2 M.R.L. Kelly, *Dalkey, Co. Dublin* (Ilfracombe: Arthur H. Stockwell, 1952), p. 24. See Chapter 4 for Dalkey castles.

3 Henry Seymour Guinness (ed.), *The Register of the Union of Monkstown (Co. Dublin), 1669–1780* (Dublin: Parish Register Society, 1908), p. v.

4 According to the *King's Inns Admission Papers 1607–1867*, edited by E. Keane, P.B. Phair and T.U. Sadleir (Dublin: Irish Manuscripts Commission, 1982), a William Bull was admitted to the King's Bench around 1734 and died on 15 November 1766. The *Index to the Prerogative Wills of Ireland 1536–1810*, edited by Sir Arthur Vicars (Dublin: E. Ponsonby, 1897), lists a William Bull of William Street in 1767.

5 National Library of Ireland MS 35,857 (2), Dopping-Hepenstal Papers.

6 See Chapter 2.

7 Arnold Horner, 'John Rennie's documents relating to the planning of Dunleary Harbour 1815–16',

Dublin Historical Record, vol. 59 (2006), pp 182–200, at pp 194–6.

8 Porter estate papers, courtesy of Brian Porter, Dalkey.

9 A.P.W. Malcolmson, *The Pursuit of the Heiress: Aristocratic Marriage in Ireland 1740–1840* (Belfast: Ulster Historical Foundation, 2006), p. 107.

10 Kelly, *Dalkey*, p. 25.

11 Charles V. Smith, *Dalkey: Society and Economy in a Small Medieval Irish Town* (Dublin: Irish Academic Press, 1996), p. 30.

12 See http://titheapplotmentbooks.nationalarchives.ie/search/tab/home.jsp.

13 *Saunders's News-Letter*, 5 May 1773.

14 Liam Clare, *Enclosing the Commons: Dalkey, the Sugar Loaves and Bray, 1820–70* (Dublin: Four Courts Press, 2004), p. 31.

15 *Irish Penny Journal*, 21 November 1840, pp 162–3.

16 *Freeman's Journal*, 21 October 1885.

17 *Freeman's Journal*, 27 October 1885.

18 *Dublin Daily Express*, 10 October 1887.

Chapter 7

1 County Dublin Grand Jury Presentments, Easter 1848, no. 355.

2 *Freeman's Journal*, 27 October 1885.

3 Incumbered Estates Court, particulars of sale, 28 March 1854.

4 County Dublin Grand Jury Presentments, Easter 1845, no. 52.

5 Sorrento Terrace property deeds, courtesy of Peter Pearson.

6 *Freeman's Journal*, 14 April 1845.

7 *Weekly Freeman's Journal*, 12 April 1851.

8 F.M. O'Flanagan, 'Glimpses of old Dalkey', *Dublin Historical Record*, vol. 4, no. 2 (1941–2), pp 41–57, at p. 43.

9 *Saunders's News-Letter*, 13 July 1844.

Chapter 8

1 Edel Bhreathnach, Joseph MacMahon OFM and John McCafferty (eds), *The Irish Franciscans, 1534–1990* (Dublin: Four Courts Press, 2009), pp 262–3.

2 *Freeman's Journal*, 2 August 1845.

3 John D'Alton, *The History of the County of Dublin* (Dublin: Hodges & Smith, 1838), p. 883.

4 Dermot O'Riordan, 'The school on Dalkey Commons', *Dún Laoghaire Journal*, no. 32 (2023), pp 45–41, at p. 46.

5 *Saunders's News-Letter*, 10 July 1824; Samuel Lewis, *A Topographical Dictionary of Ireland* (London: S. Lewis, 1837), vol. 1, p. 447.

6 National Archives of Ireland, CSO/RP/1831/422.

7 *Second Report of the Commissioners of Public Instruction, Ireland* (London: House of Commons, 1835).

8 *Dublin Morning Register*, 30 August 1836, p. 101b.

9 See article by Fr Tom Finlay SJ in *The Loreto Magazine* (Christmas 1896), pp 48–53.

10 *Irish Primary Education Report* (London: House of Commons, 1868), vol. 6, p. 117.

11 *Appendix to the Second Report from the Commissioners of Irish Education Inquiry* (London: House of Commons, 1826), pp 604–5.

12 *Saunders's News-Letter*, 11 May 1825, 12 May 1827 and 17 May 1828.

13 *Dublin Daily Express*, 20 August 1861; *Dublin Evening Post*, 16 June 1866.

14 *Irish Primary Education Report* (1868), p. 117; *Thom's Directory* for 1881.

15 *Irish Times*, 24 October 2013; *Thom's Directory*, 1912–21.

16 *Irish Times*, 28 June 1893 and 2 January 1904; *Thom's Directory*, 1896 and 1908.

17 *Second Report of the Commissioners of Public Instruction, Ireland* (1835); Census of Ireland, 1901.

18 Representative Church Body Library, architectural drawings, identifier i_gh07500101.

19 I am grateful to Brian Meyer for extracts from St Patrick's parish records.

Chapter 9

1 See Séamus Ó Maitiú, *Dublin's Suburban Towns, 1834–1930* (Dublin: Four Courts Press, 2003).

2 See Giles's map on p. 197 in Arnold Horner's article on 'John Rennie's documents relating to the planning of Dunleary Harbour 1815–16', *Dublin Historical Record*, vol. 59 (2006), pp 182–200.

3 For a full description of how the truck railway operated see Rob Goodbody, *The Metals: From Dalkey to Dún Laoghaire* (Dún Laoghaire: Dún Laoghaire–Rathdown County Council, 2010). His book reproduces extracts from the unpublished 1837 Ordnance Survey map showing the friction wheels near Dalkey quarry.

4 See Garrett Lyons, *Steaming to Kingstown and Sucking Up to Dalkey: The Story of the Dublin and Kingstown Railway* (Dublin: Londubh Books, 2015).

5 *Dublin Evening Packet and Correspondent*, 12 December 1848.

6 *Saunders's News-Letter*, 23 April 1828.

7 *Dublin Morning Register*, 26 May 1838.

8 *Thom's Directory.*

9 F.M. O'Flanagan, 'Glimpses of old Dalkey', *Dublin Historical Record*, vol. 4, no. 2 (1941–2), pp 41–57, at p. 55.

10 Strictly speaking, the gauge was 5ft 2³⁄₁₆in.

11 Dún Laoghaire–Rathdown County Council, *Newtown Villas Architectural Conservation Area Character Appraisal* (2013), p. 11.

Chapter 10

1 See William Laffan (ed.), *The Cries of Dublin, Drawn from the Life by Hugh Douglas Hamilton, 1760* (Dublin: Irish Georgian Society, 2003).

2 Peter Pearson, *The Granite Coast: Dún Laoghaire, Sandycove, Dalkey* (Dublin: O'Brien Press, 2022), p. 83.

3 Eileen O'Duffy, *Champagne, Cocktails and Crêpes Suzette: Wining, Dining and Dancing in Dún Laoghaire through the Ages* (Carrigtwohill: Lettertec Publishing, 2022), pp 31–3.

4 *Irish Times*, 20 June 1862.

5 See Chapter 11.

Chapter 11

1 *Saunders's News-Letter*, 24 May 1787 and 11 April 1829.

2 See https://libraries.dlrcoco.ie/library-services/local-history/fm-oflanagan-recorder-dalkey (accessed 4 April 2023).

3 F.M. O'Flanagan, 'Glimpses of old Dalkey', *Dublin Historical Record*, vol. 4, no. 2 (1941–2), pp 41–57, at p. 55.

4 See anonymous article, 'The inn on the hill', in Frank Mullen (compiler), *Dalkey: An Anthology*, vol. 2 (Dublin: F. Mullen, 2009), p. 38.

5 *Saunders's News-Letter*, 15 May 1837.

6 *Ibid.*, 29 July 1837.

7 *Freeman's Journal*, 6 December 1839; *Dublin Mercantile Advertiser*, 31 January 1840.

8 J.J. Gaskin and M. Simmonds, *Irish Varieties: A Victorian View of the Histories of Dalkey, Kingstown, Killiney and Bray* (Dalkey: Exchange Bookshop Ltd, 1987), p. 2.

9 *Dublin Monitor*, 21 November 1842.

10 *Saunders's News-Letter*, 20 May 1843.

11 *Freeman's Journal*, 8 July 1848.

12 For further details and photos, see chapter 6, 'Dalkey seaside hotels', in Eileen O'Duffy, *Champagne,*

Cocktails and Crêpes Suzette: Wining, Dining and Dancing in Dún Laoghaire through the Ages (Carrigtwohill: Lettertec Publishing, 2022).

Chapter 12

1 *Freeman's Journal*, 26 October 1832.

2 *Ibid.*, 12 September 1833.

3 *Ibid.*, 13 December 1851.

4 J. Stafford Johnson, 'The Dublin Penny Post 1773–1840', *Dublin Historical Record*, vol. 4, no. 3 (1942), pp 81–95, at p. 91.

5 Samuel Lewis, *A Topographical Dictionary of Ireland*, vol. 1 (London: S. Lewis, 1837), p. 447.

6 Séamus Ó Maitiú, *Dublin's Suburban Towns, 1834–1930* (Dublin: Four Courts Press, 2003), p. 25.

7 See Cunningham's profile in Chapter 15.

8 *Freeman's Journal*, 19 January 1870.

9 For details of the sewer routes and outfalls, see public notice published in the *Freeman's Journal* on 30 November 1874.

10 Ó Maitiú, *Dublin's Suburban Towns*, p. 152.

Chapter 13

1 C. Ó Conbhuí, 'The lands of St Mary's Abbey, Dublin', *Proceedings of the Royal Irish Academy*, vol. 62C (1961–3), pp 21–72, at p. 57.

2 Patent Roll 3 Henry IV, 21; see *CIRCLE: A Calendar of Irish Chancery Letters c. 1244–1509* (www.chancery.tcd.ie).

3 Robert C. Simington, *The Civil Survey AD 1654–1656, Vol. 7, County of Dublin* (Dublin: Irish Manuscripts Commission, 1945), p. 268.

4 Peter Wilson, 'A topographical description of Dalkey and the environs. In a letter to John Lodge, esq., deputy keeper of the Rolls. Dalkey Lodge, March 28, 1768', *The Gentleman's Magazine* (May 1770) [reproduced in J. Gaskin and M. Simmonds, *Irish Varieties: A Victorian View of the Histories of Dalkey, Kingstown, Killiney and Bray* (Dalkey: Exchange Bookshop Ltd, 1987), pp 61–72, at p. 69].

5 *Saunders's News-Letter*, 9 September 1818.

6 H.A. Gilligan, 'Captain William Hutchison and the early Dublin Bay lifeboats', *Dublin Historical Record*, vol. 33, no. 2 (1980), pp 42–55, at p. 47.

7 Joseph Archer, *Statistical Survey of the County of Dublin* (Dublin: Graisberry & Campbell, 1801), p. 120.

8 Arnold Horner, '"Ireland's true survay", 1630s', *History Ireland*, vol. 26, no. 5 (2018), pp 24–7, at pp 26–7.

9 Nuala Cannon, 'Mariners in the blood: pilot families of Bullock Harbour, Dalkey, Co. Dublin', *The Irish Genealogist*, vol. 14, no. 1 (2014), pp 34–45, at pp 35–6.

10 Wilson, 'A topographical description', p. 64.

11 *Calendar of the Documents of Ireland, 1302–7* (London: Longman and Co., 1886), p. 135.

12 Sir Thomas Hyde Page, Royal Engineers, *Reports Relative to Dublin Harbour and Adjacent Coast* (Dublin, 1801), pp 4–5.

13 Gerald F. Daly, 'Captain William Bligh in Dublin 1800–1801', *Dublin Historical Record*, vol. 44, no. 1 (1991), pp 20–33, at pp 25–30.

14 *Saunders's News-Letter*, 10 December 1846.

Chapter 14

1 *Saunders's News-Letter*, 10 August 1793.

2 *Ibid.*, 9 February 1832.

3 *Freeman's Journal*, 2 June 1859.

4 *Dublin Daily Express*, 29 August 1876.

5 Eileen O'Duffy, *From Dirt and Dips to Dryrobes: Bathing in Dún Laoghaire through the Ages* (Carrigtwohill: Lettertec Publishing, 2021), p. 48.

6 Dún Laoghaire–Rathdown County Council, 2018 exhibition on 'F.M. O'Flanagan, Recorder of Dalkey' (www.dlrcoco.ie).

7 See, for example, the description of the 1856 regatta in the *Evening Freeman*, 1 August 1856.

8 *Freeman's Journal*, 29 June 1850.

9 Peter Pearson, *Between the Mountains and the Sea: Dún Laoghaire–Rathdown County* (Dublin: O'Brien Press, 1998), p. 59.

10 Frank Mullen (comp.), *Dalkey: An Anthology*, vol. 1 (Dublin, 2008), p. 64.

11 See www.cualagaa.ie/historic-overview/ for a fuller account.

12 *Irish Times*, 16 May 1861.

13 Frank Mullen (comp.), *Dalkey: An Anthology*, vol. 2 (Dalkey, 2009), p. 102.

14 See the article by George Kearns and Patrick Maguire in Mullen, *Dalkey*, vol. 2, pp 200–2.

15 Conan Kennedy, *Grandfather's House: Monte Alverno, Dalkey, Co. Dublin* (Killala: Morrigan Book Co., 2008), p. 49.

16 *Freeman's Journal*, 9 October 1885.

17 *Dublin Daily Express*, 17 April 1861.

18 F.M. O'Flanagan, 'Glimpses of old Dalkey', *Dublin Historical Record*, vol. 4, no. 2 (1941–2), pp 41–57, at p. 46.

Chapter 15

1 See *Dictionary of Irish Architects* (www.dia.ie).

2 *Saunders's News-Letter*, 23 September 1839.

3 *Freeman's Journal*, 11 May 1843.

4 See, for example, Registry of Deeds 1836/12/20; 1836/13/102 and 103.

5 F.M. O'Flanagan, 'Glimpses of old Dalkey', *Dublin Historical Record*, vol. 4, no. 2 (1941–2), pp 41–57, at p. 44.

6 Harry Latham, *St Patrick's Church of Ireland Church and Parish, Dalkey, Co. Dublin* (Dalkey: H. Latham, 1993), p. 37.

7 Entry by Stephanie Jones in *Dictionary of Irish Biography*, vol. 5, pp 969–70.

8 Liam Clare, *Enclosing the Commons: Dalkey, the Sugar Loaves and Bray, 1820–70* (Dublin: Four Courts Press, 2004), p. 33.

9 A post held by my late father, Joseph S. Martin, a century later.

10 *Freeman's Journal*, 21 October 1885.

11 *Dublin Evening Mail*, 24 June 1842.

12 *Freeman's Journal*, 27 October 1885.

13 Michael Neenan, 'Martin Burke of the Shelbourne Hotel', *Tipperary Historical Journal*, no. 14 (1994), pp 113–14.

14 *Dictionary of Irish Biography*, vol. 1, pp 250–1, contributed by Frances Clarke.

15 Desmond Forristal, *The First Loreto Sister: Mother Teresa Ball 1794–1861* (Dublin: Dominican Publications, 1994), p. 109.

16 *Freeman's Journal*, 23 October 1846.

17 *Saunders's News-Letter*, 17 April 1863.

18 *Dublin Builder*, 15 September 1868.

19 *Ibid.*, 1 April 1865.

20 *Ibid.*, 1 January 1861 and 1 February 1862.

Index